Reclaim Your
Challenging Classroom

This book is dedicated to all teachers who seek to build positive, influential relationships with their students.

Reclaim Your Challenging Classroom

Relationship-Based Behavior Management

Alene H. Harris

Justin D. Garwood

FOR INFORMATION:

Corwin

A SAGE Company

2455 Teller Road

Thousand Oaks, California 91320

(800) 233-9936

www.corwin.com

SAGE Publications Ltd.

1 Oliver's Yard

55 City Road

London EC1Y 1SP

United Kingdom

SAGE Publications India Pvt. Ltd.

B 1/I 1 Mohan Cooperative Industrial Area

Mathura Road, New Delhi 110 044

India

SAGE Publications Asia-Pacific Pte. Ltd.

18 Cross Street #10-10/11/12

China Square Central

Singapore 048423

Publisher: Jessica Allan

Senior Content Development Editor: Lucas Schleicher

Associate Content Development Editor: Mia Rodriguez

Project Editor: Amy Schroller

Copy Editor: Megan Markanich

Typesetter: C&M Digitals (P) Ltd.

Proofreader: Dennis W. Webb

Indexer: Integra

Cover Designer: Gail Buschman

Marketing Manager: Olivia Bartlett

Library of Congress Cataloging-in-Publication Data

Names: Harris, Alene H., author. | Garwood, Justin D., author.

Title: Reclaim your challenging classroom : relationship-based behavior management / Alene H. Harris, Justin D. Garwood.

Description: Thousand Oaks, California : Corwin, [2021] | Includes bibliographical references and index.

Identifiers: LCCN 2020052680 | ISBN 9781071830789 (paperback) | ISBN 9781071830772 (epub) | ISBN 9781071830765 (epub) | ISBN 9781071830758 (pdf)

Subjects: LCSH: Classroom management. | Behavior modification. | Teacher-student relationships. | Mentally ill children—Education.

Classification: LCC LB3013 .H353 2021 | DDC 371.102/4—dc23

LC record available at https://lccn.loc.gov/2020052680

This book is printed on acid-free paper.

SUSTAINABLE FORESTRY INITIATIVE

Certified Chain of Custody

Promoting Sustainable Forestry

www.sfiprogram.org

SFI-01268

21 22 23 24 25 10 9 8 7 6 5 4 3 2 1

CONTENTS

WHY THIS BOOK?

The book in your hands is designed for intervening within a school year to review and revise an existing classroom management system. In it you will find a set of ideas to help you *analyze* your current classroom management system, *develop* a plan to reclaim your classroom, and *implement and assess* the effects of your plan.

In each of six areas you will find information relevant for ALL teachers and ALL students. Also, you will find information specific to students with emotional and behavioral disorders (EBDs) and trauma backgrounds because they often present the greatest challenges to teachers in managing their classrooms.

As you read this book, it is possible some of the ideas or suggestions will have you nodding in agreement and thinking, "But that's just common sense!" Consider that common sense is not always common practice. Just as your students may misbehave despite knowing you expect differently, you may find yourself engaging in authoritarian management practices that come off more dictatorial than diplomatic (and we tend to repeat behavior patterns we have experienced or witnessed in the past). Please be willing to engage in self-reflection regarding your current practices and how well—or not well—they are serving your students and you alike.

Questions You Might Have Before You Begin

Question: Is it ever too late to start over to reclaim my classroom?

Answer: Sooner is better, but teachers have found "restarting" their classrooms even as late as six months into the school year resulted in positive changes in student behavior and academic engagement for the remaining school months.

Those same teachers then began the next school year in ways that yielded significantly better student behavior and lesson engagement for the following year.

Question: Is there an optimum time to make changes to restructure and reclaim my classroom?

Answer: Yes. Teachers report it is much easier to make changes after a major break—at least after a weekend and preferably after a break of a week or more.

Question: Does it make any difference what grade I teach?

Answer: Human behavior is human behavior—whether age six or sixteen. Ideas in this book have been used successfully by teachers in K–12. You may need to adapt some ideas to students' developmental levels (for example, you greet first and tenth graders differently, but you greet both ages).

Question: So there is hope?

Answer: Absolutely! Read and reflect on this text and then make and implement your plan to reclaim your classroom. The remainder of the school year can be a better place for you and your students!

ACKNOWLEDGMENTS

The authors wish to acknowledge two independently published books—*Getting Off to a Good Start: The First Three Days of School* (Harris & Tomick, 2016) and *Maintaining Momentum: Building on a Good Start* (Harris, Tomick, & Garwood, 2018), both available from Ready To Teach—for their contributions to this book. Appreciation is also given to Carey Dincauze and Aly Martin for their thoughts and suggestions regarding earlier drafts of this work.

Publisher's Acknowledgments

Corwin gratefully acknowledges the contributions for the following reviewers:

Macquin Brockington
English as a Second Language
    Teacher (K–5)
Boston Public Schools
Boston, MA

Avis Canty-Duck
Instructional Technology Facilitator
Greenville County School District
Greenville, SC

Cindy Corlett
Principal/Educator
Littleton Public Schools
Littleton, CO

Melissa Miller
Sixth-Grade Science and Math Teacher
Farmington Middle School
Farmington, AR

Renee Ponce-Nealon
Elementary School Teacher
Petaluma City Schools
Petaluma, CA

Betty Rivinus
Special Education, TOSA
Canby School District
Canby, OR

ABOUT THE AUTHORS

Alene H. Harris, PhD, is a retired professor from Peabody College of Vanderbilt University and for fifty years was a certified teacher in both elementary and secondary (English Language Arts and Life Sciences) levels. Her background includes sixteen years of classroom teaching and twenty-three years of university teaching, including (a) more than two thousand mostly middle school students, with a smattering of elementary and high school, in urban, suburban, and independent schools and (b) more than one thousand college students—mostly graduate students returning for a master's plus teaching licensure at Peabody College of Vanderbilt University.

Her expertise includes classroom management, lesson design, and staff development. She has a background of over twenty-five years of educational research in classroom management and in lesson design and effective teaching, including federally funded research in (a) classroom management and inclusion students (elementary); (b) student self-monitoring and its effect on special education placement (elementary); and (c) lesson design, student engagement, and academic achievement (secondary and postsecondary).

As an educational consultant, she has developed and led teacher-level workshops in classroom management with more than five thousand K–12 teachers and administrators, developed and led training-of-trainers workshops in classroom management to more than eight hundred school systems staff developers, and developed and led workshops in lesson design with more than one thousand university professors and doctoral students. This staff development includes experience in more than thirty states, one American territory, and the country of Costa Rica.

Justin D. Garwood, PhD, is a current university faculty member in the College of Education and Social Services at the University of Vermont, active with the Council for Exceptional Children (CEC) across multiple divisions: Council for Children with Behavioral Disorders (CCBD), Division of Learning Disabilities, Division for Research, and Teacher Education Division. Within CCBD, he serves as secretary (a nationally elected position) on the executive board. Garwood routinely presents at the CEC national conference as well as at the annual conference for Teacher Educators for Children with Behavior Disorders. In his role as university professor, he teaches courses at the undergraduate and graduate levels focused on behavior management, academic intervention, and inclusion.

An author of more than forty peer-reviewed journal articles, Garwood's research has received national accolades. In 2018, he was awarded the CEC Early Career Publication Award for his research focused on behavior management of youth with emotional and behavioral disorders (EBDs). In 2019, he received the Research Article of the Year Award from the American Council on Rural Special Education for his study of burnout among educators serving youth with disabilities. Garwood has served as an expert witness to testify before a US Commission on Civil Rights hearing regarding appropriate approaches to disciplinary practices in schools. Currently, and with support from the US Department of Education, he is studying burnout among special education teachers serving students with EBDs.

INTRODUCTION

READ THIS SECTION FIRST

"Strive for continuous improvement, instead of perfection."

—Kim Collins
World champion sprinter

Your school year is now underway. You thought you got off to a good start, but perhaps some things have not maintained as you had hoped. Or, you got off to a rocky start, and you wish you could "reset" the school year and start over. Or, things were going well until the addition of a challenging student changed the class dynamics (or a national emergency upended your and your students' lives). However you began the school year, in some areas things are probably going well in your classroom, while in others you'd like to make changes and improvements. But how? How do you go about creating and implementing a midyear minor "management adjustment" or a major "management makeover" in your classroom later in the school year?

How Do You Go About Reclaiming Your Classroom?

In the field of engineering, the term *evolutionary operations* refers to making adjustments to improve a manufacturing process while that process is underway. Recognized for many years as a way to improve the performance of an industrial process (Hunter & Kittrell, 1966), this idea has direct application to a teacher's classroom management. Once the school year begins, it just keeps on going.

Think of your classroom as a cruise ship. You as the captain have plotted the course, the trip is underway, and you and your students are moving across the School Year Ocean. If the engine starts to miss or a berth starts to fall apart or you realize there is a better place to hold shuffleboard tournaments, you cannot stop the ship for repairs or upgrades. You as the captain must make midcourse adjustments while the ship is moving and with all passengers aboard. And the time spent in planning and making these midcourse adjustments will result in a better voyage for everyone on board—both captain and passengers!

Often, with our classroom ship underway, we are so caught up in the daily academics of school that we feel we have no time for anything else—we are too busy steering the ship to take time to adjust the engine, much less deal with rickety berths and shuffleboard location. Yet we know from looking in classrooms that teachers who take time to address thoroughly the "nonacademics" related to classroom management have students with higher academic achievement at the end of the year and better behavior throughout the year (Garwood, Vernon-Feagans, & the Family Life Project Key Investigators, 2017; Stronge, Ward, & Grant, 2011). Making room for these nonacademics in classrooms allows teachers to reach their most effective potential in helping students learn. In terms of cost-benefit ratio, investment in the nonacademics is well worth your time for the payoff in improved student learning and appropriate classroom behavior.

Today's Inclusive Classrooms

Today's classrooms contain a variety of students, some with diagnosed learning challenges—and some without the diagnosis but with the learning challenges. You cannot always tell by outward appearance the background experiences of a student. Exposure to adverse childhood experiences (referred to as ACEs and including such things as emotional or physical abuse, neglect, parental substance abuse, or mental health disorder) is becoming more and more common among children and youth today, and this new reality requires a trauma-informed approach in today's classroom (van der Kolk, 2014). In fact, it has been estimated that as many as 68 percent of children experience at least one ACE in their lifetime (Pappano, 2014). Children experiencing ACEs present a unique classroom management situation for classroom teachers, as these ACEs often result in decreases in concentration, social skills, and the ability to trust others, as well as an increase in aggressive behaviors and anxiety (Ogata, 2017; National Child Traumatic Stress Network, 2016).

So, how do you know which children are experiencing ACEs? Students in your school most likely to have gone through traumatic experiences are those with a recognized emotional and behavioral disorder (EBD) (Cavanaugh, 2016). As these students are increasingly being placed in general education classrooms, their needs are no longer the primary responsibility of special education teachers (Garwood & Van Loan, 2019). In 2017, nearly half of all students with EBDs spent 80 percent or more of their school day in an inclusive, general education classroom (US Department of Education, Office of Special Education and Rehabilitative Services, Office of Special Education Programs, 2018). Furthermore, since 1990, the placement rate of students with EBDs in the general education classroom has more than doubled (McLeskey, Landers, Williamson, & Hoppey, 2012). In sum, we know that EBD is a vastly underdiagnosed disability and that more students with EBDs are being placed in general education classrooms. With this shift in responsibility, what do we know from research involving these students that can inform the regular classroom teacher?

Many teachers mistakenly believe they must "act tough" when teaching students with EBDs for fear of being "soft" and taken advantage of by the students (Walkley & Cox, 2013). This is just flat wrong. Children and youth dealing with ACEs do *not* need strict disciplinarians; rather, they need someone to care about them and to work to build a positive (and professional) relationship with them. A goal in working with these students is to step into your own authority with kindness and compassion rather than severity.

Also, despite the popularity of behaviorist approaches to managing student behavior (i.e., a system of rewards, such as stickers or meal vouchers, made available to students through token economies), these techniques do not work well for all students, especially those with a trauma background (Parker, Rose, & Gilbert, 2016). These students desire human connection rather than edible reinforcers (Marlowe, Garwood, & Van Loan, 2017). If you find yourself working in a school with a mostly behaviorist approach to behavior management, you can still adopt a relationship-based approach to teaching.

A relationship-based approach actually aids children and youth in developing self-regulation skills. (Note: For a detailed review of trauma-informed practice beyond the scope of this book, see the work of Dr. Bruce Perry, MD, PhD.) Simple changes in how you deal with a student experiencing trauma can make a big difference. For instance, when the student misbehaves, it is much more effective to ask, "What happened to you?" instead of "What's wrong with you?" (Hosinger & Brown, 2019). This shift in word choice sends the message you are not blaming the student for the trauma experienced; instead, it assures the student that you understand he or she is dealing with a stressful life event and seek to help him or her gain the skills needed to heal (Greene, 2014). How else can you build a trauma-informed classroom? We suggest the following research-based tips (Hosinger & Brown, 2019):

1. Create a physical classroom environment built on principles of comfort and safety by considering the arrangement of desks and chairs, lighting, wall decorations, and even music. (Put yourself in a student's shoes, and imagine leaving a chaotic hallway to enter a classroom with calm music.)

2. Create and teach students the behavioral expectations for the classroom as well as the procedures they are expected to perform throughout the days and weeks ahead. Predictable environments with consistent routines are key in student self-regulation.

3. Build healthy relationships with students exhibiting behavior problems by utilizing the 2 x 10 strategy (Wlodkowski, 1983). For ten school days in a row, speak with such a student for two minutes in a brief, solution-oriented tone where you make it clear you are on the student's side and that his or her actions impact others, not just themselves (Smith & Lambert, 2008).

A final tip comes from one of the authors of this text. Although anecdotal in its evidence base, it has worked for both K–12 students and higher education students alike. At least twice per year, find or make a time to speak with each of your students on an individual basis. Be sure to do this on CLASS time (i.e., during the school day), not on the student's time (i.e., before or after school, during recess time). Ask your student two questions:

1. How is our classroom working for you?

2. How is life?

If students prefer to answer in written format, allow this option. These two questions send the message that you care about your students' experiences both inside and outside of the classroom. Their responses can open a door of understanding, communication, and relationship. Throughout this text, we offer strategies and advice we know (and research supports) works for all students, but especially for those who struggle with EBDs and trauma. In some instances, we make specific mention of these students, but in all cases, we encourage you to implement a relationship-based approach as you work with students of all abilities and varying needs.

One final note: The task of becoming a good or better or even best teacher is most effective when applied with the assistance of others. This cannot work as a solo endeavor of adhering to self-help techniques. Therefore, as you build relationships with students, be sure to lean on your colleagues for help along the way.

So What Is the Midcourse Adjustment Process, and Why Should I Do It?

Midcourse adjustment in classroom management is a sequential five-step process in each of the six interrelated areas you will find below. Each of the following numbered steps builds on the one before it; therefore, the steps need to occur in the order you see here:

1. The first step is **reflecting and self-assessing** what is and is not working in the several areas that influence classroom management and classroom climate.

2. The second step is **reviewing the research** and examining what we know from looking in classrooms to see what effective teachers do in each of these areas.

3. The third step is **making specific adjustment plans** in those areas for your own "ship," your classroom, based on your results of Step 1.

4. The fourth step is **implementing your specific adjustment plans** by putting into practice those things you think will improve your classroom ship.

5. The final step is **evaluating results** of your efforts—did it work, how well, and if not well enough to suit you, cycle back through the appropriate steps and try again.

Going through the process in each area, you may decide you need only a few adjustments in one or more areas. Or, you may decide you want a total makeover. The choice is yours.

As you work through this text and address each of the six areas, you will find ideas and techniques many teachers have used. In the Appendices you will find several resources you may duplicate and use as is or copy and adapt in some way to better suit your classroom, students, and situation. Consider how you might use—or adapt and use—any of these in your own classroom.

Why work through this process? As you read this, there are likely many more days yet to come in the school year. If you are not satisfied with the direction your classroom seems to be heading, NOW is the time to change the course. But don't just grab the wheel and turn—you may find yourself veering even more off course. Be intentional in the changes you make. Working intentionally through each of the six areas using these five steps of midcourse class management adjustment can make for a better school year for you and for your students. Both you and they will enjoy the journey much more—and there will be more of you left at the end of the school year. In the Appendices, you'll find A: A Chart to Keep Track to help you chart your journey.

Where and When Do I Begin?

Reclaiming your classroom involves six areas for examination and possible revision or overhaul—adjustment or makeover—through the five steps described above. While they are six separate areas, they work together to help you create a positive and effective classroom management system.

1. Your students' perceptions of you as their teacher

2. The physical arrangement of your classroom and materials

3. The expectations and procedures by which your classroom runs

4. The consequences you choose to use to encourage appropriate behavior

5. Your students' engagement in academic lessons

6. Your classroom climate and community

The best time to implement change is after a major break—at least a weekend and preferably a week or more. Look at your school calendar. What are the possible breaks you might follow with a management makeover?

NOTE: This symbol and others like it throughout the book indicate an activity that can help you reclaim your classroom.

DATES OF BREAK	TOTAL NUMBER OF DAYS	MY PREFERENCE (1st, 2nd, 3rd, etc.)

Start with Area One. More learning and less hassle occur in classrooms where teachers are perceived as fair, caring, and consistent. It will be easier to accomplish change in the other five areas once students have a positive perception of you as their teacher.

Then work through Areas Two, Three, and Four *in the order listed* because

- your *room arrangement* (Area Two) affects student behavior, and

- your students need to know **what** *behaviors are expected* of them and **how and when** *to do them* (Area Three) before they receive a *consequence* (Area Four) for doing or not doing them.

Areas Five and Six—*maintaining students' engagement in academic lessons* and *creating classroom community*—may come anywhere, depending on your assessment of your classroom.

By analyzing and addressing each of these five areas you will find that

- your students can be better self-controlled and more on task,

- you can be more effective as a teacher, and

- your classroom can be a more pleasant place for both you and your students.

See Appendix A: A Chart to Keep Track to help you track your progress.

STUDENTS' PERCEPTIONS OF YOU AS THEIR TEACHER

"Students don't care how much you know until they know how much you care."

—John C. Maxwell
American author and
leadership expert

Think of an administrator or teacher for whom or with whom you really enjoyed working—someone who influenced you to go the extra mile and enjoy the journey. Chances are that words and phrases such as *fair, kind, cares about me as a person, has a sense of humor, unbiased, listens well, supportive, makes it safe to share ideas,* and *establishes order without being a dictator* come to mind. If similar words and phrases come to students' minds when they think of their teacher, chances are that they will be willing to cooperate and go the extra mile. The bottom line is this: Students behave better and work harder for teachers they like and respect. Thus, their perception of you influences their behavior—and thus their learning.

> **What students think matters!**

Students of all ages tell us over and over again that they like and respect those teachers who communicate that they care about them as a person. There are specific teacher actions that cause students to believe a teacher cares about them (Jones & Jones, 2016; Nie & Lau, 2009; Philipp & Thanheiser, 2010):

- greeting students as they enter the class

- calling them by name—with the correct pronunciation

- making frequent human-to-human eye contact during class (not "the look")

- speaking to them (by name) in the hall and off school grounds

- being supportive if they get something wrong in class

As you think back over your own experiences as a student, what else might you add?

Remember that perception is reality to the person perceiving. It may or may not be accurate, but to the person perceiving, it is real and true. If students have a negative perception of you as their teacher, it falls to you to analyze the *why* of those student perceptions and then to help students change their perceptions to see you as a teacher who is caring and fair and focused on their learning. The in-class results will be well worth the effort.

How do you perceive the image at right? Do you see a woman's face or a man's full silhouette? Do you see a somewhat mysterious young woman with bangs, her head turned slightly to the left with light coming from the right and the other side of her face in shadow? Or, do you see a cartoon profile of a large-headed man, facing right and playing a musical note on a saxophone? Whatever you perceive is the reality of that image for you.

One final thought: Being *liked* by students is not the same thing as being *popular*. As a teacher once remarked, "If I wanted to win a popularity contest with students, I'd open an ice cream stand."

What do we know from research that relates to students' perceptions of teachers? Looking in classrooms reveals the following:

- Students perceive teachers more positively when they provide limits for behavior and are able to use their authority to maintain order and create a safe environment without being rigid, threatening, or punitive. The ability to be firm without using threats and public humiliation is especially important for marginal students (Cothran, Kulinna, & Garrahy, 2003; Gulcan, 2010; Schlosser, 1992).

- Students are active information processors whose perceptions affect their behavior. If they perceive teachers as supportive, then they like them and are more likely to engage in prosocial, responsible behavior; to follow classroom expectations and norms; and to engage appropriately in academic activities (Gulcan, 2010; Mitchell & Bradshaw, 2013; Schunk & Meece, 1992; Wentzel, 1997, 2009).

- Students sometimes choose to misbehave to get back at a teacher if they perceive the teacher as (1) rude, (2) mean, (3) not knowing their names, or (4) ineffective in teaching (Obenchain & Taylor, 2005; Plank, McDill, McPartland, & Jordan, 2001; Thorson, 1996).

- Students perceive teachers who use expiative punishment—that is, something with no logical connection to the misbehavior (for example, writing one hundred times "I will be respectful")—as unworthy of respect. Such punishments give students a sense that they have the right to retaliate and seek revenge (Chory-Assad & Paulsel, 2004; Dreikurs & Cassel, 1972).

- While "teacher caring" repeatedly surfaces as an important student perception that influences student behavior, higher-achieving students tend to associate caring with academic assistance while lower-achieving students tend to associate caring with personality traits (such as positive attitude, sense of humor, ability to listen) and an expression of interest and concern in students as individuals. Both groups associate teacher interest in their lives beyond the classroom as caring (Garwood & Moore, 2020; Kounin & Gump, 1961; Phelan, Davidson, & Cao, 1992).

- Students like and respect teachers who (1) use humor to get them back on track rather than resorting to more punitive tactics and (2) do not punish students for every minor misbehavior (Fovet, 2009; Stinson, 1993; Tobin, Ritchie, Oakley, Mergard, & Hudson, 2013; Wanzer, Frymier, Wojtaszczyk, & Smith, 2006).

- "Students are able to detect whether or not a teacher likes them, no matter how diplomatic teachers believe themselves to be in the classroom" (Mercer & DeRosier, 2010).

Reflect on each of the previously given items for a few moments, and think about things these findings suggest you might do or do differently to encourage students' positive perceptions of you as their teacher. Use the Reflections on Area One page at the end of this area to jot down your thoughts.

Self-Assessment #1:
Actions That Influence Students' Perception of Me

Check where you fall in each of the twelve items that follow. When the school year began, your students brought with them anxiety about who you are as a person. A YES for each item means you have addressed and are addressing their concerns. Anything less than YES is an area where you could improve your students' perception of you as their teacher and thus create a better relationship on which to build teaching and learning experiences.

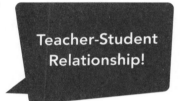

Teacher-Student Relationship!

1-2

At the beginning of the school year, I . . .	NO		SOMEWHAT		YES
1. Shared with students something about myself as a teacher—my credentials and expectations	○	○	○	○	○
2. Shared with students a little something about myself as a person—but not too much	○	○	○	○	○
3. Shared with students my enthusiasm for the coming school year	○	○	○	○	○
4. Communicated I would be honest and fair as their teacher	○	○	○	○	○
5. Communicated that I value and respect each student as an individual	○	○	○	○	○
6. Communicated that I value a positive community in our classroom	○	○	○	○	○
7. Participated with students in some sort of classroom icebreaker activity that allowed them to get to know me a bit better	○	○	○	○	○
Now into the school year, I . . .					
8. Stand at the door and greet my students as they enter	○	○	○	○	○
9. Know the first and last names of all of my students	○	○	○	○	○
10. Call my students by name in the classroom—and when I see them in nonclassroom settings	○	○	○	○	○
11. Make an effort to interact with my students in nonacademic settings—for example, attend a game or music recital	○	○	○	○	○
12. Maintain a professional relationship with students—a friendly teacher, but not their "friend"	○	○	○	○	○

Communicating a Positive Perception of Yourself as a Teacher

Think back to your college days, and recall questions you had about your professors. Remember how your anxiety lessened (or increased!) as they revealed themselves to you as human beings as well as professors. The same is true for your students.

Your students come to you with various background experiences. Some trust adults—and especially teachers—while others do not. Some have had positive past classroom experiences while others have not. It is probable that some were emotionally nurtured by teachers; it is possible that others were emotionally devastated. Your goal is to convince your students that you are a human being who can be trusted to interact with them in ways that are both fair and safe. This paves the way for them to follow as you guide them in their learning.

Consider how you could improve your *communication* of each of the following with your students. What could you SAY and DO in your classroom that you have not said and done thus far to address each area and cause students to perceive you as a positive and caring and competent teacher?

Myself as a Teacher	Myself as a Person
My Enthusiasm for This School Year With This Class	**My Honesty and Fairness**
My Values for Students as Individuals	**My Values for Our Class as a Community**

Source: Adapted from Harris and Tomick (2016).

See the Appendices for B: Communicating a Positive Perception of Yourself as a Teacher: Ideas From Teachers for sample responses shared by teachers who have participated in workshops with one of the authors of this book.

The Value of Relationship in Developing Positive Perception

From the moment you first encounter your students in the classroom, whether consciously or not, you begin to form relationships—and those relationships influence students' perceptions of you. Daily interactions within your classroom—perhaps numbering in the hundreds or even more—shape the strengths and weaknesses of your connections with your students. Being proactive in these interactions leads to better relationships. While some teacher-student relationships flower on their own accord, others take effort.

Relationship is intervention!

One group of students, in particular, requires a conscious effort on the part of the teacher to develop a high-quality relationship with them. These are students dealing with adverse childhood experiences (ACEs) and who often struggle with emotional and behavioral disorders (EBDs). Such students lack the ability to develop positive relationships with others and need an adult model and a mentor. As they are often lacking adults in their lives who model functional behaviors and healthy relationships, to you as the teacher falls the opportunity and responsibility to be that functional adult who proactively engages with them in a healthy (and professional) relationship.

So, how do you get started? First, when working with children who have experienced trauma and/or are struggling with EBDs, it is crucial to develop a mindset of patient understanding. Think of yourself as part of a team, with you and the student working together against the student's undesirable behaviors (Marlowe & Hayden, 2013), rather than thinking of yourself as the student's opponent who is periodically dispensing rewards.

Unlike the *behavioral* model that seeks to change student behavior through extrinsic motivators (for example, stickers, edibles, homework passes), the *psychoeducational* model of education suggests the most important intervention for a student is, in fact, the relationship between teacher and student (Marlowe, Garwood, & Van Loan, 2017). "Behavioral change comes not only from the manipulation of environmental variables . . . but from the development of a better understanding of oneself and others (the 'psycho' part), and the practice of new ways of reacting (the 'education' part)" (McIntyre, 2011).

If a teacher develops a relationship with a student—a relationship that the student cares about and values—then it increases the chance that the student's behavior will improve because of the student's desire to maintain that positive relationship with that teacher. And this desire is intrinsic motivation—much more likely to result in long-term behavior change than extrinsic motivation (Ryan & Deci, 2000).

To put it another way, any intervention, whether academic or behavioral, that a teacher implements will be more effective if the student has a positive relationship with that teacher.

To put it ANOTHER way . . . relationships ARE the intervention.

Building Positive Teacher-Student Relationships With Challenging Students

So how do you go about building positive relationships with challenging students? The teacher skills and beliefs that follow are suggested as a prerequisite for developing a positive teacher-student relationship (Marlowe & Hayden, 2013):

Skills

- Exercising self-awareness about one's own actions *and* how students perceive those actions.
- Seeing the student's behavior from the student's perspective.

Beliefs

- We as people (teachers and students) are all more alike than we are different.
- A student who misbehaves is not a bad student but simply engaged in an undesirable behavior—in other words, a student is not defined by his or her actions.
- No one wants to be unhappy. Some students just go about trying to be happy in really ineffective and counterproductive ways.
- Every student CAN change. (Note that we do not suggest every student WILL change—only that everyone has the potential for transformation.)
- As a teacher we fail only when we give up trying to help a student; our success is not defined by the student's success but by our attempts to help the student succeed.
- All behavior is on a spectrum (think Einstein's theory of relativity).

A useful way to think about building relationships with your students is to envision yourself and your student as gears trying to connect. As you seek to shift gears to a high-quality relationship, be careful with your "speed" (Van Loan, Cullen, & Giordano, 2015; Van Loan, Gage, & Cullen, 2015). If you come at students too fast (for example, you attempt to be the student's buddy from day one and he or she doesn't even know you), you strip the gears and make it harder to connect. The student may see you as not being genuine and therefore not trust your attempts to build a relationship. If, on the other hand, you wait too long to attempt to build a relationship (i.e., to connect the gears), the student can spin out of control; then, when you try to engage, both you and the student suffer. While the student may have known you for some time as the teacher, if you have not related on a human-to-human level in some way, an attempt to build connections months into the school year will also seem ungenuine.

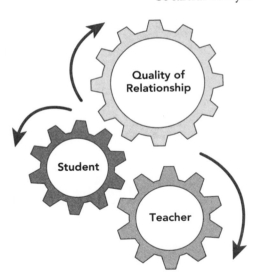

As illustrated in the diagram you see here, it is the teacher who bears responsibility for the quality of the relationship. How a teacher engages with a student determines development of the relationship. True, some students bring gears somewhat bent and stripped from prior painful experiences. The more you can learn about the "shape" of a student's gear, the better you can choose words and actions to engage with that student.

Source: Christopher L. Van Loan, PhD, Appalachian State University.

One way to begin gauging relationship quality with your students uses the acronym TAN (Van Loan & Garwood, 2020a). TAN stands for methods to move **T**oward or **A**way from your student, while being mindful of your and your student's **N**eeds.

The best way to move **T**oward your student (desirable) is to develop trust, and the best way to build trust is to be perceived as fair, reliable, and predictable in your interactions.

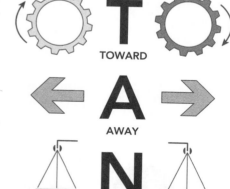

Every interaction you have with a student . . .

is a chance to model appropriate behavior.

To keep from moving **A**way (undesirable) from the student, avoid power struggles. Instead, proactively listen, de-escalate, inquire to understand, and speak with a neutral tone and volume rather than reactively lecture, demand, insist, and yell.

Finally, to check if **N**eeds (mutual) are being met, periodically ask yourself, "Are my *student's* needs being met? Are my *own* needs being met?" If the answer to either is no, the relationship is out of balance. Teachers often forgo their own needs for the sake of their students. While this is commendable, if you burnout, you will not be able to help and support your students. One of the reasons you must have a life outside of school and your job is to help you maintain a balance.

For challenging students, especially those struggling with EBDs, choice can be a powerful tool in promoting desirable behavior (Jones & Jones, 2016). Typically, these students are repeatedly told what to do in school (for example, be quiet, sit still, don't move, go to the principal's office) and rarely get the chance to make a choice or have a say in their education. Something as simple as a choice between two activities or a choice in the order of doing activities can avoid pushback and power struggles (key in moving **T**oward your students and preserving the quality of the relationship).

A focus on choice can also be a tool to help students understand they have the power to take control of their own actions—and this is a key to self-monitoring. When a student misbehaves, emphasize the choice the student is making rather than lecturing about why that choice is undesirable. Suggest that there are more positive choices the student can make, and lead the student to recognize what the likely desirable outcomes may be if the student makes a better choice. It is also helpful to ask a student engaging in undesirable behavior, "What is your best prediction for how this will end if you don't make a better choice? Will it help you?" This encourages the student to self-reflect, which is an effective de-escalation technique.

Offering students with EBDs choices is also a way of instilling in them a sense of agency. For the first time in a long time, they may finally feel as if they have a say in their own lives. You, their teacher, can be the one who reminds them of their power. They will likely be grateful for the autonomy you provide—and that gratitude contributes to a positive relationship with you.

Adjusting a Student's Perceptions

Each student in your classroom has a perception of you as his or her teacher. Whether you agree or disagree with that perception, to that student perception is reality. But what if that perception is negative and interfering with your teaching and the student's learning? How can you change that student's perception?

The first step in changing a perception is identifying it. (Note: For a student who is exhibiting negative attitudes or behavior, this is best done in a one-on-one, nonpublic setting; for measuring a class's perception, it can be done with an anonymous survey.) Step 2 is identifying why the student sees you that way. Sometimes the underlying cause may be something as simple as the student's mishearing something you said. Sometimes the cause may be your own lack of clarity in distinguishing expectations from procedures (see Area Three) or your own lack of consistency in following through. Or, sometimes the cause may be linked to a cultural difference or to a prior experience that actually has nothing to do with you. Step 3 is honestly and forthrightly addressing the underlying cause of the misperception.

Consider the following four vignettes, and see if you can identify a possible underlying cause for the person's (mis)perception. What would you recommend for each?

VIGNETTE #1	VIGNETTE #2	VIGNETTE #3	VIGNETTE #4
"Ms. Anders, you're not fair!" third-grader Sam accused as the teacher reprimanded him for talking out without raising his hand for permission. "How am I not fair?" asked the teacher. "Well," Sam replied, "Shamika talks out lots of times without following the rule, and she never gets in trouble." This was true. Sometimes in class discussions students could contribute an idea as long as they did not interrupt one another.	A middle school student complained to a parent that the teacher ridiculed his struggle with a new math concept. "She said it's easy, and it isn't easy for me, so she's saying I'm stupid!" What the teacher said was "Once you get the first three steps, it's easy to calculate the final step."	Four high school students requested that the guidance counselor change their class schedules and remove them from the third period French I class. Each student gave this as the reason: "The teacher just doesn't like me." Further investigation revealed that all four students sat in the far-right row, and the teacher was extremely left-eye dominant. In the first four weeks of school, she had never called on or even made eye contact with those four students.	One December, two young men who had grown up as classmates in Nashville, Tennessee, reunited and met in a small city park where they had often played. "Oh, how green and fresh everything is!" exclaimed the man coming from Fort Sill, Oklahoma. "Oh, no, how brown and dead everything is!" replied the one coming from the Florida Keys. Whose perception was accurate?

One way to assess students' perceptions is to allow them an anonymous way to give opinions (Jones & Jones, 2016). A possible way to do this is to provide students with a checklist of some sort. Samples of three charts follow—one each for early elementary, upper elementary/middle school, and secondary levels. You'll find the complete charts for duplication and use in the Appendices (C: Some Thoughts About Our Classroom [Early Elementary], D: Some Thoughts About Our Classroom [Upper Elementary/Middle School], and E: Some Thoughts About Our Classroom [Secondary]). Note that for students who cannot yet read, someone can read the statements to them, and they can mark the chart. If you choose to use one of these charts, after tabulating the results, do reflect on them by finishing the following statements (Evertson & Harris, 2003):

I learned that . . .   I was pleased that . . .

I was surprised that . . .   I was disappointed that . . .

Sample From C: Some Thoughts About Our Classroom (Early Elementary)

Ask students to circle the smiley face if they really agree, the neutral face if they are not sure, and the frowny face if they really disagree.

STATEMENT	AGREE	NEUTRAL	DISAGREE
1. My teacher cares about me.	☺	😐	☹
2. My teacher is fair.	☺	😐	☹

Sample From D: Some Thoughts About Our Classroom (Upper Elementary/Middle School)

Ask students to mark the words or phrases in the chart as follows:

Always true: Circle the word or phrase   Seldom true: Draw a line through the word or phrase
Often true: Check the word or phrase   Never true: X out the word or phrase

Likes me	Caring	Friendly	Fair	Helpful	Kind
Patient	Humorous	Calls on me	Gentle	Likable	Cheerful
Respectful	Looks at me	Generous	Creative	Listens to me	Loving

Sample From E: Some Thoughts About Our Classroom (Secondary)

Ask students to check the column that shows their opinion of how their teacher would rate if the classroom were a basketball court.

My Teacher . . .	NEVER Personal Foul	ALMOST NEVER 0-Point Air Ball	SOMETIMES 1-Point Foul Shot	ALMOST ALWAYS 2-Point Basket	ALWAYS 3-Point Basket
1. Is nice to me	○	○	○	○	○
2. Treats all students fairly	○	○	○	○	○
3. Has a sense of humor	○	○	○	○	○

> I'll promise you perfect students when you can promise students a perfect teacher.

1. Imperfect Students Are Typical—You Were Not a Perfect Student Either

Let's face it: You may have a class of students, each with one or more behaviors you would rather they left outside your classroom door. Guess what? You have a class of typical students! Would you be surprised to learn that, when given a class roll and asked to write ten adjectives after each student's name, teachers will write at least one undesirable adjective among the ten for practically every student? Think back. If your teachers had been asked to do the same thing with *your* name, would there have been at least one undesirable attribute listed?

2. Every Student Has Value—Find Something Positive in Each Student, and Focus on It

Let's face it: Some students are easier to like and enjoy than others. For those whose positive attributes are not as obvious, you have to search and focus. Often you can see potential in students that the students themselves cannot see. It may be a child or adolescent who has been told throughout life thus far that he or she is stupid or ugly or worthless. These students desperately need your help to allow them to see their value as a human being. But before you can show it to them, you have to learn to see it yourself.

3. Students Can Spot a Phony—Be Authentic in Your Interactions With Them

Let's face it: Students are turned off by playacting. While it is important to interact in positive ways that let students know you care, the ways in which you do this must be authentic and not contrived. Students—especially adolescents—have a built-in "garbage detector," and contrived sincerity sets it off and turns them off.

What ARE You Communicating to Your Students?

The seven questions that follow can be used (1) first as a way to recognize negative perceptions you are communicating to your students and (2) then as a way to identify things you can do to improve students' perception of you as their teacher (Evertson & Harris, 2003).

1. Do I make frequent and positive eye contact with every student?
2. Do I use a normal, pleasant voice in both tone and volume?
3. Do I speak with a calm and controlled voice, even when irritated by student behavior?
4. Do I make more positive statements to students than negative ones?
5. Do I avoid questions that could be intimidating to students (for example, Why are you so slow/careless?)?
6. Do I forgive past behavior and allow students a "fresh start" each day?
7. Do I accept a student for who he or she is, not holding the child or youth responsible for behavior of a sibling or parent or guardian?

Words of Wisdom: "You don't have to like every student in your class, but you must LOVE the adventure of teaching them." —Justin Garwood

Adjusting Your Own Perceptions—Two Teacher Mindsets

Perhaps the students who frustrate us most as teachers are the ones we call "academically unmotivated." We believe these kids could do well, but they don't. But wait! The question is WHY—and what we believe about that WHY influences our perceptions of (and therefore attitudes toward and interactions with) those students. Do we believe . . .

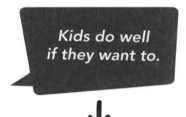

Kids do well if they want to.

Assumption: Students simply do not want to do well.

Kids do well if they can.

Assumption: Students are lacking one or more skills needed to do well.

Dr. Ross Greene (2008), a clinical psychologist in the Department of Psychiatry at Harvard Medical School, who has worked with children for over thirty years, says it well:

> The "kids do well if they can" philosophy carries the assumption that if the kid could do well, he would do well. If he is not doing well, he must be lacking the skills needed to respond to life's challenges in an adaptive way. What's the most important role an adult can play in the life of such a kid? First, assume he is already motivated, already knows right from wrong, and has already been punished enough. Then, figure out what thinking skills he is lacking so you know what thinking skills to teach.
>
> "He's not motivated" . . . is . . . (a) very popular characterization that can be traced back to the "kids do well if they want to" mentality, and it can lead us straight to interventions aimed at giving a kid the incentives to do well. But why would any kid not want to do well? Why would he choose not to do well if he has the skills to do well? Isn't doing well always preferable? (p. 162)

Consider it highly likely that a student who seems "unmotivated" is in fact lacking development in one or more of the following mental processes that help students succeed in learning and become motivated to learn more:

- focusing attention
- planning and problem-solving
- organizing oneself

- remembering information
- learning from mistakes
- managing impulses

Identifying underdeveloped needed skills can change your perception of a student from "unmotivated" to "doing the best he or she can" and in need of your help to do better. Once you identify the underdeveloped skill(s), an analysis of underlying causes can guide you to help the student develop the skill(s). Searle (2013) provides an analysis tree for each of these processes that can give you a head start on the diagnostic process.

Some Dos and Avoids to Encourage Positive Perceptions

Consider this old adage: "Students don't care how much you know until they know how much you care."

DO meet students with a smile at the door as they enter.

DO greet students by name as they enter.

DO make, periodic, frequent eye contact with students (pleasant, human-to-human eye contact).

DO call students by their names during class—and with correct pronunciation.

DO use courteous, positive language and pleasant voice tone.

DO survey students' perceptions of you as their teacher. Consider using one of the options provided in Appendices C: Some Thoughts About Our Classroom (Early Elementary), D: Some Thoughts About Our Classroom (Upper Elementary/ Middle School), and E: Some Thoughts About Our Classroom (Secondary); tabulate the results; and complete the four sentence stems on page 19.

AVOID intimidating questions and accusative language.

AVOID trying to be students' "buddy and friend." They have friends and buddies their own age. What they need is a TEACHER.

Key Takeaways: New and/or Reinforced Ideas on Student (and Teacher) Perceptions

Possible Applications: Things I Plan to Try in My Classroom

Please use the following space to jot down (1) key ideas you want to remember—whether new or a reinforcement of your current knowledge and beliefs—and (2) ideas you want to remember to try in your classroom. In the second column, it may help to keep track if you consecutively number the ideas to check them off as you try them.

KEY TAKEAWAYS:	POSSIBLE APPLICATIONS:
New and/or Reinforced Ideas	Things I Plan to Try in My Classroom

PHYSICAL ARRANGEMENT OF THE CLASSROOM AND MATERIALS

"Out of clutter, find simplicity.
From discord, find harmony.
In the middle of difficulty
lies opportunity."

—Albert Einstein

The *What* and *Why* of Room and Materials Arrangement

Room arrangement literally sets the stage for how the "play" of a daily class will unfold. Organization of the physical components of a classroom contributes to the drama, comedy, and real-life adventures that will occur in that room. Decisions you make in locating and spacing desks, chairs, shelves, pencil sharpeners, computers, file cabinets, and so on will either support or hinder teaching and learning in the classroom and contribute to or detract from a smoothly running classroom. There is no such thing as a neutral room arrangement, and there is no such thing as one perfect arrangement for all types of instruction.

Carefully set the stage!

What is the best room arrangement? It depends. It depends on a number of things: the number of students you have (and who those students are), the type of instruction in which you plan to engage students, the amount (and shape) of space in the room, the type and size of class furnishings and equipment you inherit, the types of materials you have available for use, and on other factors you can likely add to this list.

Consider four of the five physical senses—*sight, hearing, smell,* and *taste*—in arranging your classroom. Students fare better in classrooms where they (1) can see the teacher and instructional materials, including both unobstructed paths of vision and adequate light to read by; (2) can hear instructions, facilitated by both low noise levels (motors and other students) and minimal hard-surface echoes; (3) are not distracted by smells, either unpleasant or overly delicious; and (4) are surrounded by "tastefully" decorated furnishings, neither too bare nor overly embellished.

Keep in mind that your room arrangement sends visual signals of expectation to students—they take one look and make assumptions based on what they see.

IF	THEN
If students' desks are touching (here is the fifth physical sense of touch, but applied to furniture), . . .	. . . then students expect to talk with one another.
If open aisles are by at least one side of every student desk, . . .	. . . then students expect you could walk beside them at any time.
If classroom shelves are messy and disorganized, . . .	. . . then students assume neatness and order are not valued and messy work is okay.
If some areas of the room are hidden from your vision, . . .	. . . then students assume they may do whatever they please in those spaces.

Rooms communicate! Consider that an orderly room sends a different message from a disorderly one; a room with adequate personal space sends a different message from one with crowded desks and little personal space; and displays that include student work send a different message from displays of all commercially prepared materials. It is important that the unspoken room signals are a match for your expectations (Grube, 2013).

Space, Behavior, and Lesson Engagement

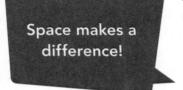

Space makes a difference!

In any room arrangement, space is a major constraint, especially in light of the repeated findings on the human need for personal space (for example, Capizzi, 2009). This need is present in all students, and for students with an emotional and behavioral disorder (EBD), more personal space is linked to two desirable outcomes: (1) appropriate behavior and (2) academic engagement. Providing adequate personal space for such students decreases the chances of peer-to-peer conflicts (Kauffman, Bantz, & McCullough, 2002). Decrease the opportunity for conflict, and you decrease the possibility of misbehavior. When such students feel a lack of personal space, it can disrupt their ability to stay on task (Burke & Burke-Samide, 2004). Increase the sense of personal space (and thus of safety), and students are less distracted and better able to focus.

In a self-contained classroom for students with EBDs, the smaller number of students allows more flexibility in providing students personal space. However, with increased inclusive instruction (i.e., all students being educated in the same classroom throughout the day), teachers must be creative in creating for these students the personal space that can decrease conflict and increase lesson engagement. Two possibilities are supported by research—one that a teacher can directly implement and one that depends on a school's financial resources for class furnishings.

The first possibility is to think of yourself as an air traffic controller responsible for maintaining safe distances between aircrafts (students) and monitoring arrivals and departures of many planes (students) at one time (Mundschenk, Miner, & Nastally, 2011). Establishing "flight zones" can be done for a student's own space and for shared class spaces. It is possible to provide a personal flight zone (i.e., personal space) by placing a border of colored tape on the floor around a student's desk and making it clear that the student stays in that space until "cleared for takeoff" by teacher permission—*and* no other student may enter that space unless "cleared" by the student. Flight zones may also be common spaces shared by all students (again marked with tape if deemed necessary for a visual boundary) in which the student may "land" and enter only with permission (Mundschenk et al., 2011). All this possibility requires is a roll of painter's tape.

A second option to consider for students with EBDs is flexible (or alternative) seating, which preliminary evidence suggests can improve on-task behavior (Williams, 2020); and improved on-task behavior leads to improved students' engagement and academic achievement (Drobnjak, 2017). The use of flexible seating (such as beanbag chairs, standing desks, exercise balls, wobble chairs, area rugs) (Hill & Nickels, 2018) is justified by research suggesting there is a mismatch between students' physical body dimensions and the seats, tables, and desks they are asked to use in school (Castellucci, Arezes, Molenbroek, de Bruin, & Viviani, 2017; Parcells, Stommel, & Hubbard, 1999). This option requires school and possibly district financial support for alternative furniture purchases.

What do we know from research that relates to arranging the classroom? Looking in classrooms reveals the following:

- Research suggests that more effective teachers (defined as teachers whose students demonstrate lower incidents of misbehavior and higher academic on-task rates) begin with more traditional room arrangements as they learn names, teach expectations and procedures, administer diagnostics, and so on. They then change the arrangement to support various types of instruction as the year progresses (Capizzi, 2009; Weinstein, 2007).

- Students who are (1) visible to the teacher and (2) physically accessible to the teacher stay more engaged in the lesson (Emmer, Evertson, & Worsham, 2003; Harris, Shapiro, & Garwood, 2015).

- Students who can easily see instructional displays relating to the task are more likely to stay on task (Emmer et al., 2003; Sterling, 2009).

- Students have a need for personal space. Crowding students contributes to undesirable student behavior. Adolescents are more sensitive to crowding than younger children. Crowded adolescent males tend to become aggressive; crowded females tend to withdraw (Capizzi, 2009; Dixon, 1995; Sinha, Nayyar, & Mukherjee, 1995).

- Students stay more engaged in instruction when seating arrangement supports the type of instruction—separated desks for independent work, paired desks for partner work, and touching desks or tables for group work (Lambert, 1995; Muthyala & Wei, 2013).

- Aesthetically pleasing environments influence desirable student behavior, and students are more likely to use materials if those materials are easily accessible and visually pleasing (Horowitz & Otto, 1973; Morrow & Weinstein, 1982; Sommer & Olson, 1980; Sterling, 2009).

- Classrooms have "action zones," typically across the front and down the middle of the classroom (especially those with desks in rows), and students seated in these zones get more teacher attention (Doyle, 2006; Wannarka & Ruhl, 2008).

- As technology increases, e-books and tablets are replacing textbooks and binders, and although most teachers try to keep cell phones out of the classroom, some choose to incorporate their use into academic instruction. There is a growing area of research addressing teacher concerns on managing students' use of electronic devices. For more information on this topic, please see Chapter 25 in the *Handbook of Classroom Management* (Bolick & Bartels, 2015).

Please reflect on each of the previously given items for a few moments, and think about things these findings suggest you might do to make your room arrangement work better for you and your students. Use the Reflections on Area Two page at the end of this area to jot down your thoughts.

Self-Assessment #2:
Analyzing the Physical Classroom Setting

Check where your current room arrangement falls in each of the following items. Any one of these areas can negatively affect student behavior and academic learning and your own peace of mind. A YES in each item means you have proactively addressed that possible problem and paved the way for success. Anything less than YES is an area where a change could create a better stage for teaching and learning experiences to take place.

Make the room work *for* you!

I Have Arranged My Room and Materials so That . . .	NO		SOMEWHAT		YES
1. I can see all students from any teaching area in the room.	○	○	○	○	○
2. I can make eye contact with all students from any teaching area in the room.	○	○	○	○	○
3. Each student can easily see the board areas.	○	○	○	○	○
4. I have quick physical access to each student (for example, I can reach any student in five giant strides).	○	○	○	○	○
5. I can easily reach all of my needed teaching materials.	○	○	○	○	○
6. Each student can easily reach all needed materials.	○	○	○	○	○
7. Aisles are clear for easy traffic flow.	○	○	○	○	○
8. The room arrangement allows special needs students easy accessibility in and out of the room.	○	○	○	○	○
9. The room arrangement allows students dealing with emotional and behavioral issues added personal space.	○	○	○	○	○
10. Students are seated facing away from doors and windows.	○	○	○	○	○
11. Students are seated away from distracters (for example, students are not seated next to a gerbil cage, close to a computer, in the noisy airflow path of an air conditioner, or beside a pencil sharpener and/or wastebasket).	○	○	○	○	○

Source: Adapted from Evertson and Harris (2003).

Your room is your first line of communication with your students. It speaks loudly. In fact, if you say one thing and the room says another, the room wins! If you say, "Be neat," and the room is messy, then messy wins. If you say, "Do your own work," and the touching desks say, "Collaborate," collaboration wins. If you say, "Pay attention," and colorful fall leaf mobiles hang from the ceiling, fluttering with each air current and visually singing out, "Look at me, look at me," the leaves win.

Match message and expectations!

Your room sends a visual message of what you expect. Orderly rooms send a different message than disorderly rooms; academic displays send a different message than unrelated displays; calm colors send a different message than loud colors; rooms with adequate student personal space send a different message than crowded desks with little personal space. Some displays of student work send a different message than all displays of commercial posters.

Think a moment about your room. What are some messages you WANT it to send, and why?

2-3

_____

_____

_____

_____

_____

Now stand just inside the door and look around—physically or in your imagination. What DOES your room say, and why?

_____

_____

_____

_____

_____

Bravo if the these two are a match! If they are not the match that you want, look for ideas in the following pages to help the match happen.

Creating a Supportive Classroom Arrangement

Whether you have tables and chairs, desks and chairs, or one-piece desk-chair combinations; whether you have a floor plan that is oblong, square, round, or "creative"; whether you have high technology or just a board and some chalk, there are three areas you must address (Evertson & Harris, 2003):

1. *Visual access.* The old adage "out of sight, out of mind" is true in the classroom. Ask yourself these two questions:

   a. Can I make eye contact with each student?

   b. Can each student easily see the board and/or screen and any other needed information (such as posted class expectations)?

2. *Physical access.* Any student who is more than five giant strides away from you may feel a sense of security not conducive to on-task behavior. Needed materials that are not easily accessed by your students will be seldom used and/or used with lesson disruption. The same is true for your own teaching materials. Ask yourself these three questions:

   a. Can I easily reach each student?

   b. Can I easily reach my needed materials?

   c. Can students, including those with special needs, easily reach needed materials?

3. *Minimal distractions.* Many things will compete with you and your planned instructional activities for students' attention in the classroom (for example, a window overlooking the ball field, a jittery gerbil in a cage, mobiles twisting overhead, hall activity visible through a door). Ask yourself these three questions:

   a. As I look around my room, what things could entice student attention away from instruction?

   b. How can I adjust any of these in some way to lessen the distraction?

   c. Have I identified students likely to be distracted and seated them away from any distracters I cannot control?

A SUGGESTION:

Sit in each student seat and ask yourself
what life as a student would be like for you
in that space in terms of vision, access, and distractions.

It is likely that you may decide to rearrange your classroom furniture. Moving furniture is much easier with your computer mouse than with your shoulder. At the companion website (**resources.corwin.com/ReclaimYourClassroom**) you will find a set of electronic templates in PowerPoint for (1) classroom floor space and (2) classroom furniture that can help you plan a room "on paper" before you ever move a desk. The furniture is sized to scale for the floor space diagram (based on furniture measurements found on the School Outfitters website). Templates represent traditional classroom furnishings; if you have some "untraditional" pieces, you will need to measure them and create additional templates for those pieces.

Save your energy!

Step 1. Begin by measuring the length and width of your room. Then go to the floor space PowerPoint slide, and block out any "extra feet" that are not included in your room space. (Note that the dotted lines indicate the average US classroom size of twenty-four by thirty-two square feet; this template provides a few extra feet for those who may have a larger room.)

Step 2. Next measure in your classroom, and draw in the diagram those things that cannot move—windows, door(s), whiteboards or screens, bulletin boards, shelving affixed to walls, wall heaters, and possibly a sink.

Step 3. Then go to the second PowerPoint slide of furniture. Select the set of classroom furniture appropriate for your classroom (lower elementary, upper elementary/middle, middle/high school). From that set, *copy* items onto your floor space slide and *duplicate* them to make as many as needed to match the number you have in your room.

Step 4. Now click and drag furniture pieces into arrangement. When finished, analyze the arrangement in three areas on the previous page.

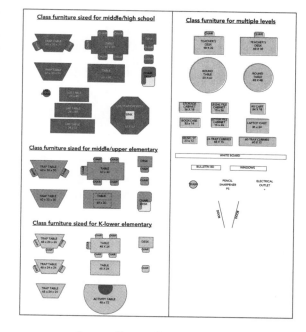

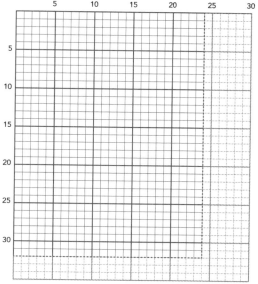

Caution! Students sitting at tables and at desks with a separate chair *seldom* sit scooted up under the table or desk. Rather, their chairs are pushed back somewhat—often for leg room—and the aisle space you thought you had is reduced by 20 percent to as much as 50 percent. Make sure you have a more-than-adequate aisle width to allow you to reach each student easily and without bumping up against seated students.

Enhancing Your Visual and Physical Access

Visual access. Having an open line of vision with each student and making frequent, normal eye contact (think "pupil-to-pupil eye contact"—pun intended) nips a lot of behavior problems in the proverbial bud. The student who's thinking about misbehaving is usually watching to see if you're watching! (At times, you may need to use your "teacher evil eye." Practice in front of a mirror until it cracks—*but* then use this technique sparingly for greatest effect.)

Carefully set the stage!

What ideas do you have to avoid these typical visual access problems?

- Two of the students in each of five small groups of four sit with their backs to the board and screen. Sometimes one tips over in the chair in leaning back and trying to see; often, several of the students with their backs to the board ask a group member what is on the board while others in the small group are trying to listen.

- In alphabetical seating, the shortest student sits at the back of a row. With a basketball player seated in front of her, she has difficulty seeing you and the board.

- The room is deep, and students seated far from the whiteboard and screen squint as they try to see what is there.

- Some students are unable to see the faces of other students speaking and have difficulty following a class discussion. (It's easier to engage in a class discussion with classmates' faces than with the backs of their heads.)

- A student slips out the door without your seeing her leave.

Physical access. Having hip-width aisles (and that width varies), clear of book bags, beside *at least one side* of every student desk prevents problems, as does placing materials and equipment students use (such as reference books, scissors, calculators, turn-in baskets, wastebaskets) where they can easily access them. Also, having your own materials easily accessible cuts out downtime.

What ideas do you have to avoid these typical physical access problems?

- Resource materials on a back shelf are inaccessible to everyone except students sitting in the back row; other students using them walk past one or more class members both there and back—sometimes detouring to drop off a note or speak to another student.

- The turn-in basket sits on a file cabinet behind the teacher's desk, and things periodically disappear from the top of the desk.

- At the pencil sharpener by the door, some students stand and sharpen pencils to a nub as they look out the door.

- There is a frequent traffic congestion at the single wastebasket.

- The tight space where students pick up and return calculators causes problems.

Check the Appendices for possible solutions for these ten access problems. See F: Avoiding Typical Visual Access Problems and G: Avoiding Typical Physical Access Problems.

Some Teacher-Tested Ideas for Improved Visual and Physical Access

Four Problems Solved!

Placing Class Expectations in Students' Line of Vision

When I realized the importance of posting class expectations, I wrote them in large letters and hung the poster on the back wall—where the expectations reinforced me throughout the day. Not the best place.

When I moved them to the front of the room, they were in the students' line of vision and easily referenced.

A colleague of mine may have an even better idea—he places his expectations beside the classroom clock!

Clarifying Student Access to the Class Library

Hanging a shower curtain across our extensive in-class library allowed me to easily signal when library access was and was not allowed.

When the library was "open," I pulled the shower curtain back; when it was "closed," I pulled the shower curtain across to cover the bookshelves.

Keeping Clear Aisles

Plastic laundry baskets solved the problem of aisles cluttered with backpacks.

I labeled three large laundry baskets A–H, I–R, and S–Z and placed them at the front of the room.

As students enter, they remove those things needed for the day's class and then place backpacks in the appropriate basket by their last name.

It requires my keeping track of the time to allow students an extra minute at the end of class to begin getting their packs, but it is well worth it.

Improving Student Access to Dictionaries

Numbering and relocating dictionaries reduced student traffic.

Using clear contact paper, I laminated three-inch-tall red paper numbers on the front of each book of our class set of dictionaries. Then I placed a dictionary in each desk, in number order.

Students no longer need to get up and move to the bookshelf (and sometimes detouring to visit a friend) to use a dictionary—now they can just reach in their desks.

(And although classroom items will sometimes "disappear," I've never lost a dictionary.)

Minimizing Classroom Distractions

Students today have a harder time focusing than in years past. Research shows that student attention spans have decreased in the past ten years (Vidyarthi, 2011), and the number of students diagnosed with ADD-ADHD has risen dramatically (Jensen & Steinhausen, 2015; US Department of Education, National Center for Education Statistics, 2015). Consider that student brains in your classroom have been shaped by an influx of shorter and shorter rapid-fire media images—indeed, the average shot length of Hollywood films has shortened from 8.2 seconds in 1950 to 3.8 seconds in 2010 (Miller, 2014). So what can you do to help your students focus? The first step is identifying the competition, and the second step is neutralizing it.

Consider the following comments from real-life teachers:

> "With five students dealing with ADD, I realized that multiple hanging mobiles were not the best idea."

> "When I turned students' desks so that no one faced out the windows or could see out the door, it made a difference."

> "Whoever sat in the desk by the computer was frequently disengaged. I decided it wasn't the student but the location."

> "I gave up trying to keep cell phones out of class and just required students to place their phones facedown on the right top corner of their desks—where I could see them at all times."

> "A periodic pillowcase over the tarantula cage gave everyone a break, including the spider."

> "I didn't realize that the air conditioner noise in the back of the room made it hard for students seated there to hear me."

> "Then it dawned on me: As the teacher, I can assign seats; sitting with a friend should be an earned privilege, not an inalienable right."

> "Using masking tape on the floor to make arrows to designate a 'one-way traffic' flow for entering and leaving the lab supplies area saved class time and stopped students from jostling one another."

Go "Sherlocking" in your classroom for potential distractors. What things do you identify as your competition? What plans of action will you make to neutralize as many as possible?

_____

_____

_____

_____

Some Teacher-Tested Solutions for Challenging Room Problems

Four More Problems Solved!

Computer Screen Surveillance

The odd floor plan and limited power outlet options of my newly assigned computer lab space (formerly a teachers' lounge) meant that one row of computers sat in an area where seeing all screens at any given time was impossible.

Taking a cue from a local grocery, I strategically placed a full-length mirror (sideways, slightly angled, and high on the wall) so that I could monitor those screens. I had only to glance at the mirror to see what was on every screen.

Middle School Teacher, TN

Creating More Board Space

My portable had one whiteboard and one bulletin board—not nearly enough.

With my principal's permission, I added two whiteboards by attaching (Liquid Nails) pieces of shower wallboard to the side walls. I added bulletin boards by placing several squares of self-sticking cork tiles together. This gave me much-needed work and display space.

Elementary School Teacher, CA

Adjusting Furniture for a Day

As a sub, I soon saw a connection between my control of a class and how well the room arrangement I "inherited" for the day allowed me to make eye contact with all students and to move and stand quickly beside each desk.

I made a point of arriving early to assess a room in which I would be subbing and see if it would allow me to do these two things. If not, I made a few snapshots of the room and then moved student desks to meet these criteria.

At the end of the day, I used the pictures to put everything back as I found it.

High School Teacher, OH

Masking Recreational Distractions

My windowed classroom overlooked the ball field, and a game outside was often more fascinating to students than the academic task at hand. I tried turning desks so students' backs were to the distraction, but lack of air-conditioning meant that the windows were open on warm days, and the sounds of the game floating through the air caused heads to turn.

By sitting in several student desks in my room, I found that the line of vision was primarily through the bottom two panes of each of the six stacked four-paned windows.

I next cut twelve panels of white butcher paper, each slightly larger than a glass pane, and had students draw illustrations on them of historical events we were studying. I then taped the student illustrations to the frames of the bottom twelve panes. This reinforced content and limited distraction.

Middle School Teacher, SC

Arranging Teacher and Student Desks (and Computers)

> Location!
> Location!
> Location!

Two room arrangement questions teachers often ponder are "Where is the best place for my desk?" and "What's the best arrangement for my students' desks?" The answer to both of these is the same: "It depends." There is no one best room arrangement for all types of teaching and learning. Your room should support the type of instruction in which students are to engage. The best location for furniture depends on your goals for your class.

"Where Is the Best Place for the Teacher's Desk?"

It depends on how you want to use it.

IF	THEN
If your desk will be a place for students to pick up and turn in materials, . . .	. . . then students need easy physical access and you need easy visual access.
If your desk will sometimes be used as a one-on-one tutoring station, . . .	. . . then students need easy physical access, but not easy visual access.
If your desk will be the place where you store teaching manuals and materials, . . .	. . . then you need easy physical access.
If your desk will be the place to keep graded papers and confidential materials, . . .	. . . then students should not have easy access and you need easy visual access.
If your desk will sometimes be used as a "place reward" where a student may sit and do work, . . .	. . . then students need easy physical access and you need easy visual access.
If your desk will serve as a "borrowing station" where students may (with permission) borrow items such as a stapler or scissors, or get a tissue, hand sanitizer, and so forth, . . .	. . . then students need easy physical access and you need easy visual access.
If you plan to sit at your desk for extended periods of time grading papers while students work, . . .	. . . then change your plans! Get up from your desk and find another time to grade papers—a teacher on the feet is worth several on the seat!

"What's the Best Arrangement for Students' Desks?"

It depends on what you want students to do.

IF	THEN
If students are to work independently, . . .	. . . then use traditional rows or a horseshoe or double-horseshoe arrangement (always with open corners for access) with at least six inches between desk sides. If the room has four-top tables, gender-mixed seating may help; if trapezoid tables, place one student at each end.
If students are to work with a partner, . . .	. . . then push pairs of individual desks together side by side or front to front; for trapezoid tables, place students side by side at the long side or adjacent to or across from one another.
If students are to work in small groups, . . .	. . . then use four-top tables, push two trapezoid tables long sides together, or move individual desks into groups.
If students are to engage in a whole-class group discussion, . . .	. . . then seek an arrangement where students can see one another's faces. (It's difficult to have a discussion with the back of someone's head!)

Whichever arrangement you choose, remember the importance of student personal space as you arrange desks and equipment. Studies with both elementary and secondary students bear out repeatedly the negative influence of crowding. Allowing less "teacher space" in order to give more "student space" can pay off with better behavior.

"And What About Desks With Computer(s)?"

It depends both on how your room is wired and on your students' seating.

IF	THEN
If there are limited outlets in the room, . . .	. . . then your placement may be limited. Check with a knowledgeable authority before running any type of extension cord.
If there are chalkboards and/or a manual pencil sharpener in the room, . . .	. . . then keep computer(s) away from chalk dust and/or pencil shavings as these can cause damage.
If there is bright light in the room, . . .	. . . then place computer screen(s) to avoid any glare.
If you want to be able to see where students are going on the web, . . .	. . . then place computer(s) where screens are easily visible to you. (Consider using an angled wall mirror to help.)
If you do not want students not at the computer to see what is on the screen, . . .	. . . then place computer(s) where the screens are not easily visible to the remainder of the class.
If you want students to work in pairs or trios at the computer, . . .	. . . then make sure there is enough chair room and leg room for all students. (A trap table can work well.)
If you have multiple computers and wish to set up a center, . . .	. . . then try using a U-shaped arrangement where computer users are facing out and you can easily monitor all of them by walking inside the U.
If you must have computer screens facing away from your line of vision, . . .	. . . then mount a mirror on a wall and at an angle that allows you to view those screens.

Consider the amount of space in your room. If you have one of the large or extra-large teacher's desk, downsizing it is a way to create more walkway space and/or personal space for your students. Some teachers find that changing to a workstation designed for computer work is more useful than the traditional teacher's desk.

Preserving Teacher-Desk Privacy

A centrally located, empty student desk solved the problem of students repeatedly asking for (or borrowing/taking) things from my teacher's desk.

On it I placed items students frequently such as a loaded stapler, paper clips, scissors, tissues, hand wipes, paper towels, and a container of sharpened pencils (used ones collected from the floor at the day's end). Students now have a "class desk" of their own from which they may borrow or take as needed.

Teacher-Tested Ideas to Prevent Computer-Related Problems

LOCATION

Locate computers away from chalkboards and pencil sharpeners to avoid dust particles that can clog and harm a computer. Keep the rear of the computer free of clutter to avoid overheating.

Locate computers to the side or back of the room to avoid visual distractions for other students.

SAFETY

If electrical outlets are limited and you must run extension cords, check first with administration about electrical building codes.

If you are allowed to run extension cords, place them in a sleeve that can be purchased for this purpose and affix the sleeve to a baseboard.

Wind excess cord from printers and computers around a table leg where the equipment sits so cords do not dangle where students' feet may become entangled.

Use two-sided Velcro to create a loop and bind multiple loose cords together. Or, use gaffer's tape to tape down cables (like duct tape without the residual goo, used in stage plays and studio work).

DISTRACTION

Use earphones to cut down on noise distraction. If two students are sharing a computer, use a cable splitter (about $10 at an electronics store) to accommodate up to four students.

Mask colorful and distracting screen savers by using Velcro to attach a "Sleeping Now" sign onto the screen frame. Or, use a blank screen saver.

When working with a class on a specific research project, find websites ahead of time, and add them to "favorites" to save valuable time and keep students focused.

Design—or have a student design—a tutorial that takes students step by step through programs such as PowerPoint and Excel.

FACILITATION

Color-code program CDs and DVDs as possible to help students quickly find and file disks. Color-coding disk storage boxes can also assist in keeping programs organized.

Post expectations and guidelines at each computer station—for example, make visible to students *how many* at a time, *how long* they may stay, and *how loud* they (and the computer) may be.

Note: Hundreds of teachers report that extra computer time is a privilege/ reward that students actively seek. Use this knowledge to your and your students' benefit.

Books, handouts, student work, professional materials—if you can't place your hands on materials you want in under thirty seconds, consider them lost. Even if you eventually find them, your time is lost in searching—and TIME is a commodity that there is no way to replace.

Save your time!

Your teacher manuals/materials. Place these in a location quickly accessible, where you do not have to turn your attention and eye contact away from students to retrieve them. As many teacher texts contain answer keys, consider placing these where students will not be tempted to "borrow" them.

Papers you are handing out to students. A rule of thumb is to make three extra copies of each handout for students—one to keep as a record and two extras in case the copy machine misfed or you miscounted. To keep track of class handouts over the course of a grading period or semester or year, make a teacher's master notebook for that class. Place a dated copy of each handout in sequential order in a three-ring binder; you may wish to add any special lecture notes for that day as well. This can serve as (1) a reminder of handouts and information you have provided when you are planning, (2) an excellent way for returning absentees to see what they missed, and (3) a record to inform your teaching in coming years of what things you have used in past lessons.

Classroom sets of books used daily. Select a location in the classroom easily accessible for students to retrieve and replace books without disturbing classmates. Three steps can let you know at a glance if all books in the set are there:

1. Line all the books in the set on the bookshelf.
2. Measure the shelf space length the set occupies when every book is there.
3. Place a strip of colored cloth or plastic tape that same length on the front edge of the shelf.

When books of the set are placed back on the designated tape-marked shelf, there should be a book spine above every inch of the tape. If not, the set is incomplete.

Classroom sets of sequential reference books. Again, select a location easily accessible without disturbing other students. Again, three steps can let you know at a glance if all books in a set are there and are shelved in order for easy retrieval and reference:

1. Line all the books in the set in the correct order on the bookshelf.
2. Run a strip of a contrasting colored plastic tape angled diagonally across the spines of the entire set, starting at the top of the first book and ending at the bottom of the last book.
3. Then use a single-edge blade to slice the tape between each book and trim the two ends even with the edge of the spine.

When all of these books are in order on the shelf, you should see one solid diagonal line. If there is a break in the diagonal line, then a book is missing or out of place.

Organizing Students' Materials: Supplies, Journals, and Papers

There may be student supplies and student work that your students need to access almost daily. Also, throughout the year, you take up work from students. Some papers you keep in the room for students to use periodically, some you may keep on file for the year to document student progress and your assessment of that progress, and some you may periodically send home for parents to see.

Supplies you keep in the classroom for students. In some classes, teachers may provide sets of materials that their students are to use and leave in the classroom. This is true of art supplies for an elementary classroom, rulers and protractors for a middle school math class, and science equipment for a biology or physics or chemistry lab. Consider these three suggestions:

- To save time, assemble sets of needed materials and place in a container ready for a designated student in a group to pick up and return (for example, glue, scissors, rulers). Plastic zip bags work well. (To help bags lay flat, barely snip a bottom corner for air to escape.)

- To keep track of items, number the items and number the students or student pairs or student groups. Have students use only those items with the same number as their student number or pair number or group number.

- To keep sets complete and items working, provide a checklist for students to examine materials and equipment in their set, and determine if everything is there and working before they put that set away. Students can sign and turn in this list to you.

Also, some teachers find having a designated spot on a shelf for a "student set" of things that students often ask to borrow from the teacher's desk allows them to tend to their needs without interrupting the teacher or handling items on the teacher's desk. Such a set might include items such as a loaded stapler, a staple remover, a pencil cup, a bottle of hand sanitizer, a box of tissues, a hole punch, and a ruler.

Journals you keep in the classroom for students. Teachers who have students journal in class find this works better when journals are kept in the classroom. Consider two possibilities for organizing and storing journals:

- For lightweight journals (such as a folder with a few sheets of paper), string a clothesline along a wall, and have students use a pincher clothespin to hang up journals.

- For weightier journals, use a storage container such as a milk crate. For multiple classes, use a different colored container for each class. Place crates where they are easily accessible to students.

Papers students use in class. Some teachers use folders to help students organize and keep track of work completed in class. Each student has a two-pocket folder clearly labeled with their name. Possible organization systems include the following:

- One pocket may be designated to hold papers that the student is to complete that day, and the other pocket is to receive the work as it is completed.

- One pocket may hold graded work returned to the student and the other pocket work to be done; here, as the student completes a paper, it is moved to the back of the materials in that pocket.

(Note that for either of these, if the folder has center brads, these can be used to affix assignment directions or content materials.)

Papers you take up from students. Three criteria in collecting student work are accountability, organization, and speed. You want to make sure that (1) no student work slips through the cracks ("I turned it in—you must have lost it."), (2) when papers are turned in, you have a system to keep straight what was turned in when, and (3) valuable class time is not lost in collecting papers.

Some Accountability Ideas

1. *Paper from every student present.* For every written assignment, collect a paper from each student present. If a student lacks the assignment to submit, ask the student to take a piece of paper, head it appropriately, and write the reason for the missing work. Explain that this is to help you as the teacher keep track of work and makeup work. A student's reason may simply be "I do not have the assignment because I was out sick yesterday"; if this is the case, you now have an additional written record to help you keep track of the student's absence. Or, you may read "I do not have the assignment because Mother said I had to wash the dog last night"; if this is the case, you may have a useful piece of documentation for parent conference time—especially if the parent tells you the family has no dog.

2. *Designated paper monitors.* If students pass papers up or across rows, ask the last person in each row, designated as the row's paper monitor, to check that there is a paper from each student in that row. If a paper is missing, the paper monitor requests the written assignment or written explanation (see #1 above). The same is true for papers coming in from students seated in small groups, with one person in each group serving as paper monitor.

3. *Stapled paper sets.* When a class turns in a set of papers, immediately staple that set together. This eliminates the possibility of a paper going astray and your losing a student's work. If the assignment was turned in on time, then it will be in the stapled set of papers. This can help eliminate the "I turned it in, but you must have lost it" ploy.

4. *Initialed class roll.* For independent turning in of papers, have a designated basket for the specific assignment with a printed class roll beside the basket. Each student initials his or her own name or marks it with a provided highlighter before placing the assignment in the basket. You can tell at a glance who has and has not yet submitted work.

Some Organizational Ideas

1. *Student roll numbers.* Teach students a paper heading that includes name, date, title of assignment, and student roll number. Have each student write his or her roll number in the upper left-hand corner of each paper. For a self-contained class, this is simply the number beside each student's name in your roll book. If you teach multiple classes, use a fraction where the roll number is the numerator and the class period is the denominator (for example, $\frac{12}{3}$ would be the twelfth student on third period roll, $\frac{1}{6}$ would be the first person on sixth period roll).

2. *Paper set labels.* As a set of papers comes in, have a designated student paper clamp on the top of the stack a labeled, color-coded three-by-five-inch card that identifies the papers—by subject area if self-contained and by class period if departmentalized. A yellow card with a "3" on it or a blue card with "Math" clipped to the top of a set of papers allows you to tell at a glance what each set of assignment papers is.

3. *Passing papers across.* If students are seated in rows, consider Wong and Wong's (1991) suggestion of having students pass papers across to one designated side (either left or right) of the room rather than to the front of the row (see diagram at right). This allows students to see easily when papers are coming their way, and it eliminates the opportunity for students to whack the person in front of them with a stack of papers in passing them forward. The final student can then either hand the papers to the teacher or clip them together as described in #2.

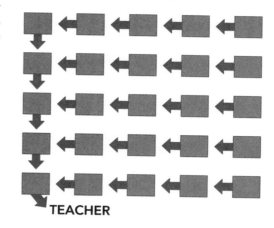

TEACHER

Papers you keep for students (student portfolios). Whether creating official student portfolios or simply keeping together student work for documentation, organization is the key to filing those student materials quickly and accurately so that you can easily access them.

Physical Organization Ideas

1. *Hanging file folders.* One way to organize student work is with a series of hanging folders. If cleared out periodically, you can store three students' interior file folders in each hanging folder; if you keep a whole year's worth, one hanging folder per student may be needed. If you teach one group of students multiple subjects, you may wish to have multiple folders for each student—one for language arts, one for math, and so on.

2. *Color-coded files.* Whether you are self-contained or departmentalized, color-coding can help in organization. For example, if departmentalized with multiple class periods of different students, then use a different colored hanging file (with matching colored folder label) for each—for example, red for first period, blue for second. If self-contained with the same students for multiple subjects, use red for math, blue for language arts, and so forth.

Some Thoughts on Portfolio Content

A portfolio allows the four purposes of assessment: keeping track, checking up, finding out, and summing up. Goals of a portfolio include documenting student growth, providing justification for grades, and having something tangible to share with parents at conference time. Consider carefully what things you will place in the folder to create a "paper trail" of a student's progress.

Papers you send home. Sets of papers sent home weekly are a good method of home-school communication. But here is a word of caution: Teachers report that for some students only the "good" papers make it home for parents to see—the less-than-good ones somehow evaporate between school and home. You can solve this problem by designing a parent or guardian signature sheet affixed to the cover of the packet that has a space for you to write in ink the number of assignments that should be found in the take-home packet for the week.

SIGNATURE SHEET FOR WEEKLY STUDENT WORK		
DATE	# PAGES	PARENT/GUARDIAN SIGNATURE
9/01	3	*Harriet Smithson*
9/08	5	*Harriet Smithson*

Papers you want students to keep for a set period of time—student notebooks. Some teachers want students to keep an organized folder of notes, class work, and homework throughout a specific grading period. Students often need help in organizing skills—some more than others. One way to help students is to keep a master folder yourself of all notes, handouts, assignments, and so on. This becomes a class folder for reference that you can then lend to students to check and see if they have everything dated and organized in their own folders. (It also serves as a reminder for you of what has been assigned and given out when. If you teach multiple classes, keep a folder for each class—even though you may teach three classes of Algebra I or American History, all classes often do not progress at the same pace.)

Folder organization could take several strategies—for example, divisions of homework, handouts, notes, and quizzes; or spelling, grammar, literature, and vocabulary; or math, reading, social studies, and science.

Organizing Classroom Sets of Equipment for Students' Use

A complete classroom set of equipment is wonderful—one of "something" for every student in the class to use. However, a classroom set with one or more items missing is frustrating. Maintaining complete "sets of stuff" that are easily accessible to students improves students' behavior and the quality of learning. Here are some ideas teachers report work well for them:

Organize sets of "stuff!"

MANIPULATIVES SETS

My students frequently use sets of manipulatives at their desks. I prepare one set of manipulatives for each student (plus extras for any new students), place each set in a plastic zip bag, and use a permanent marker to label bags with consecutive numbers. (I snip a corner tip, squeeze out the air, and bags lie flat.) I set out the bags in order in a tote bin. My students know and use their class number to indicate which bag to pick up and take back to their desks, and they replace their bag in number order also. A designated student or I can quickly check through bags to see if all are there.

GROUP TOTES

For small-group activities, I prepare a Group Tote, with the group designated by color or a bold number on the side. I place in it the appropriate number of scissors, rulers, glue sticks, math counters, and so forth students in that group will need. One student in each group is assigned the weekly task of bringing that tote to his or her group each day, for checking to see that the appropriate number of items are in the tote at the end of the activity, and for returning the tote to its appropriate cupboard space.

THE PENCIL POT

For me, the most basic piece of equipment in the classroom is a pencil, and my goal is to engage students academically rather than fuss about pencils. So, I instituted the "pencil pot." In an attractive flowerpot, I placed about a dozen sharpened pencils—discards picked up from the floor over a few days plus a couple of new ones I found. I taped a card with two lines to the pot: NEED ONE? TAKE ONE! / GOT AN EXTRA? DROP IT IN! Students knew that if they needed a fresh, sharpened pencil during the period, they could exchange their dull or broken one. During homeroom, different students were assigned the task of sharpening the pencil pot pencils for the day. It works!

Teacher-Tested Ideas for Flexible Student Desk Arrangements

Sometimes you want an arrangement that is flexible and allows students to engage as a whole group with you, in partners with one another, and/or in small groups. The arrangements that follow show how three teachers have accomplished this. (Note that teachers who change desk arrangements during the day or class typically have a "home arrangement," with proper placement of each right front desk leg marked in some way on the floor.)

Butterfly Desks—Independent Work, Partners, Collaborative Groups of Four

A middle school teacher used a "butterfly" desk arrangement. The inner front legs of each pair of desks rested in a small empty coffee can. Pairs of desks could swing out at a 45-degree angle for student independent work; pairs could swing together side by side or front to front for study partners. For group work, desk pairs would first swing front to front, and then each two pairs scoot together to form a group of four.

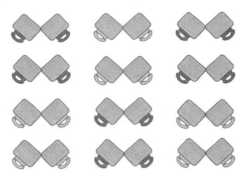

Hip-Width Aisles—Independent Work, Partners, Collaborative Groups of Three or Four

A high school teacher had too many desks in too small a room. He arranged desks in pairs with six inches between each pair, and with a hip-width walking aisle between the pairs of desks. This allowed him direct physical access to each student during independent work. For partner work, students moved pairs of desks together. For group work, the first and third rows turned around, and each facing foursome scooted together while students on the back row turned and formed two groups of three.

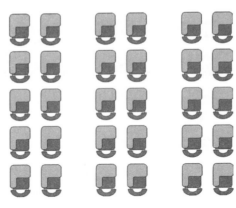

L-Shaped—Independent Work and Collaborative Groups of Four

An elementary school teacher wanted students to transition quickly between whole-group instruction and collaborative group work. She used an "L-formation" of four desks to allow eye contact with all students for content delivery. Then for group work, the extended desk in four outside groups would swing around 90 degrees and moved up to touch the center desk. In the center group, the two end desks would swing around 90 degrees and scoot in to form a square.

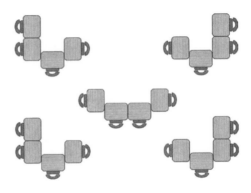

Consider that your room and materials arrangement sends a constant message to students; also consider that any arrangement either supports or hinders your instructional efforts.

DO keep your needed teacher materials close at hand and organized.

AVOID overdecorating!

Bright, fluttering mobiles and lots of loud colors compete for students' attention.

DO allow each student as much personal space as possible.

AVOID crowding students close together, allowing little or no personal space.

DO make sure you can see and reach all students (hip-width aisles!).

AVOID allowing students' book bags and backpacks to congest the aisles.

DO adjust the room arrangement to support the type of teaching and learning you want to occur in that classroom space.

AVOID seating students in desks that touch or at group tables and then telling them "no talking."

When you and the furniture send mixed messages, it is confusing.

Source: Harris and Tomick (2016, p. 15).

Key Takeaways: New and/or Reinforced Ideas on Room and Materials Arrangement

Possible Applications: Things I Plan to Try in My Classroom

Please use the following space to jot down (1) key ideas you want to remember—whether new or a reinforcement of your current knowledge and beliefs—and (2) ideas you want to remember to try in your classroom. In the second column, it may help to keep track if you consecutively number the ideas so you can check them off as you try them.

KEY TAKEAWAYS: New and/or Reinforced Ideas	POSSIBLE APPLICATIONS: Things I Plan to Try in My Classroom

EXPECTATIONS AND PROCEDURES BY WHICH YOUR CLASSROOM RUNS

"The greatest sign of success
for a teacher is to be able to say,
'The children are now working
as if I did not exist.'"

—Maria Montessori
Educator and physician

The *What* and *Why* of Expectations and Procedures

Once you have optimally set the stage for learning, the next step is to consider how you want the players to interact with one another and to get things done. You have arranged the classroom to send visual signals of behavior expectation; now, the task is to make these expectations visible and clear with words and actions. These expectations fall into the categories of *class expectations* and *class procedures*—and possibly *class goals* as well. (Note that we use the term *expectations* in place of *rules* to focus on communicating desirable behaviors in a positive framework that encourages responsibility.)

Visible Expectations!

Students are familiar with expectations (also referred to as rules, and in some secondary classrooms as policy), and with procedures (also referred to as routines), and with goals through games they have played. Whether tag, Monopoly, or chess, every game has its rules and expectations. In Monopoly, if you land on Boardwalk and another player owns it, you are expected to pay "rent" to the owner; if you pass Go, you expect to get $200. Every game has its procedures. In Monopoly, if the play is moving clockwise and if a player gets confused and starts to play out of turn, you correct and remind the player of the correct direction of turns. Every game has goals. In Monopoly, a goal is to own board spaces all of one color, and when you reach that goal you get rewarded by getting more rent.

A smoothly running classroom is based on students' understanding of the behaviors expected of them and knowing how and when to do those behaviors. A well "thought out and taught out" (1) set of class expectations and (2) collection of class procedures increase the probability that students will be successful in following expectations and procedures—and thus, everyone enjoys a more pleasant classroom, and more teaching and learning occur. Keep in mind that few students have ever passed "Mind Reading 101" (including yourself!), and unless you explicitly explain, demonstrate, and rehearse desired behaviors, students will not be able to do them.

Expectations (or rules) and procedures (or routines) provide the framework for student interactions within your classroom. When students understand this framework, they begin to understand how to "build" interactions with other students and how to get things done. Your consistency in adhering to the expectations and procedures of your classroom will highly influence how successful your students are at following them. This is especially true of students dealing with emotional and behavioral disorders (EBDs).

Consider this after-school student exchange:

"Come join us in a game of confustication Saturday afternoon?"

"Sure thing! But . . . how do you play?"

"Oh, you make up the rules as you go along—"

"Huh?"

"And then you yell at the players when they don't understand."

"But that's not . . . Oh, I get it. . . . It's like last year's classroom."

What do we know from research that relates to expectations and procedures? Looking in classrooms reveals the following:

- In classrooms where expectations and procedures are specifically taught and consistently reinforced, those students are less off task, more academically engaged, and have higher academic achievement (Evertson & Emmer, 1982; Johnson, Stoner, & Green, 1996; Simonsen, Fairbanks, Briesch, Myers, & Sugai, 2008).

- Five is the average number of class expectations; from three to five is an optimal number for those challenging students exhibiting behavior problems. Having too many expectations can lead to unintentional violations or the feeling of an overly controlling environment from a student's point of view. The number of procedures, however, may be much larger (Boostrom, 1991; Kostewicz, Ruhl, & Kubina, 2008).

- In classrooms where students engage in discussion for developing and/or defining the class expectations, they are more likely to follow them (Capizzi, 2009; Schaps & Solomon, 2003).

- In classrooms where teachers focus more on the rationale for having expectations than on the punishment for breaking them, those students demonstrate a better self-control (Rohrkemper, 1984; Way, 2011).

- In both elementary and secondary classrooms, off-task behavior is typically twice the class average during a transition. However, teachers who plan and teach transition procedures reduce student off-task behavior and increase academic learning time (Arlin, 1979; Evertson, 1985, 1989; Haydon, DeGreg, Maheady, & Hunter, 2012; Hine, Ardoin, & Foster, 2015).

- Providing students with cues decreases undesirable behavior in middle school classrooms, elementary school recess, and high school hallways (De Pry & Sugai, 2002; Lewis, Colvin, & Sugai, 2000; Oswald, San Fran, & Johnson, 2005).

- In classrooms where teachers first give students a time frame for an activity or routine and then give a two-minute warning before it is to end, students are more likely to complete the activity or routine and make the transition to the next activity in a timely manner (Codding & Smyth, 2008; Kern & Clemens, 2007; Kounin, 1970).

- Ignoring student misbehavior, once lauded as an effective method of handling student misbehavior, may be effective in the short term; however, students themselves have reported the method ineffective. Ultimately, ignoring violations of rules and expectations will undermine a classroom management system (Boysen, 2012).

Reflect on each of the previously given items for a few moments, and think about things these findings suggest you might do or do differently to have expectations and procedures function smoothly in your classroom. Use the Reflections on Area Three page at the end of this area to jot down your thoughts.

Check where you fall in each of the items that follow. Any one of these areas can make a definite difference in students' understanding and following class expectations. A YES for each item means you have addressed an important component of classroom expectations. Anything less than YES is an area where a change could improve students' understanding of the class expectations.

Communicating Expectations!

Concerning the Expectations for My Classroom . . .	NO		SOMEWHAT		YES
1. There are no more than six of them.	○	○	○	○	○
2. Every expectation is something that is true at *all* times.	○	○	○	○	○
3. Every expectation is stated positively.	○	○	○	○	○
4. Every expectation is stated behaviorally—beginning with an active verb telling students what to DO.	○	○	○	○	○
5. Every expectation is stated in clear and meaningful language for my students.	○	○	○	○	○
6. I have these expectations posted in my room—large enough to read and in students' line of vision.	○	○	○	○	○
7. Every student has a copy of these expectations in his or her possession.	○	○	○	○	○
8. I have on file for each student a copy of the expectations signed by a parent or guardian.	○	○	○	○	○
9. I involved my students in developing our classroom expectations.	○	○	○	○	○
10. I involved my students in giving specific examples of what each expectation would look, sound, and feel like in our classroom.	○	○	○	○	○
11. I engaged my students in a discussion of why each expectation is valuable to them in our classroom.	○	○	○	○	○
12. I spent time having students role-play positive examples of following our class expectations.	○	○	○	○	○
13. I would be willing to live by these expectations if I were a student.	○	○	○	○	○
14. I am positive that each expectation is really an expectation and not a *procedure* or a *goal*.	○	○	○	○	○

Self-Assessment #3b:
Analyzing Current Classroom Procedures

Teaching the "How-Tos"!

Check where you fall in each of the items in the following chart. A YES for each item means you have addressed an important component of classroom procedures. Anything less than YES is an area where a change could improve students' understanding of the class procedures.

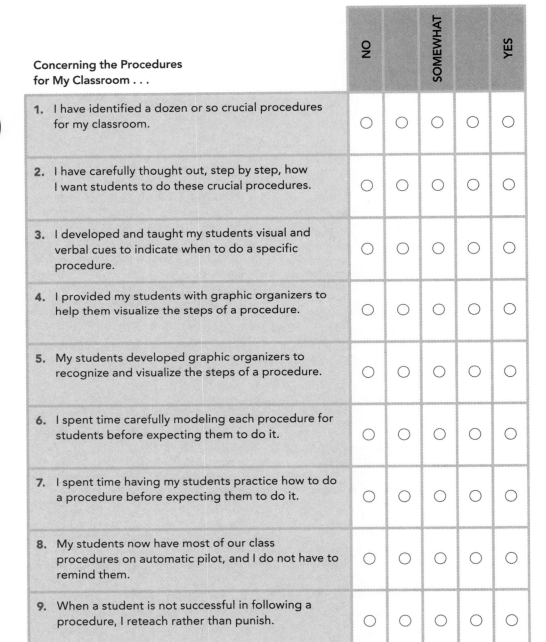

Concerning the Procedures for My Classroom . . .	NO		SOMEWHAT		YES
1. I have identified a dozen or so crucial procedures for my classroom.	○	○	○	○	○
2. I have carefully thought out, step by step, how I want students to do these crucial procedures.	○	○	○	○	○
3. I developed and taught my students visual and verbal cues to indicate when to do a specific procedure.	○	○	○	○	○
4. I provided my students with graphic organizers to help them visualize the steps of a procedure.	○	○	○	○	○
5. My students developed graphic organizers to recognize and visualize the steps of a procedure.	○	○	○	○	○
6. I spent time carefully modeling each procedure for students before expecting them to do it.	○	○	○	○	○
7. I spent time having my students practice how to do a procedure before expecting them to do it.	○	○	○	○	○
8. My students now have most of our class procedures on automatic pilot, and I do not have to remind them.	○	○	○	○	○
9. When a student is not successful in following a procedure, I reteach rather than punish.	○	○	○	○	○

The Value of Spending Time on Teaching Expectations and Procedures

So you're into the school year, things are a bit (or more) bumpy, and you wish you could get more time just to *teach*. Do you remember the mechanic in the oil filter ad some years ago who advised car owners that "You can pay me now . . . or pay me more later"? The message was that you could either pay the cost of a somewhat-expensive oil filter to begin with, or you could pay the cost of a much more expensive engine repair later. The fact is, if you did not spend a goodly portion of the first few weeks of school teaching and having students actually practice how to follow the expectations and procedures successfully, then chances are you are now paying for it in lost teaching time. (And what is a "goodly portion"? Some studies indicate up to 37 percent for elementary teachers and 25 percent for secondary teachers.)

> It's worth the time!

Looking in classrooms reveals that teachers who dedicate time at the beginning of the school year to develop, teach, and consistently reinforce class expectations and procedures reduce student off-task behavior by more than half for the remainder of the year and get back more time to teach the remainder of the year; as a result, their students show higher academic achievement at the end of the year (Good & Brophy, 2008). Moreover, the classroom is a more pleasant place for both teacher and students.

In the past twenty-five years, over two thousand teachers participated in class management workshops (with workshop follow-up) with one of the authors of this book. Again and again, these teachers (from forty-three states and one American territory) identified the teaching and rehearsing of class expectations (or rules) and procedures as the area that made the greatest positive difference in their classrooms. They repeatedly reported that the cost-benefit ratio of the time they invested in these nonacademics and the resulting increase in time to teach the academics was well worth their efforts. Without having constantly to correct and reprimand students for undesirable behavior, and with procedures on automatic pilot, students got more work done and teachers experienced less stress.

The beginning of the year has come and gone, but it is never too late to invest time in teaching the nonacademics to get back more time to teach the academics for the remainder of the year—not to mention a more pleasant class climate for everyone. Taking time NOW to revisit, revise, and teach or reteach class expectations and procedures is a win-win for everyone.

Research has pointed to the importance of revisiting classroom expectations throughout the school year (Wong, Wong, Rogers, & Brooks, 2012). Teachers who have chosen to revisit, review, and revise as needed report that they are able to make changes that result in a positive difference even as late into the school year as after spring break.

Guidelines for Class Rules for Students With and Without an Emotional and Behavioral Disorder

Guidelines for Class Rules!

In a review of fifty years of research, Alter and Haydon (2017) discovered seven features of classroom rules and their effective implementation:

1. While there is no magic number for class rules, from three to five is the recommendation.

2. Creating rules with students in a collaborative manner is often recommended, but some (with a more behaviorist and less relationship-based approach) have argued against this practice.

3. When possible, rules should be stated positively. It is better to tell students what TO do rather than what NOT to do. (The brain processes the verb; thus, the lifeguard shout "Please, walk!" is often more effective than "Don't run!")

4. Rules should be stated in specific rather than general terms. If rules are generic, be sure to explain what it "looks like" to follow the rule. (No student has ever passed Mind Reading 101!)

5. Rules should be publicly displayed, easily seen (location), and easily read (font size).

6. Similar to #4, students should be taught the rules (refer to pages 55–56). It is not enough just to display them in the classroom.

7. There should be both positive (for following) and negative (for violating) consequences tied to rules, and these should be reviewed beforehand so as not to be a surprise (this is especially important for negative consequences).

Specific to students with EBDs, a decision-making guide with six questions follows for teachers to use when creating classroom rules (Kostewicz et al., 2008). You will note the guidelines for rules regarding students with EBDs are fairly similar to the guidelines for all students.

1. **Who creates rules?** Because students with EBDs respond better to environments with established boundaries, it is best for teachers to create rules for students, using prior knowledge of students' needs (from personal experience, research, and/or other teachers) as they do so.

2. **For what behaviors should there be rules?** Rules should be in place to address severe student behaviors (such as physical aggression) and chronic minor behaviors.

3. **How should I word the rules?** Positively stated, behavior-specific rules are best for students with EBDs.

4. **How many rules do I need?** Three to five is best for students with EBDs.

5. **How do I let students know the rules of the classroom?** Display them in a public place for all to see, and teach them using direct instruction (such as teacher modeling of examples and nonexamples).

6. **How do I support students in following rules?** After teaching a rule, observe students carefully and look for any struggles that may be due to preskill deficits. Then, provide more individual attention to students based on their needs.

Your answers to four crucial questions determine the effectiveness of your classroom expectations:

1. Are each of your classroom expectations truly "expectations"—or are they really something else masquerading as an expectation?

2. Do your students buy in to the expectations as valuable to them personally?

3. Do your students know what each expectation looks like, sounds like, and feels like in action?

4. Are you consistent in your reinforcing of the expectations?

What are your answers?

We said earlier that more learning and less hassle occurs in classrooms where teachers are perceived as fair, caring, and consistent (Jones & Vesilind, 1995). That "fair" thing is a big thing. One of the most common reasons students will choose to challenge a teacher's authority is if they perceive the teacher as "unfair." (Think about it: How do YOU feel when you think something or someone is unfair?) A common cause of the perception of "unfairness" occurs when we as teachers blur together class expectations, procedures, and goals. Why? It relates to what students—and adults—expect to be linked to each (more about that in a few pages . . .).

Here are a dozen statements that are a combination of expectations, procedures, and goals. Before reading any further, make your best guess if each would be considered an expectation (E), procedure (P), or goal (G) by writing the letter on the line before each statement.

1. _____ Think and make wise choices.

2. _____ Use a purple crayon to correct your work in any class-checking session.

3. _____ Speak at appropriate times, and use appropriate voice and language.

4. _____ Sharpen pencils before class; if yours breaks, borrow one from the pencil pot.

5. _____ Be in your chair and ready to begin when the bell rings.

6. _____ In whole-class discussion, raise your hand and wait to be called on.

7. _____ Show respect to others and to yourself.

8. _____ Follow directions correctly the first time.

9. _____ Bring all needed materials to class.

10. _____ Keep hands, feet, and objects to yourself.

11. _____ In computer lab, place the red plastic cup on top of the yellow and green ones to signal a need for assistance.

12. _____ Bring a positive attitude to class.

After you complete this area, please revisit these statements and make any changes you wish. Then see Appendix H: Expectations, Procedures, and Goals for an explanation of each item.

Distinguishing Among Expectations and Procedures and Goals

(Are the Expectations Truly Expectations?)

Separate these three!

It is crucial to differentiate among these three categories for two reasons: (1) It helps you organize your thoughts about your expectations of students, which then helps you communicate them better. (2) It helps students understand which things stay the same at all times and which ones change in different situations. This second reason is a crucial factor in your students seeing you as a "fair" teacher. The primary cause of a student's challenging a teacher's authority is if the student *perceives* the teacher as "unfair."

As previously stated, frequently this perception comes from a teacher's failure to distinguish among expectations, procedures, and goals. Consider some of the distinguishing features of each group in the following chart.

EXPECTATIONS IN YOUR CLASSROOM (the Have-Tos)	PROCEDURES IN YOUR CLASSROOM (the How-Tos)	GOALS IN YOUR CLASSROOM (the Hope-Tos)
Expectations address relationships with others, time, space, and materials.	Procedures address ways to get things done.	Goals address areas of attitude and mental behavior.
Expectations are general behavioral expectations.	Procedures are specific ways of "how to do it."	Goals are generic desirable emotional and mental attributes and activities.
Expectations probably number from three to six.	Procedures probably number over one hundred.	Stated goals for students may number from zero to about five.
Expectations are in place at all times.	Procedures change with the situation.	Goals are desirable at all times.
A student's not following an expectation results in a disciplinary consequence.	A student's not following a procedure results in a reteaching consequence.	A student's nearing or achieving a goal results in a positive consequence of verbal praise.

Sources: The first two columns are adapted from Evertson and Harris (2003), and the third column is adapted from Harris and Tomick (2016, p. 28).

Look at that bottom row in the chart. Remember we said that students—and adults—have different expectations linked to these three categories? When they are not a match, things are "not fair." Note that the word *consequence* refers to a logical result of a previous act—not necessarily a negative experience.

Expectations (rules) are the "have-tos" of your classroom. They address student (and teacher) relationships with others, time, space, and materials (for example, *talk at appropriate times and use appropriate voices* or *keep hands, feet, and objects to yourself*). Expectations are posted on classroom walls and sent home for parent signatures. Failure to follow an expectation may result in a negative consequence. Consider the following chart:

EXPECTATIONS SHOULD BE . . .	BECAUSE . . .
Easily observed	It should be quick and easy for you to tell objectively if a student is following an expectation.
Simply stated	The KISS principle (keep it short and simple) increases the likelihood of students' understanding.
Positively stated	The brain hears the action word—if you say "no running" or "do not yell," the brain processes *running* and *yell*.
Behaviorally stated	Telling students what to DO, using an action verb, communicates much more than telling them how to "be."
Physically doable	You cannot override physical discomfort—and you cannot legislate bladders.
Always true	That's what makes it an expectation.

Procedures are the "how-tos" of your classroom. They address ways to get things done (for example, *place finished papers in the yellow basket* or *line up for lunch*). Procedures are demonstrated, explained, and practiced. Failure to follow a procedure may result in reteaching through demonstration, explanation, and practice. Note that specific procedures (such as *in class discussion, raise your hand and wait to be called on; during a test, do not talk; in small-group work, use your quiet voice; when presenting to the class, speak so everyone can hear you*) can help students follow a more general expectation (*speak at appropriate times and use appropriate voice and language*) in a designated situation.

Goals are the "hope-tos" of your classroom. They are *not* "going-to-school" skills, but they *are* target attitudes and mental behaviors you hope students will master—things like *bring a positive attitude to class, follow directions the first time, think and make wise choices,* and *always do your best.* Goals are seldom made public in a classroom, although some teachers choose to involve students in developing goals and creating a public display of them as a reminder. Success in nearing or achieving a goal may result in a positive consequence of verbal praise.

Beware of statements in the category of "goals" trying to sneak in as expectations. Goals are fine things to have. We praise students when they move in the direction of a goal. But admit it. Even you do not successfully achieve all four examples listed in the previous paragraph every day, so they surely could not be expectations for students!"

Two Sample Goals Bulletin Boards

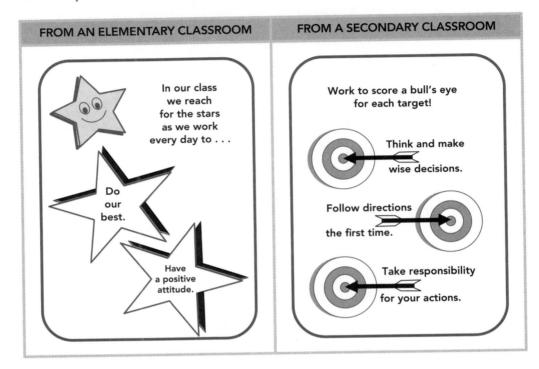

FROM AN ELEMENTARY CLASSROOM	FROM A SECONDARY CLASSROOM
In our class we reach for the stars as we work every day to . . . Do our best. Have a positive attitude.	Work to score a bull's eye for each target! Think and make wise decisions. Follow directions the first time. Take responsibility for your actions.

Some Classroom Expectations Common to Effective Classrooms

COMMON TO ELEMENTARY CLASSROOMS	COMMON TO SECONDARY CLASSROOMS
1. Show respect to all people.	1. Show respect to all people.
2. Show respect to other people's property.	2. Show respect to other people's property.
3. Talk at appropriate times, and use appropriate voices.	3. Talk at appropriate times using appropriate language.
4. Keep hands, feet, and objects to yourself.	4. Bring all needed materials to class.
5. Follow all school rules/expectations.	5. Be seated and ready to begin when the bell rings.
	6. Obey all school rules.

Source: Adapted from Evertson and Harris (2003).

Developing Student Buy-In to Class Expectations

(Do Students Feel an Ownership of the Expectations?)

Students are much more likely to buy into class expectations if they have had a part in some way in the development and/or defining of the expectations. Teachers report again and again that involving students in some way—either developing or defining classroom expectations, or both—has many benefits, and these can be summarized with two generalizations:

> **Involve students as is possible.**

1. **Student ownership.** When students are involved in developing and/or defining class expectations, they are more willing both to abide by the expectations themselves and to encourage others to abide by them as well.

2. **Teacher knowledge.** When you engage students in developing and/or defining class expectations, it allows you to see what students value—their picture of a good classroom.

As yours is the signature on the contract, you are the one responsible for the classroom. Involving students in development of class expectations is NOT about abdicating this authority; rather, it is about inviting students to have—or perceive that they have—a part in shaping the "constitution" under which they will live. Teachers tell us again and again that there are multiple benefits of involving students in developing classroom expectations and that the school year proceeds more smoothly when students have had this involvement.

Teachers report different levels of personal comfort in involving students in developing class expectations. It depends on the teacher (personal beliefs of how students learn best and past experiences with students), the school (school philosophy and community norms and expectations), and the students (personalities, past experiences, and maturity levels). Let's consider two possible approaches to involving students in class expectations. The first, a revision activity presented as a lesson outline, is one that one of the authors of this book has used with some classes. The second, a defining activity, is also one she has used with some classes; it depended on the class.

The lesson outline on the next two pages uses a "think-write-share-then-categorize" technique developed by Hilda Taba (Taba, Durkin, Fraenkel, & McNaughton, 1971) that many teachers of Grades 3 through 12 report using at the beginning of the school year, slightly revised for midyear use. (Teachers in Grades K–2 use a similar technique but omit the "write" step.) Interestingly, teachers who have multiple sets of students each day (such as art, music, PE, departmentalized middle school, departmentalized high school) report that when they use this process, their several classes still end up with the same set of expectations. Some have criticized this lesson plan as having the teacher still in control of the expectations, not the students. Yes. That is the signature on the contract. It is the *teacher* who has responsibility for student order and safety and learning in the classroom.

Involving Students in Revising Expectations—
A Possible Lesson Plan

(The following is suggested as written for Grades 3 and above; for Grades K–2, a teacher-scribed version is possible.)

One Way of Involving Students in Revising Class Expectations

1. Set the rationale with your students.

    Explain to the class: *It's time we revisited our classroom expectations. We may keep some of them, we may change some of them, but it's time we took a look at them. Since we all work together throughout the school year, our classroom needs a set of expectations that helps everyone feel safe and comfortable in our room and lets everyone know what is expected of them.*

    Elicit and accept student comments on rationale: *Can anyone think of any other reasons classroom expectations could be important for us?*

2. Have students individually generate ideas of what class expectations could cover.

    Say: *Please take paper and pencil, and write down at least three things you think our class expectations should cover. (Allow three minutes for students to think and write; walk around among all students as they write.)*

3. Have students share ideas with the class, and write them on the board.

    Say: *Let's make a list of all the things that came to mind. Will someone please start our list with something you think is important, and we will continue until all our ideas are listed? (Accept and write each student response; follow each response with "Why do you think that is important?" Continue to encourage students to share ideas and build the written list. If no student lists a concern that is important to you as the teacher, such as "bring all needed materials," remind students that you are a member of the class, too, and add the item you value and tell why.)*

4. Have students group items that could go together because they are alike in some way; have them give a title to each group.

    Say: *As you look at all the things we listed, do you see some things that could go together because they are alike in some way? (Go to the board, and begin making groups of the items as students suggest which ones could go together. As a student suggests a group, ask, "Why do you think those could go together?" and "What might be a title for this group?")*

5. You finalize the class expectations. (After all, *you* are the teacher—the one who is legally responsible for the classroom.)

    Say: *We have listed many important things about working together in our class. Tonight I'm going to read over all of the things you said and tomorrow bring back a list of a few expectations that will cover all of the things you mentioned. We'll go over the list tomorrow and see if it covers everything you've said. (Take a picture of what is on the board for reference.)*

6. THE NEXT DAY: Show the class expectations on the board, and project the image(s) of the picture(s) of the original list of ideas on the board from yesterday.

    Ask: *Does anyone see anything on our original list that might not be covered in the expectations on the board? (If a student asks about a specific item, show how that item is included in the expectations—or better yet, ask another student to explain where it fits.)*

7. THE NEXT STEP: Engage students in role-play to teach and reinforce what the desirable behaviors look like, sound like, and feel like (see the next page).

A more conservative approach in involving students in class expectations is to decide ahead of time what the several classroom expectations will be (typically three to six*), and then as you present each, spend several minutes engaging students in describing in their own words what each expectation would look, sound, and feel like in various situations in their own classroom. This allows you to check if the image of acceptable behaviors in your students' minds matches the image in your own, and it provides you the opportunity to teach what is expected in various classroom situations.

The next step would be to engage students in role-play to demonstrate the desired behaviors (see Teaching Classroom Expectations Through Role-Play on the next two pages).

Caution! If you have more than six expectations, you probably have some goals and procedures masquerading as expectations.

Teaching Classroom Expectations Through Role-Play

(Do Students Know What Each Expectation Looks and Sounds and Feels Like in Action?)

> The most difficult behavior for a child to do is the one he or she has never seen.

Consider the words on the sign at left. Imagine you enter your PE class and the teacher announces, "Today, you will play tennis." You've heard the word *tennis,* but you've never seen a tennis game, much less ever played. How do you feel? What are your chances of success? Wouldn't you like a chance to practice the game a bit before you are held accountable for playing it?

Now imagine you are a student in your classroom. There is a classroom expectation stating, "We will show respect to others and ourselves." You've heard the word *respect,* but you are not sure just what the statement means for *this* classroom. How do you feel? What are your chances for success? Wouldn't you like a chance to practice some of the typical behaviors expected of you before being held accountable for them?

Ideas on class expectations thus far have engaged visual and auditory modalities. But as Dewey said, we *learn by doing.* After demonstrating an example of "respect" in the classroom, give students the opportunity to role-play the desired behaviors in several typical classroom situations. Students get a chance first to "see it in action" and then to "do it"—thus engaging the tactile/kinesthetic modality. (And you get a chance to see your students' interpretation of respect.) The following are possible classroom scenarios you might use to have students demonstrate respect:

1. Two students go to the door and show what respect looks and sounds like when both want to go through the door at the same time.

2. Three students come up and show what respect looks and sounds like when the teacher is talking with one person and the two others each want to be next.

3. Two students come up and show what respect looks and sounds like when one person accidentally picks up another's book or bumps another's desk or drops a jacket.

4. Two students go to the computer and show what respect looks and sounds like when one person's turn is over, but he or she has lost track of the time and the other person's turn is due.

5. A student models respect for others in asking to borrow something (such as pencil, sheet of paper, ruler, eraser) from another student.

In the following chart, first list three or more of the class expectations you wish to use in your classroom; these may be expectations you already have, current expectations you revise and reword in some way, or new expectations you plan to use. Then for each expectation, brainstorm three or more scenarios you could use to have some of your students role-play specific behaviors that show this expectation in action.

EXPECTATION	SCENARIO
1.	1a.
	1b.
	1c.
2.	2a.
	2b.
	2c.
3.	3a.
	3b.
	3c.

Begin by asking those students who you think will know how to do a desired behavior to role-play the scenario. Then call another set of players who are students you think may have difficulty knowing and doing the desired behavior—who have likely just seen it for the first time—to show it again. This gives the second set of students opportunities both to see and to do the desired behavior.

Caution! Teachers report that students often beg to role-play an undesirable behavior as a negative example. This is *NOT a good idea*! Things can get out of control. However, if you as the *teacher* act out the inappropriate behavior, it can appear even *more* inappropriate to make the point—plus you as the teacher remain in control of the "misbehavior situation."

Maintaining Teacher Consistency

(How Can I Stay Consistent in My Expectations and Reinforcement?)

Consistency is the key!

Once you have developed and taught your classroom expectations, success now depends on your consistency in reinforcing them. Four things will help you do this:

1. **Make sure the expectations are really expectations.** The most common reason students will challenge a teacher's authority is if they perceive the teacher is unfair, and a confusion of expectations (rules) with procedures or goals is often the underlying cause of this perception.

2. **Be aware of student behavior.** To be consistent, you must be consciously aware of each of the expectations you have for your students and consciously aware of their behavior. How do you increase your awareness of how students are and are not following expectations? One answer is using your eyes and feet: Your eyes must be able to see all students at all times, with clear lines of vision and no hidey-holes. Your feet must be able to reach any student in a few strides, with walkways clear and free for easy access.

    If you are periodically making eye contact with each student multiple times during a class session, and if you are frequently walking around the room so that you pass beside each student's desk, then your eye contact and physical presence will (1) cause students to focus on what they should be doing and (2) enable you to be more knowledgeable about students' behavior. This combination leads to greater consistency in your reinforcement of expectations.

3. **Be aware of your own behavior.** To be consistent, you must be aware of your own tendencies to be inconsistent. Some days you just feel more mellow and lenient and others more frazzled and strict. Consciously monitoring yourself for consistency can prevent the "slot machine syndrome" from playing out in your classroom. People plunk coins into slot machines in response to that most powerful of reinforcers—intermittent reinforcement (Freeland & Noell, 2002; MacDonald, Ahearn, Parry-Cruwys, Bancroft, & Dube, 2013; Menendez, Payne, & Mayton, 2008). If you are inconsistent in what you *say* you require of students and what you *actually require* of them, then the mixed messages sent make you like the slot machine—because once in a while there is a "payout" of acceptance for an undesirable behavior. And like the slot machine, even a "low percentage payout" is enough to reinforce that undesirable behavior and cause future repetition of it.

4. **Prevent rather than punish.** Consistency does not equate with cruel dictatorship. The goal is not to punish behavior caused by teacher inconsistency but to be consistent to prevent the undesired behavior.

Consider that the more visible your expectations are, the better chance students have to understand them. Student role-play increases visibility of expectations.

DO write expectations that begin with action verbs.

DO make sure each expectation is really an expectation and not a procedure or goal.

DO state expectations positively.

DO develop expectations that align with school expectations.

DO take time to teach the expectations.

DO allow students opportunities to practice desired behaviors.

DO post the expectations in a location constantly visible to all students.

DO provide a copy of your class expectations to your principal, parents, and each student.

DO follow classroom expectations in your own behavior—model for your students what the expectations look like in action.

AVOID assuming students "ought to know how to behave."

AVOID assuming your definitions of *respect* and *appropriate* are the same as your students' definitions.

Source: Harris and Tomick (2016, p. 42).

Think WD-40!

WD-40! Isn't that stuff wonderful in the way it prevents friction and makes things move smoothly? A stuck drawer, a rusty hinge, a squeaking wheel . . . a spray of this magic stuff and the problem is solved—or at least greatly improved. Think of procedures as the WD-40 of your classroom, for they, too, prevent friction and make things run smoothly. Every classroom holds many potential "points of friction" where "things can get stuck"—and these possible problems can be "oiled." What procedures do your students need to know how to do and when to do them for your classroom to run more smoothly? Look at the following suggestions listed by teachers as important student skills in their classrooms. What else would you add for *your* students?

1. Walk quietly into the classroom.

2. Sit properly in a chair at a desk or table.

3. Listen when you give instructions—for example, assume a "listening position" (sitting straight, making eye contact with teacher, mouth closed, hands on desk).

4. Speak audibly in addressing the whole class.

5. Participate appropriately in whole-group discussion.

6. In some instances, raise a hand and wait to be called on to respond.

7. At other times, take turns and avoid talking on top of another person.

8. Or, wait and respond when your name is called from an equity card (see Appendix I: Equity Cards—Not Craft Sticks for this technique to assure fair student participation).

9. Speak in a quiet, conversational voice in small-group work.

10. Use a very quiet twelve-inch voice in paired discussion or peer tutoring.

11. Know when and how to sharpen a pencil.

12. Write legibly.

13. Head a paper.

14. Take notes.

15. Turn in a paper.

16. Line up for lunch (stand, push chairs, form a line, use low voices or keep lips together).

17. Go to and return from lunch (walk, keep hands to selves, use low voices or lips together).

18. Share materials with classmates.

19. Use a pleasant tone of voice with one another.

20. Take turns at or in an activity.

21. Go to and from the restroom.

22. Follow the class opening routine.

23. Follow the class closing routine.

24. _____

25. _____

Look back at the last page, and consider the "successfully doing school" skills your students must master to be their most successful in your classroom. Rate each one by placing one of the following six marks in front of it:

X = This is not relevant to my class or grade level or school.

+ = All my students have it on automatic pilot—no lost class time and I love it!

✓+ = Most students get it most of the time—some lost time but I can live with it.

✓ = It's a little rough—too much lost time and I want to improve it.

✓- = It's ragged—way too much lost time and it's driving me crazy.

✱ = I never thought of it—but it's a great idea, and I want my students to learn it!

Now make a list of what you consider the most important ten to twelve of those skills you marked with a check, check-minus, or asterisk.

✓	SKILLS MY STUDENTS NEED TO KNOW HOW TO DO IN OUR CLASSROOM
	1.
	2.
	3.
	4.
	5.
	6.
	7.
	8.
	9.
	10.
	11.
	12.

In the chart above, rank the skills in the order you plan to (re)teach them, and then check off each one as you cover it in class. (If you teach multiple classes, create additional check-off columns for each class to the left of the chart.)

Teaching Procedures—Step by Step

Students, when you head a paper, write your name on the right top line . . .

There is one key concept to keep in mind in teaching your students classroom procedures: TELLING ≠ TEACHING.

If a teacher speaking the sentence at left stops after only telling students what to do, no actual teaching has taken place, and a frustrating number of papers will repeatedly be headed incorrectly.

Teaching a procedure should follow the same lesson outline as teaching any academic content. It starts with telling—but it does *not* stop there.

1. You start by explaining four things about the skill—what, why, how, and when . . .

	ACADEMIC SKILL EXAMPLE	PROCEDURE EXAMPLE
What is it that students are to do?	We're going to learn how to add.	*We're going to learn how to head a paper.*
Why is the skill worth doing (from the student's point of view)?	Adding is useful when you want to know how much of something you have.	*Heading a paper correctly helps make sure you get full credit for your work.*
How (step by step) do you do it?	Start with the top number . . .	*Start by writing your name . . .*
When do you do it?	Whenever you see the plus sign . . .	*Whenever you write an assignment . . .*

2. You then have students practice the skill.

ACADEMIC SKILL EXAMPLE	PROCEDURE EXAMPLE
Let's work these problems together . . .	*Let's take out a piece of paper and practice . . .*

3. You observe and tell students how they did.

ACADEMIC SKILL EXAMPLE	PROCEDURE EXAMPLE
It looks like we still need some work on . . .	*It looks like we still need some work on . . .*

4. You reteach as needed.

ACADEMIC SKILL EXAMPLE	PROCEDURE EXAMPLE
Let's look again at what we do . . .	*Let's look again at what goes on the top line . . .*

At right you see the several steps needed to teach a procedure.

Concrete definition. A short, simple, clear statement of what the procedure is that students are about to learn shows them the target they are about to learn to hit.

WIIFM rationale. Students are much more willing to follow a procedure if they believe it is of personal benefit to them—hence the WIIFM rationale: **W**hat's **i**n **i**t **f**or **m**e? (And aren't *you* more willing to do something if you believe it is in your own best interest?) Teacher statements of "because I said so" or "because it makes my life easier" carry no weight—and will even backfire with some students. In developing a WIIFM rationale for students, work to remove yourself as the teacher and authority figure from the rationale statement.

Demonstration step by step. Show students what the procedure looks like in action. This can be done by you or by one or more students in your class. If the procedure is a complex one, break it down into manageable steps.

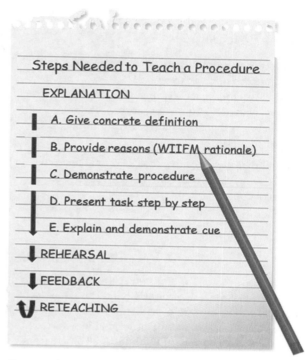

Steps Needed to Teach a Procedure

EXPLANATION
A. Give concrete definition
B. Provide reasons (WIIFM rationale)
C. Demonstrate procedure
D. Present task step by step
E. Explain and demonstrate cue
REHEARSAL
FEEDBACK
RETEACHING

Source: Adapted from Evertson and Harris (2003).

Cues. Visual and auditory cues literally "cue" students when to do a procedure. We use such cues every day—a red light cues drivers and pedestrians to stop, a flag up on a mailbox tells the mail delivery person to pick up an outgoing letter, an ambulance siren cues drivers on the road to pull over, and the ding of the oven timer tells a cook the biscuits are ready.

Rehearsal. We would *never* teach a new athletic skill and not allow students some time to practice that skill! Yet, in teaching procedures, we often skip that very vital step. Can you imagine a coach explaining a play—and maybe even demonstrating the play—and then NOT having players get out on the field or court and *practice* that play! What chance would the players have for successfully using that play in a game? Probably that of the proverbial snowball!

You may be asking, "Do students need to practice every procedure?" The answer is "Only the ones you want them to do." It's rather like the sign that hangs on the wall of a Nashville dentist:

You don't have to floss all your teeth—
only the ones you want to keep.

Feedback. Tell students what they did well and what needs improvement.

Reteaching. Cycle back, clarify, and go through the steps again.

A Few Thoughts on Cues

Voice Level Signals

For noise control, I use a five-step color code to signal voice level for an activity. Purple = silence, blue = whispering (no vocal cord vibration), green = low talking, yellow = presenting, and red = cheering.

I remind students of the "color" of an activity and display an appropriate colored square as a visual cue.

Cue From a Fellow Student

Although I always told them to get ready, Kim was never ready to take social studies notes. One day she exclaimed, "Mr. Smith, I figured out how to be ready! Andre keeps his social studies notes in a red notebook, and if I watch when he gets out that notebook, I know when to get ready for social studies notes."

A Visual Cue for Raised Hands

For two students who could never remember to raise hands and wait to be called on, I made a large, bright red cardboard, raised hand and explained that in group discussion if the big red hand was standing in the board rail at the front of the room, it meant you had to raise your hand and wait to be called for a turn to talk. It took six weeks of my consistently remembering to put up the hand when I wanted students to raise hands, but the results for the remainder of the year were well worth it.

Kitchen Timer for Class Closure

I use a kitchen timer to cue myself and my students for the end of class.

The end of class often sneaked up on me, and I found myself scrambling to give last-minute homework instructions while my students were scrambling to get materials together and leave.

My procedure is to set a timer to sound five minutes before the end of the period. This auditory cue gives me time to close class in an orderly fashion and my students time to write down any assignments, pack up, and leave calmly.

Three-Color Help Signal

Twenty-five-plus students repeatedly calling my name for help in computer lab was frustrating. I made thirty stacked sets of three paper cups, one each red, yellow, and green, and placed a set upside down beside each computer.

If stuck and needing immediate help, a student placed the red cup on top; if no help needed, the green; if student could keep working until I got there but had a question, the yellow.

A Lesson Plan Outline for Teaching a Procedure

Here is a Procedures Lesson Plan Outline enumerating and explaining each of the ten steps needed to develop and teach a classroom procedure (Harris & Tomick, 2016). Begin by selecting a procedure you marked with a check, check-minus, or an asterisk on page 69. Head a sheet of paper with the title of your selected procedure, and write down something for each step. Teach your lesson plan, and see if it makes classroom life smoother for both you and your students.

Procedures Lesson Plan Outline

1. **Procedure and time frame:** What is the procedure you wish to teach, and how much class time do you think it will take to teach it?

2. **Teacher benefit(s):** What do you see as the personal benefit(s) to YOU if all students do this successfully?

3. **Materials and preparation:** What materials will you need, and what prior preparation must you do?

4. **Concrete definition:** What is the most succinct way you can complete this sentence: *Class, today we are going to learn how to . . .* ?

5. **Student rationale—personal WIIFM for students:** What succinct statement can you provide to show students how doing this is of personal benefit to them? (Avoid reference to yourself—making your life easier is not a student motivator.)

6. **Step-by-step demonstration with explanation:** How will you allow the class to *see* what this looks like—either by doing it yourself or having a few students do it?

7. **Cue:** What visual and/or auditory signal can you provide to let students know now is the time to do the procedure?

8. **Rehearsal:** How will you have the class practice the desired procedure?

9. **Feedback:** What will you say to students, depending on how successfully they rehearse the procedure.

10. **Anticipated areas of reteaching:** Where do you think students may have difficulty doing the procedure, and how might you reteach?

Continue selecting from your list on page 69 those procedures you think are important for all students to follow successfully. Sketch out a plan to teach each one. (Remember that sign hanging in the dentist's office?)

Note: Some teachers have found it helpful to create a permanent Word template of these ten steps and use it repeatedly to help in their planning and teaching of procedures.

Read through the following case study, and jot down a list of the specific things you identify that the teacher did to engineer success.

#		
	Subject _____ Your Name	
◯	Assignment _____ Date	

Teaching Students How to Head a Paper

From a Third-Grade Teacher—Suggested Use With Adaptation for All Grades

Before teaching this lesson to his class, Mark LaBlanc prepared and displayed on a side bulletin board in easy visual access of all students a chart page that was an enlargement of a piece of notebook paper like his students will use in class (see above). He began the lesson:

CUE. *"Class, when I say "Turn into group tables," that is your cue to begin. Ready?" (Heads nod.)*

CONCRETE DEFINITION. *"Class, today we are going to learn how to head papers so that you and I can easily identify each assignment that you do. Your heading will include the subject you are working on, the title and/or page number of the assignment, your name, the date, and your own special roll number*.*

RATIONALE. *"We need to head each paper completely so that both you and I can tell what has been done. Complete headings help me make sure you get credit for your work, and they make it easy for you to organize and keep track of papers that you get back.*

DEMONSTRATION STEP-BY-STEP. *"Please take out two clean pieces of notebook paper and a pencil and put everything else off of your desk. (He walks around the room, among the students, and watches as students do this.)*

"Now look at the headed-paper display on the side bulletin board. If that paper were at your desk, please answer out if you can tell me if the holes are on your left or right. (A few students chorus a response of "my left.") Yes, the holes are on the left. Raise your left hand. (Students do this.) The holes of your paper are on the side where your hand is raised—the "windows" side of our classroom.**

"Let's make a pattern page for heading papers. On the <u>left</u> side of your paper, on the top line, write the word 'Subject.' This is where you write the title of Math or English or Science or Spelling or Social Studies——or whatever it is we are doing. (He walks around the room and looks over shoulders to make sure each student has written 'Subject' in the correct area.)

"On the <u>right</u> side of your page on the top line, where you see the words 'Your Name' in the example, write <u>your name</u>—John Smith, Latanya Haversham (here he calls out several students' actual names). (He walks and monitors.)

"On the <u>left</u> side of your page on the <u>second</u> line, under the subject, write 'Assignment.' This is where you would write the page number and/or assignment title—things like 'page 18' or 'Nouns I Saw This Morning.'

"On the <u>right</u> side of the page on the <u>second</u> line, under your name, write 'Date.' Here you will write the date that you actually do the work. (Again, he walks and monitors.)

"In the top left corner, above the holes, write your own special class roll number I gave you this morning.

<u>CUE</u>. "Class, for the first two weeks, I'll have two turn-in baskets—a yellow one labeled "Papers Headed Correctly" and a blue one labeled "Papers NOT Headed Correctly." Check to see which box is the right one for your paper—and if it is the blue box, fix it and put it in the yellow box.

<u>REHEARSAL</u>. "Please take the second piece of paper on your desk and let's do a practice heading. This will give you practice and let me see if I've explained this well for you. For your practice heading, the subject is 'Reading,' the assignment is 'My Favorite Topic,' and the date is today, August 20. After you have headed your paper correctly, please write the following sentence and finish it." (On the board he writes: My favorite thing to read about is _____ because _____.)

<u>FEEDBACK & RETEACHING</u>. (He walks around the room, looking over shoulders as students head papers and write. He commends those who do it right, and re-explains to those who do not.)

(He tells students to place the one they did together as a class in their notebooks for future reference. He instructs them to place the completed papers in the appropriate basket—and winks.)

He also gives students a copy of the graphic organizer shown on the following page to put in their folders for future reference. (Harris & Tomick, 2016, pp. 54–56)

*A student's roll number is the line number where that name is written in the teacher's roll. For multiple classes of students, use a fraction with the roll number on the top and class period on the bottom—for example, $\frac{12}{3}$ is the twelfth person on roll in third period class.

** For students with difficulty distinguishing left from right, a room feature reference helps.

Teaching Procedures With Graphic Organizers

It helps to
see it!

Graphic organizers are an effective tool in teaching procedures (Rock, 2004) as they can be used to spell out a process step by step. Graphic organizers not only help *students* "see" the several ordered steps they must do to complete a given task, but they also make clear to *teachers* the many details their students must master.

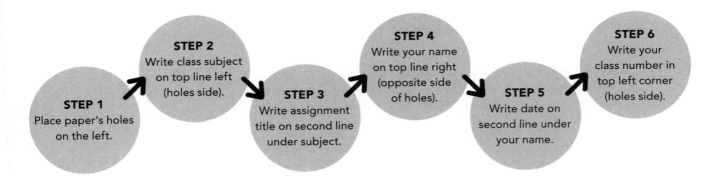

STEP 1
Place paper's holes on the left.

STEP 2
Write class subject on top line left (holes side).

STEP 3
Write assignment title on second line under subject.

STEP 4
Write your name on top line right (opposite side of holes).

STEP 5
Write date on second line under your name.

STEP 6
Write your class number in top left corner (holes side).

Many things you now do on automatic pilot were once actions you had to learn step by step. Ever learn how to drive a stick shift car? To use a new computer program? You learned specific actions and the specific order in which they must be done. You practiced, you made mistakes, you learned from your mistakes, and eventually with more practice you mastered the skill. This is what your students must do when they learn classroom procedures. For visual learners, a graphic organizer helps them see each step and see it in the sequence in which it should be done. Consider how the graphic organizer just shown could help a student "see" the several steps of the procedure for heading a paper described on the previous two pages.

Some teachers use the graphic organizers to clarify their own lesson planning. For example, a graphic organizer can be a useful aid in planning out a class play or field trip. Others have students fill them in with predetermined steps—or even have students work together to generate a step-by-step map for success in mastering a specific "going-to-school skill." The fact that this is also teaching generic sequencing skills is an added classroom bonus! (Note that teachers report handing students an already-filled-out graphic organizer and telling them to follow it has little or no effect on students successfully following a procedure.)

Not only do graphic organizers take students step by step through a process, but also they provide a visual image and visual reinforcement of that process. Engaging students in both auditory and visual directions (i.e., telling *and* showing) offers a double chance at understanding. And when they are writing the steps out on the page, the tactile/kinesthetic modality is also engaged.

Look back over the list of procedures on page 69. Which ones do you think might benefit from teaching with a graphic organizer? What others can you think of that are not on the list?

You'll find four graphic organizers in the Appendices (J: Three-Step Graphic Organizer, K: Four-Step Graphic Organizer, L: Five-Step Graphic Organizer, and M: Six-Step Graphic Organizer) that you may wish to use with your students. Have each student fill out his or her own copy. For a procedure that you want to reinforce consistently for the first few weeks, such as heading a paper, you may choose to enlarge and post the completed graphic organizer as a wall poster.

A Review on Class Expectations and Procedures

To check yourself on some of the key ideas in this area, please take a few minutes to complete the following sentences. Feel free to look back if you need a reminder. When finished, compare your completed sentences with those on N: A Review of Expectations in the Appendices.

1. The most common reason students will challenge a teacher's authority is if they perceive the teacher as _____.

2. The primary reason a teacher may be perceived as unfair is not clearly separating or distinguishing among _____.

3. Spending class time deliberately teaching class expectations (rules) and procedures *and* being consistent in reinforcing these has been shown to produce three results: _____.

4. Relationships with others, time, space, and materials are addressed by _____.

5. Ways to get things done are addressed by _____.

6. Statements that relate to desirable student attitudes and mental behaviors are _____.

7. An expectation is true (when?) _____.

8. A procedure is true (when/where?) _____.

9. Classroom expectations generally number from _____ to _____, while class procedures can number _____.

10. The logical result of a student's not following a classroom expectation is _____.

11. The logical result of a student's messing up on a procedure is _____.

12. The logical result of a student's nearing or achieving a goal is _____.

13. A major benefit of involving students in developing class expectations is _____.

14. The most difficult behavior for a student to do is _____.

15. Students can learn what following an expectation looks like and sounds like in your classroom by (doing what?) _____.

16. The steps for teaching a procedure are _____.

17. Students are much more likely to follow a procedure if they believe there is a _____ _____ (WIIFM).

18. A _____ lets students know *when* to do a procedure.

19. One value for students in using a graphic organizer to teach a procedure is that it _____ _____.

20. The only procedures students need to practice are _____.

Some Dos and Avoids of Teaching Procedures

Consider that the time you spend teaching procedures will multiply in time paid back in academic activity and student learning throughout the remainder of the year.

DO invest time in teaching procedures.

AVOID assuming that if you told them, they understand and can do it.

DO give a WIIFM reason (rationale) why each procedure is worth doing.

AVOID trying to teach too many procedures at one time.

DO have students practice each of the procedures that you want them to do.

DO teach and use cues to signal students when to do a procedure.

DO prioritize procedures, and teach first the ones that students need to know first.

DO sketch out a lesson plan for teaching each important procedure.

DO remember that it takes some students longer than others to master a procedure.

Source: Harris and Tomick (2016, p. 62).

Key Takeaways: New and/or Reinforced Ideas on Teaching Expectations and Procedures

Possible Applications: Things I Plan to Try in My Classroom

Please use the following space to jot down (1) key ideas you want to remember—whether new or a reinforcement of your current knowledge and beliefs—and (2) ideas you want to remember to try in your classroom. In the second column, it may help to keep track if you consecutively number the ideas so you can check them off as you try them.

KEY TAKEAWAYS: New and/or Reinforced Ideas	POSSIBLE APPLICATIONS: Things I Plan to Try in My Classroom

CONSEQUENCES YOU CHOOSE TO USE TO ENCOURAGE APPROPRIATE BEHAVIOR

"Don't look back; you're
not going that way."

—Mary Engelbreit
Artist and author

The *What* and *Why* of Behavior and Consequences

As teachers, we hold two goals. In the immediate here and now, we want a smoothly running classroom with academically engaged students who are interacting respectfully with one another and with their teacher. In the long term, we want intrinsically motivated, self-regulated learners who interact with society as responsible and respectful citizens. How do we help our students achieve both of these goals?

> **What is a consequence?**

Consequences play a part. But keep in mind that a consequence is a *logical result of a previous act,* and that can be either a positive thing (encouraging praise or tangible reward), a negative thing (punishment or corrective discipline), or a "teachable moment" thing. Some consequences are more effective than others in achieving a desired goal, and some consequences will backfire badly.

Let's start with that definition of the word *consequence*: *A consequence is the logical result of a previous act.* In life there are always logical results of our previous acts. Take toothbrushing, for instance. Consider the logical consequences in the following three scenarios as they lead to three different types of logical results:

SCENARIO 1	SCENARIO 2	SCENARIO 3
You choose to brush your teeth twice each day.	You choose never to brush your teeth.	At age three you go to bed without brushing your teeth. Mama calls out, "Good night. Did you remember to brush your teeth?" Honest child that you are, you reply, "No, Mama."
↓	↓	↓
You have no cavities, fresh breath, and more friends.	You have cavities, bad breath, and fewer friends.	Mama says, "Get up and go brush them." And you choose to do so.

Knowledge of consequences shapes human behavior, and these consequences can be identified as *natural* or *planned* and *intrinsic* or *extrinsic*. All are a part of life. But what works with our students? Planned and extrinsic consequences—both positive and negative—result in only short-term behavior change and do little or nothing to cause students to make any internal change (Ryan & Deci, 2000). They fail to increase academic, social, and emotional learning over the long term or to encourage development of self-control and self-discipline. In other words, rewards and punishment do not work to establish continued, long-term desired change.

Now notice that the word *discipline* is not included in that last sentence—for there is a big difference between the effectiveness of discipline and of punishment, with the first possibly productive and the second definitely counterproductive. Nor do you find the term *appropriate praise* (some call this *encouragement*) in the sentence—for this is distinct from rewards (and generic praise) in effectiveness. Both of these can be useful tools in a well-managed classroom (Marshall, 2005).

Positive Consequences of Praise and Rewards

- An overreliance on rewards and positive feedback undermines children's moral motivation (Mader, 2009).

- Intrinsic motivation is an effective motivator across cultures (Haichun, Haiyong, & Ang, 2013; Yun-Jeong & Kelly, 2013).

- Tangible rewards can enhance intrinsic motivation *when* linked with praise that focuses on student effort and reflects the value of the accomplishment (Covington & Müeller, 2001).

- Different types of praise influence students' (1) beliefs about themselves as learners, (2) motivation, and (3) ability to cope with setbacks.

  - *Ability praise* focuses on students' intelligence or skill (for example, "You're so good at this!" or "You must be smart at this kind of problem.") Ability praise implies that a positive evaluation is based on an innate set of abilities over which a student has no control, so failure therefore means a lack of ability. Repeated ability praise statements lead students to value performance over learning and undermine student persistence.

  - *Process praise* focuses on students' efforts, thinking, and strategies (such as, "You must have worked hard on those problems!" or "You discovered a good way to do that."). Process praise implies that skills are malleable, so failure therefore means low effort, not low ability. Repeated process praise statements cause students to see that their efforts and use of effective strategies pay off, and this encourages student persistence.

    In other words, process praise leads students to value learning opportunities and to keep trying, even in the face of setbacks; ability praise leads students to attempt to protect their self-esteem by avoiding challenging tasks (Dweck, 2002; Kamins & Dweck, 1999; Mueller & Dweck, 1998; Rathvon, 2008).

- Positive feedback can be delivered in both oral and written modalities. Written comments allow a student to save and review that comment. Such comments are best kept brief and should be within a student's reading ability (Brookhart, 2008; Yun-Jeong & Kelly, 2013).

Please reflect on each of the previously given items for a few moments, and think about things these findings suggest you might do or do differently in using praise and rewards in your classroom. Use the Reflections on Area Four page at the end of this area to jot down your thoughts.

Negative Consequences and Discipline

- Four downsides of applying negative consequences are (1) they may increase the undesired behavior, (2) the undesired behavior may continue if you are not present, (3) mild negative consequences do not permanently eliminate undesirable behavior, and (4) severe and immediate negative consequences that may be permanently effective are illegal and ethically forbidden (Little & Akin-Little, 2008).

- The following guidelines for "disciplinary" action can help students develop self-control: (1) separate the deed from the doer; (2) teach students they have the power to choose their actions; (3) encourage reflection, self-evaluation, and problem-solving; and (4) teach the rationale for choosing to do a different and acceptable behavior in similar future situations. (Jones & Jones, 2016).

- Students tend to associate expiative punishments (see page 95) with the person giving the punishment rather than with their own misbehavior. Such punishments provide students with the sense that they have the right to retaliate and seek revenge (Jones & Jones, 2016).

- Aggressive management strategies (such as yelling, deliberate embarrassment, group punishment, and sarcasm) increase students' negative perception of the teacher, and even small amounts of such strategies are magnified in students' perceptions (Romi, Lewis, Roache, & Riley, 2011).

- For adolescents, "Firm and fair enforcement of expectations with a dash of humor will work better than rigid requirements for compliance" (Nucci, 2006, p. 726).

- Future confrontations with combative students are minimized when the teacher (1) frequently moves around the room (teacher presence influences behavior), (2) provides expectation reminders in a calm voice, (3) uses frequent, normal eye contact, and (4) provides temporary escapes (such as noticing a student is "about to explode" in anger or frustration and allowing the student to get up and move around or bringing up a topic not related to the lesson to put the student at ease) (Allday, 2011; Lampi, Fenty, & Beaunae, 2005).

- While reprimands are generally ineffective in changing student behavior and can contribute to negative classroom environment, teachers use them. Six elements have been shown to enhance reprimand effectiveness: (1) *promptness* (even a two-minute delay makes it ineffective), (2) *brevity* (student's name and no more than two words), (3) *softness* (audible only to the target student), (4) *proximity* (within three feet of the student), (5) *calmness* (teacher tone shows no emotional upset), and (6) *eye contact* (normal, not the teacher "evil eye") (Rathvon, 2008).

Please reflect on each of the previously given items for a few moments, and think about things these findings suggest you might do or do differently in disciplining students. Use the Reflections on Area Four page at the end of this area to jot down your thoughts.

Self-Assessment #4:
Analyzing Current Classroom Consequences

Check where you fall in each of the items that follow. Any one of these areas can make a definite difference in students' understanding and engaging in appropriate behavior. A YES for each item means you have addressed an important area that leads to student behavioral success. Anything less than YES is an area where a change could improve students' understanding of the behavior desired and motivation to behave in desirable ways.

Behavior and Consequences!

Concerning Behavior and Consequences in My Classroom . . .	NO		SOMEWHAT		YES
1. My students and I have mutually clearly defined what each classroom expectation looks like, sounds like, and feels like in our classroom.	○	○	○	○	○
2. I have carefully separated expectations, procedures, and goals in our classroom.	○	○	○	○	○
3. I have protected my students' dignity and have not yelled, used sarcasm, embarrassed, or shamed anyone publicly.	○	○	○	○	○
4. Thus far this year, I have considered the underlying cause of students' misbehavior before responding.	○	○	○	○	○
5. Thus far this year, I have responded to student misbehavior with a disciplinary rather than punitive approach (see page 96).	○	○	○	○	○
6. I have had my students use graphic organizers or diagrams to visualize the steps of some procedures.	○	○	○	○	○
7. I spent time having my students practice how to do a procedure before I expected them to do it.	○	○	○	○	○
8. When a student has not been successful in following a procedure, I have retaught rather than punished.	○	○	○	○	○
9. My students now have most of our class procedures on automatic pilot, and I do not have to remind them.	○	○	○	○	○
10. When I have praised a student, I focused on the student, the product, and/or the behavior choice and not on my opinion of those.	○	○	○	○	○
11. I have sometimes provided spontaneous rewards.	○	○	○	○	○
12. If I used a tangible reward, I linked it with words of praise that focused on the student's effort.	○	○	○	○	○

In this section, we will first revisit what is meant by the term *consequence* and what types of consequences are appropriate for what situations. Then we will examine four research-proven influences on student behavior and suggestions for the application of each:

1. *Practice consequences*

2. *Positive consequences*

3. *Negative consequences*

4. *Proactive interventions*

For each of these we will consider specific things you can do in your classroom that can help develop a positive classroom climate and encourage students to engage positively with academic instructional activities, with other students, and with you as the teacher.

- In the practice consequences section, we will look at appropriate teacher responses when a procedure is not being followed.

- In the positive consequences section, we will consider the pluses and minuses of tangible rewards and a more effective way to encourage students than the typical teacher praise patterns used when a student is nearing or achieving a goal.

- In the negative consequences section, we will distinguish between punishment and discipline, consider more effective ways to deliver a negative consequence, and examine the pros and cons of using the typical punishments we find in schools today for failure to follow rules or meet expectations.

- In the proactive interventions section, we will consider a hierarchy of teacher responses to nip misbehavior in the bud before it can blossom.

Caution! A key thing to be aware of in classroom management is that we tend to do to our students that which was done unto us. Some—or many—of the research-based ideas for teacher management strategies in these materials may be different from what you yourself experienced as a student in your own K–12 years. How you were treated as a student and how you witnessed your peers being treated have formed a soundtrack in your head that will play back in your own words and actions unless you make a conscious effort to erase and replace it.

The fact is that human beings repeat familiar patterns, so if you experienced a teacher who yelled at you and/or your classmates, you are "experientially predisposed" to yell at your own students. You may need to work to erase some files recorded on your "mental hard drive" throughout your own K–12 schooling experiences. Otherwise, you may be shocked to observe yourself in an unguarded moment, saying or doing things you would not choose to say or do.

A Word About Consequences

Appropriate Consequences!

Would you be surprised to learn that interviews of over 180 students from public, private, urban, suburban, and rural schools revealed two things those students associated with their own good behavior? They are (1) clear classroom expectations and consequences and (2) caring and respectful relationships with teachers (Cothran, Kulinna, & Garrahy, 2003).

Relationships were addressed in the first section of this manual. Now, let's consider clear consequences. Keep in mind that a consequence is the logical result of a previous act, and a consequence can be either *positive* (such as receiving affirming words from the teacher for a task well done), *negative** (such as losing computer privileges for a week for misusing the equipment), or *practicing* (such as practicing how to enter a classroom calmly, to move desks into small-group formation, to pass in papers, or to prepare for leaving the room when one of these is not done successfully). We noted in the chart on page 58 that each of the three types of consequences is logically attached to either expectations, goals, or procedures—remember the bottom row?

EXPECTATIONS IN YOUR CLASSROOM	PROCEDURES IN YOUR CLASSROOM	GOALS IN YOUR CLASSROOM
A student not following an expectation results in a *disciplinary* consequence.	A student not following a procedure results in a *reteaching* consequence.	A student nearing or achieving a goal results in an *appropriate praise* consequence.

And we alluded to the fact that giving a student a negative consequence for messing up on a procedure causes them to cry "unfair!"

Consider three guiding questions for choosing an appropriate *positive consequence* for progressing toward a goal or *disciplinary consequence* for violating an expectation (Harris et al., 2018):

1. Is it in line with school norms and district policy?

2. Is it appropriate for the situation?

   a. Offense appropriate—Using an elephant gun to go after a gnat or a flyswatter to deal with a charging rhino is not ideal.

   b. Age appropriate—Sitting beside you may be a privilege for a third grader but a punishment for a ninth grader.

   c. Student appropriate—Staying after school with you is a pleasure for the student who goes home to an empty house and a penalty for the student who is anxious to get to sports practice or an after-school job.

3. How would you feel if it were applied to you—or your own child?

*A negative consequence may be a *disciplinary measure* (likely to promote a positive change in future student behavior choice) or a *punishment* (unlikely to promote a positive change in future student behavior choice and likely to cause student rebellion). Refer to page 96 for distinction between these two.

The old joke asking *How do you get to Carnegie Hall?* with the response of *Practice, practice, practice!* holds true for students mastering procedures. It takes several practices (multiple sources indicate twenty-one) for a procedure to become habit, and habits fade if they are not regularly practiced and reinforced. Thus, students may experience problems in successfully following procedures during the first several weeks of school and again in the first few days after a break of a week or more—and even after a weekend.

Consequences for Procedures!

There is also an old saying that "Practice makes perfect." However, repeated *im*perfect practice does not accomplish the goal. When your students practice a procedure, observe carefully to determine that they understand and are performing the procedural steps correctly.

When a student fails to perform a procedure correctly (or at the appropriate time), *how* you provide the corrective feedback and practice makes a huge difference in that student being willing to hear what you have to say and continuing to perceive you as fair and kind as you say it. Poet William Carlos Williams, a contemporary of Robert Frost, said it well:

> It is not what you say that matters, but the manner
>
> in which you say it; there lies the secret of the ages.

How you say it matters. A corrective and teaching *practice* consequence should be given in a way that . . .

- maintains a neutral and nonaccusatory tone (both verbally and visually—no "staring daggers" at the hapless student),

- maintains the dignity of the student (nix the sarcasm), and

- focuses on what to DO rather than on what not to do (when a human brain hears an action verb, it stimulates brain cells that carry out that muscular action [Hank, Johnsonrude, & Pulvemuller, 2004]—thus saying "Please walk" is more effective than "Do not run").

Note that for some students the use of a visual or auditory cue may help a classroom procedure become a behavioral habit. These are often students who know what to do but are not sure when to do it. Such students should not be thought of as "clueless" but rather as "cueless," and the teacher can provide the needed cue. Consider this after-school student exchange:

"What's with the long face?"

(Long sigh . . .) "*I messed up on my homework and lost points.*"

"What happened?"

"*Last year Ms. Taylor said to write our answers in a word or phrase. But this year Mr. Bell says to write them in a complete sentence.*"

"So?"

"*Some days I just forget which year it is.*"

Choosing Appropriate Practice Consequences

Consider what would be an appropriate teacher response to each of the following and why and what would be an inappropriate or less effective teacher response and why. Please refer to O: Choosing Appropriate Practice Consequences in the Appendices for a discussion of some possible teacher responses.

STUDENT BEHAVIOR The procedure is to . . .	POSSIBLE APPROPRIATE TEACHER RESPONSE AND REASON(S) TO DO THIS	POSSIBLE INAPPROPRIATE TEACHER RESPONSE AND REASON(S) NOT TO DO THIS
1. Pass papers to the left, and Paula passes hers to the right.		
2. Push chairs in before leaving for lunch, and Sam leaves his out.		
3. Head papers in a certain way, and Juan writes his name on the wrong side.		
4. Sign your name, date, and time in and out on the bathroom pass sheet, and Maria forgets to write in the times.		
5. Close out all programs when leaving the computer station, and Roberto leaves some open.		
6. Exchange a broken pencil with a sharp one from the pencil pot, and Sureka goes to the pencil sharpener and begins grinding away.		
7. Place backpacks under the desks, and Mark leaves his in the aisle.		
8. Place your music folder on your music stand, and Carlos puts his under his chair.		
9. _____ _____ _____ _____ _____ (Fill in a procedure from your classroom.)		

Responding Appropriately With Positive Consequences for Desirable Student Behavior and Academics

When you observe students "going in the right direction," how do you communicate this in a way that causes them to stay on course and hopefully pick up the pace? Tangible goodies and stickers will not do it—and can in fact have the opposite effect of what was intended! Praising students for being "good" has no lasting effect. Telling them you really like something they did doesn't stick—and again can have the very opposite of the intended effect! When students receive rewards and/or praise not linked to their performance, they may perceive they have no control over the action— they were just lucky that day (Haydon & Musti-Rao, 2011). So what works?

Right Direction!

According to research (Haydon & Musti-Rao, 2011; Lampi et al., 2005), three factors influencing the power of praise are the *when*, the *what*, and the *how*:

WHEN: Encouraging praise has the most impact if it comes close in time after the behavior— immediately, if possible. This immediacy helps students to develop positive feelings associated with the desirable choice in the behavior you are praising—and thus to develop their intrinsic motivation to do it again.

WHAT: Encouraging praise has the most impact if it (1) causes the student to link his or her effort with a positive outcome and (2) focuses on the student and not on your opinion of the student.

Students who believe their success is caused by their efforts are more likely to put forth more effort (for example, "The choice you made to hold your temper shows a mature self-control" or "That A on your test shows you really studied"). Praise that focuses on the teacher's opinion (such as "I really like the way that you used self-control") takes away student ownership of that praise AND can backfire if the student does not wish to be seen as a "teacher pleaser."

HOW: Your choices here are public vs. private and oral vs. written. Some students respond well to public praise—especially younger ones. Some students are averse to public praise—especially adolescents. Even if you follow the guidelines for *when* and *what*, if you give the praise where others can hear it, then some adolescent students are embarrassed, and the praise has an unintended negative effect. The problem is that for spoken praise to be time contingent, it is hard not to be public.

HOWEVER, many teachers find that a small sticky note with a few words can follow the praise guidelines of *when* (be close in time), *what* (focus on the student and link effort with outcome), and *how* (be private). The added bonus of a written note is that it lasts. A student can reread your written words again and again to reinforce and reaffirm something he or she did right. (And don't we as teachers keep those special notes from students and parents through the years for that same reason?)

Source: Adapted from Harris et al. (2018, p. 31).

Rethinking Effective and Encouraging Praise Statements

Challenge: Audio record yourself, and listen to the teacher praise that is coming out of your mouth. If you are like most teachers, you are using the same type of praise that your teachers used with you, and it is a statement that begins with the phrase *I really like the way that . . .*

Now think a moment: When you say *I really like . . .* , what have you just validated? Your students or yourself? Look at the subject of that sentence: the word *I*. What are you affirming? *Your opinion* of something. If you teach younger children, many of whom are still "teacher pleasers," knowing they have pleased you may make them momentarily happy. If you teach adolescents—many of whom are often averse to any authority figure—making you as their teacher happy is likely low on their list. In both cases, such a statement has little or no effect on developing long-term, self-regulated desirable behavior. The bottom line for all ages is this: If your goal is to help your students develop internal motivation to continue "going in the right direction," then something else is needed beyond an "I-statement" of what you like.*

Whether you use the comparison terms of *effective praise* vs. *ineffective praise* or *encouraging praise* vs. *praise*, characteristics of the first category in each pair are the same. These positive statements that encourage a student to "keep on keeping on" do one or more of the following:

1. Focus on the effort rather than the outcome.

2. Help the student see a link between effort and outcome.

3. Focus on the feelings of the student rather than those of the teacher.

4. Provide specifics so the student knows what it is that is worthy.

5. Anchor in reality and do not exaggerate for the sake of effect.

INEFFECTIVE PRAISE	EFFECTIVE AND ENCOURAGING PRAISE
"How pretty you look!"	"The scarf you chose is a great match for your jacket."
"You have a good grade on the test."	"That good grade on your test shows you really understand fractions."
"I am proud of you."	"You can be proud of yourself."
"Good paper!"	"The clear organization of your paper makes it easy for the reader to follow your ideas."
"You are the best!"	"You are definitely getting better."

*As I-messages place the value of the action with the teacher rather than the student, they are of little (or counterproductive) value as effective praise for long-term effect. However, research supports their use for immediate correction of some undesirable behaviors (Jones & Jones, 2016). For example, if a student is talking to a neighbor during teacher-led instruction, you might say something like the following: "When you talk with your friend as I am teaching, I am worried you are not able to hear what is being said. This means you will not be able to learn from the lesson and you may also be distracting other students in our class. Please wait to talk to your friend until I have asked you to do so in small-group discussions." In this instance, it is appropriate to place the value with yourself because it lets the student know in a direct manner that the student's actions are having a negative effect on you and on other students.

Develop a more effective praise and encouragement statement for each of the following situations and on the following page. Work to link student choice and/or effort with the desirable outcome. You may refer to P: More Effective Praise/Encouragement Statements in the Appendices for some possible more effective statements.

LESS EFFECTIVE AND/OR INEFFECTIVE PRAISE	EFFECTIVE PRAISE AND ENCOURAGEMENT
Carmen wore a blue scarf. "Carmen, I like your scarf."	"Carmen, the color of the scarf you chose today matches your outfit beautifully."
Steve completed a difficult assignment (elementary). OR Steve correctly completed a complicated science lab experiment (secondary). 1. "I'm so proud of you."	
After receiving Cs on the last two math tests, Alene finally made an A. 2. "You made an A? It must have been your lucky day."**	
Asim made the winning foul shot. 3. "You're the best player on the team!"	
Laronda brought a finished art project to you, saying, "What do you think?" 4. "Lovely!"	
Saul showed up to the ball game with his face painted in school colors. 5. "Saul, I like that school spirit!"	
Kim stayed after school to help a returning absentee classmate catch up with lessons missed (elementary). OR Kim stayed after school to help three new band members learn the music for an upcoming marching competition (secondary). 6. "You are so good!"	

(Continued)

(Continued)

LESS EFFECTIVE AND/OR INEFFECTIVE PRAISE	EFFECTIVE PRAISE AND ENCOURAGEMENT
Nancy *finally* turned in an assignment on time. 7. *"I like the way your work is on time for a change!"*	
The chorus stayed on key throughout the entire piece of music. 8. *"I enjoyed the way you were on key that time."*	
Marcus was absent with the flu for a week and made up all of his missed work in three days. 9. *"Marcus, I appreciate your getting all your work made up quickly."*	
Every student in your class turned in a field trip permission slip on time (elementary). OR Every student in your class turned in a research paper on time (secondary). 10. *"Great! I am so pleased that everyone will get to go"* (elementary). OR *"Great! I am so pleased that no one will lose points for being late"* (secondary).	

*Both academic and behavioral

**Actual feedback experienced by one of the authors—who studied really hard for that test and still remembers the teacher's comment with resentment.

Source: Adapted from Evertson and Harris (2013).

One way to think about negative consequences for misbehavior is to consider three categories (Brady, Forton, Porter, & Wood, 2003; Dreikurs & Cassel, 1972; Jones & Jones, 2016; Mancuso & Allen, 1976; Nelsen, Lott, & Glenn, 2000):

Choose carefully!

1. Natural negative consequences

2. Logical negative consequences

3. Expiative punishments

The goal of natural and logical negative consequences is to *teach* students to understand, anticipate, and make decisions based on the consequences of their actions in the real world. The purpose of an expiative negative punishment is to cause the guilty party to experience a discomfort that results in the person's not doing the misbehavior again.

Natural negative consequences occur naturally and without any intervention from the outside (for example, a child plays roughly with a favorite toy and breaks it). The natural consequence of a child's playing roughly with a toy and breaking it is that the child's toy is now ruined, and there is no need for an external punitive intervention—learning occurs from the direct consequence of the mistake. However, if the misbehavior substantially affects others or if a potential natural consequence would be too severe (for example, a secondary student abuses a computer that other students use as well; a kindergarten student refuses to stay within the playground fence next to the street), then a logical negative consequence is needed.

Logical negative consequences are undesirable stimuli imposed to reduce the student's undesirable behavior (for example, a student misuses or mistreats a computer, and that student's computer privileges are withheld for a period of time). Logical consequences have three basic features. They are

- related (the consequence is logically related to the misbehavior),

- reasonable (the severity of the consequence equals that of the offense), and

- respectful (the teacher is calm and speaks in a matter-of-fact voice).

Expiative punishments have no logical connection to student misbehavior (for example, writing one hundred times "I will be respectful," copying words from the dictionary, running laps); therefore, they give students little information to help their social development and maturation. Moreover, the negatives of these punishments outweigh their usefulness, as students tend to associate such punishments with the person assigning them and not with their own misbehavior. Indeed, such punishments can give students a sense that they have the right to retaliate and seek revenge on that person (Dreikurs & Cassel, 1972; Jones & Jones, 2016). Thus, the morality of the situation is turned upside down as the student guilty of misbehavior now views himself or herself as the injured party. Expiative punishment can transform the environment of a classroom into one of ill will that supports students' continued misbehavior (Nucci, 2006).

Punishment and Discipline

There is a big difference!

Punishment and discipline—while the terms are often used interchangeably, the two are NOT synonymous. Consider their origins:

ENGLISH WORD	LATIN ORIGIN	ORIGINAL MEANING
punish	*punier*	*to cause pain for an offense*
discipline	*disciplina*	*teaching; instruction*

Consider the differences between punishment and discipline as set out in the following chart:

	PUNISHMENT	DISCIPLINE
Purpose	To inflict pain or discomfort intentionally on a student in the hope of changing the student's behavior	To teach self-control and confidence in the hope of developing self-discipline within the student
Focus	Past undesirable behavior	Future desirable behavior
Teacher's attitude	Frustration with (and possible hostility toward) the student	Care and concern for the student
Student's resulting feelings	Resentment toward the teacher	Sense of security in the classroom
Goal	Student complies with teacher's request	Student self-disciplines his or her own behavior

Source: Adapted from Ingram (2006).

Whether or not a negative consequence is perceived as a punishment or as discipline depends on why and how you as the teacher deliver it. And how you deliver it reflects whether you believe that "kids do well if they want to" or "kids do well if they can" (Greene, 2008). The first assumes that the student needs motivation to do well; the second assumes that the student is lacking thinking skills and needs to learn to respond to life's challenges in an adaptive way (please refer back to page 21).

A Reminder of Two Things We Know About Punishment

- Punishment may increase the undesired behavior.

- Punished behaviors may continue if the punisher is not present (Jones & Jones, 2016).

The Pros and Cons of Typical Negative Consequences

 Here is a chart of teachers' nine most frequently used negative consequences and a summary of comments made by over two thousand teachers who have brainstormed possible pros and cons of each of these. (What might you add to these lists?) Please note this chart is a REPORT, NOT a recommendation. You will have to decide which ones are possibly worth using to help you meet your goals, both for effect and affect. Note that most items have significantly more negatives than positives. . . . What does this tell you?

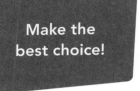

Make the best choice!

1. Loss of privilege—For example: The student loses the privilege of using a computer for five days.

Pros	Cons
• It is logically connected to the infraction. • It tends to be seen as fair by other students. • It causes the student to recognize value of lost privilege—without access, the assignment is more difficult to do. • It takes little teacher time and effort.	• The student may need computer access to do the assignment. • The student may be ostracized by other students by being excluded from computer time.

2. Stay after school—For example: The student must stay after school.

Pros	Cons
• This gives teacher one-on-one time to conference.	• The student may not have transportation home. • The student may have after-school responsibilities (for example, care for sibling or a job). • This takes teacher time after school. • After-school detention hall "quality" varies greatly.

3. Restitution—For example: The student must replace a lost textbook.

Pros	Cons
• Instructional materials are available for that student and for the next student.	• Financial hardship: The student or family may lack funds to replace the book. • Financial largess: Parents may pay for book replacement with no disciplinary measure or involvement of student. • Student may choose not to comply as a point of rebellion.

4. Confiscation—For example: The teacher takes away a student's toy cell phone.

Pros	Cons
• The student is no longer distracted by the item or temptation to use it.	• The teacher is then responsible for the item, and if it is stolen, the teacher must replace it. • Unless clear expectations with a rationale are previously set,* student may refuse to surrender the item.

*Example: "Because I care about you and about your learning, if something you bring to class is interfering with your or others' learning, know that I will ask and expect you to place it in my keeping until the end of class so you can focus on the lesson. You can reclaim it at the end of class."

5. Repetitive writing—For example: The student must write a set piece of words or numbers a certain number of times.

Pros	Cons
• None	• The student resents being assigned a menial, punitive task. • The student develops a negative attitude toward writing—sees writing as punishment. • The student pays the other student to do the write-offs and turns them in as his or her own work. • This makes no change in student behavior.

6. Reflective writing—For example: The student must describe in writing his or her actions, feelings, and plans for positive change in the future.

Pros	Cons
• The student is able to self-reflect and demonstrate empathy and/or regret for his or her negative actions in a sincere way. • The teacher can better understand thinking and feelings of the student.	• The student does not take the assignment seriously and uses it as an opportunity to justify actions or to rant.

7. In-school suspension (ISS) or sent to another room—For example: The student goes to an ISS class (high school) or other teacher's class (middle or elementary school) for a set time period.

Pros	Cons
• The behavior problem is removed from your classroom.	• The student misses out on the instruction. • It falls to the teacher to help the student catch up. • Going to detention may be a "badge of defiant honor." • Quality of supervision and instruction in ISS class or other teacher's class varies. • The student may want to get out of the teacher's class.

8. Principal's office*—For example: The teacher sends the student to the principal's office.

Pros	Cons
• The behavior problem is removed from your classroom.	• The teacher abdicates or undermines his or her own authority. • The student may want to get out of class. • The teacher appears weak to the administration. • The principal may or may not do anything.

Suggestion: To gain administrative support for a problem behavior, document, document, document! Keep a written record of dates, value-free descriptions of a student's behavior, and your disciplinary response. Then request an appointment with your administrator "to ask your advice on a next step you suggest I take in dealing with this problem behavior." Come to the meeting with documentation in hand, maintain a calm and professional voice, and read off the list of incidents and your disciplinary efforts. This approach is much more likely to result in your being perceived as a professional and to receive additional support.

9. Lowered grade—For example: The student has points deducted from his or her grade.

Pros	Cons
• None	• This is illegal except for performance classes such as band or debate, where "behavior" is a part of the academic content. In other subjects, teachers are open to legitimately angry parents and lawsuits.

Source: Nine typical consequences reported in Evertson and Harris (2003).

Not all students always successfully follow all expectations. Do you? Have *you*—or a friend—ever broken a speed limit? Why? Was it ignorance, misunderstanding, an accident, an emergency, or deliberate disobedience? And do the law's representatives deal with you any differently depending on your reason?

> **Identify the underlying cause!**

Unless it is a dangerous behavior that must be stopped immediately for safety's sake, the first step in dealing with a student's misbehavior is to ask *why*: *Why do I think the student is misbehaving in this way?* How many different reasons are there that could underlie a student's misbehavior? And how does the underlying cause of a student's undesirable behavior influence what is an appropriate response from you? Many textbooks on behavior management for students with and at risk for emotional and behavioral disorders (EBDs) discuss the importance of addressing the *why* through functional behavior assessment (FBA) (Horner & Yell, 2017). An FBA is a multistep process undertaken by a team of people (such as general education and special education teachers, school administrators, counselors, student, parents) to discover not only what a student did but why he or she did it. The logic of an FBA is that if we can determine *why* a student performed a certain behavior, then a better understanding of the motivations behind it can guide us in choosing appropriate consequences to decrease (or increase, in some cases) the rate of the behavior being performed. Steps involved in an FBA include the following (Alberto & Troutman, 2016):

1. Verify that the behavior is serious enough to require an FBA. Have other, less invasive strategies been tried to change the behavior?

2. Define the problem behavior in observable and measurable ways. Just saying the student is "unmotivated" does not help. What does the behavior LOOK LIKE?

3. Collect data on the occurrence of the behavior. What happened before it occurred? What did the actual act look like? What happened afterward?

4. Review the data, and come up with some hypotheses as to the function of the student's behavior.

5. Develop an intervention to change the behavior.

Note that the traditional FBA process is rooted in behaviorism and does not consider relationship quality between teacher and students as a means of changing behavior. However, we contend, and research suggests (Marlowe, Garwood, & Van Loan, 2017; Mihalas, Morse, Allsopp, & McHatton, 2009; Van Loan & Garwood, 2020a), that any behavior intervention derived from an FBA and delivered by a teacher will be more effective if the relationship quality between teacher and student is warm and close rather than distant and hostile. Furthermore, while we do not deny the importance of FBA, research suggests teachers struggle with the laborious process and the amount of time required to implement such an assessment (Hirsch, Bruhn, Lloyd, & Katsiyannis, 2017; Oram, Owens, & Maras, 2016). For those comfortable with FBA, we applaud this decision. For others, we offer suggestions on ways to consider the *why*.

The following chart summarizes the responses of over 2,500 teachers and administrators throughout the US when asked to identify underlying causes they have observed for student misbehavior. Are there other items you could add in any of the categories? Have you observed additional categories not represented in the chart?

Self-Esteem or Power	Academic Work-Related	Home Life	Physical Problems
• Seeks teacher's attention • Shows off for peers • Challenges the teacher (related to perceiving teacher as unfair or weak) • Work avoidance (related to fear of failure and resulting embarrassment)	• Bored (work is too easy) • Frustrated (work is too hard) • Disinterested (sees no relevance or value of assignment) • Nothing to do (no assigned work)	• Divorce in family • New sibling • New stepparent • Family member arrested • Witnessed or experienced physical abuse • Determined to be different from older sibling	• Vision loss • Hearing loss • Hunger • Sleep deficit • Medicine side effects • Food allergies • Drugs
Knowledge or Maturity	**Inconsistent Consequences**	**Other School Situations**	**That "Tough Kid"**
• Does not know what desired behavior is • Does not know how to do the desired behavior • Does not know when to do the desired behavior • Immature, poor self-monitoring skills	• Thinks teacher will not catch them • Sometimes student gets away with it • Student always gets away with it at home	• Angry over something that happened in another setting (for example, another class, on the bus)	• Likely a combination of three or more items from the other seven areas of this chart

As you consider items in the chart, how many of those could you as the teacher address *in some way*? Some examples (bored, does not know the desired behavior, sometimes gets away with it) are directly within your sphere of influence; others (vision loss, food allergies) are things that if you knew they were the cause, you could help connect the student to appropriate resources; still others (witness of physical abuse, anger over something outside of your class) could best be addressed by a referral to a counselor. Take a few minutes to review the chart, placing a *T* beside any underlying cause you could directly address in some way and a *t* beside those you could indirectly address in some way. What do you discover?

Understanding why a behavior is occurring does not change the behavior, but it can inform your approach in addressing it. And often when you understand what is occurring in the life of a "tough kid," you will likely wonder how the student is managing to do as well as he or she is.

A good mantra to remember when you observe an undesirable behavior is . . .

ACT, DON'T REACT!

Whatever underlying reason you hypothesize, you want to deal with the undesirable behavior in a proactive rather than a reactive way. What's the difference? It is the difference between being calm or upset, logical or emotional, rational or irrational, consistent or inconsistent, in control of the situation or the situation in control of you. Ask yourself these three crucial questions to help you maintain a proactive response:

1. WHY?

Why do I think the student is behaving in this way? Can you pinpoint the reason the student is acting in this way? (And does there seem to be a pattern of when or with whom it occurs?)

STEP 1. Evaluate the cause of the behavior.

Once you have identified a plausible *why,* the second question is *what.*

2. WHAT?

What is my ultimate goal—for the student, for me, and for the rest of the class? Your answer to this may vary from time to time. Yet another question in this *what* category is "What kind of a thirty-five-year-old do I want?"; then consider how what you choose to do is shaping the future adult and citizen whom you desire to be gainfully employed and contributing to your future Social Security.

STEP 2. Assess your goals for the student, the class, and yourself.

Once you have identified the *what* of your goal, the last question is *how.*

3. HOW?

How shall I choose to respond? Where do you start with possible choices? Use the "Law of Least Intervention" (Cummings, 2001), and start with a strategy that does the following:

1. Causes the least disruption to the academic lesson
2. Takes the least teacher time and energy
3. Creates the least negative classroom vibes—in other words, the strategy choice maintains a positive classroom climate

STEP 3. Choose an appropriate teacher response.

The place to start is with your eyes and feet—your use of these two can really help students stay appropriately academically engaged. If you see an undesirable behavior beginning to emerge, make eye contact with the student and increase your physical proximity. It is amazing how much "power" is in a teacher's normal eye contact and physical presence.

Source: Adapted from Harris et al. (2018).

Practice in Developing a More Proactive Response

4-8

Your answer to the *why* and *what* will determine your response to the final question of *how*: *How shall I choose to respond?* On the following chart, what proactive response might you suggest for each of the six misbehaviors in the first column? See Q: Developing a More Proactive Response in the Appendices for some possible proactive teacher actions.

MISBEHAVIOR	WHY? PROBABLE CAUSE	WHAT? TEACHER GOALS	HOW? TEACHER ACTION
A pencil rolls off student A's desk, and student B picks it up. Student A calls out, "Dirty thief!"	Typical pattern of interaction from past experience	Have the student substitute appropriate language in future similar situations. Keep the classroom climate positive. Don't waste class time or energy on anger.	
A pencil rolls off student A's desk, and student B picks it up. Student A calls out, "Dirty thief!," grabs the pencil out of student B's hand, hits him with it, and smirks at the teacher.	Seeks to establish power and dominance over weaker student and over teacher	Bring home the facts that student A will treat others with respect, that hitting is never acceptable, and that the teacher is the one in charge in the classroom. Keep the classroom climate positive. Don't waste class time or energy on anger.	
Student C closes up her book and begins social chatting with a nearby student who is still working.	Has finished all assigned work—and has nothing to do	Redirect the student to an appropriate academic task. Keep all other students working. Don't waste class time or energy on anger.	
Student C is making derogatory comments to a student sitting nearby.	Enjoys tormenting other students and getting them upset	Bring home the fact that unkind language and hurting other people's feelings are not acceptable. Cause other students to feel emotionally safe. Don't waste class time or energy on anger.	
Student D is late for class, saunters in, and says with a grin, "Looks like I'm late again."	Has been goofing off in the hall and wants to be sent to the principal's office	Cause the student to get to class on time. Encourage all students to get to class on time. Don't waste class time or energy on anger, and don't let the student out of class.	
Student D is late for class, comes in obviously upset, and mumbles an apology to you on the way to his seat.	Something happened between classes—causes the student to be upset and late	Help the student get emotions under control. Get class started and all other students engaged. Find a way to help or counsel or get help for the student.	

Eyes and Feet

Think about it—the student considering misbehaving is usually looking to see if you are looking. Develop the habit of frequently scanning the faces of all students and making momentary eye contact, and students get the message that you are aware of their behavior. Develop the habit of walking around the classroom so that every student periodically experiences your physical presence beside him or her, and students get that same message—plus it lets you see up close what students have on their desks and are actually doing. (However, do be sure to stop and stay in place at least ten seconds after several steps; otherwise, students will focus on following *you* instead of following the lesson.)

A Hierarchy of Suggested Intervention Strategies

A. As you go right on with the lesson, work down through the following:

   1. Ignore it—but only if (a) the student quickly self-corrects or (b) the student's purpose is to annoy you and the behavior does not interfere with other students' learning.

   2. Make eye contact with the student—"pupil to pupil."

   3. Increase your physical nearness—if possible, stand beside the student (you may even come close enough to touch lightly against the chair or desk).

   4. Academically involve the student by saying his or her name (neutral voice), giving a one-sentence review of the current lesson topic, and asking an open-ended question you feel sure the student can answer.

B. But if none of the first four are working or workable, then interrupt the lesson and work your way down through the following:

   5. Remind the student of the expected behavior.

   6. Tell the student to do the expected behavior.

   7. Ask the student to see you after class, and question the student about the misbehavior—but only later IN PRIVATE to avoid a power struggle.

   8. Follow through with an appropriate negative consequence when you have exhausted all of the options above. (More on these later.)

Source: Adapted from Evertson and Harris (2003).

Four Counterproductive Strategies (Don't Go There!)

Note that four strategies *not* in the previously stated list are *warning, threatening, lecturing,* and *nagging*. If you've seen the TV special *A Charlie Brown Christmas*, then you know the sound of the teacher's voice: "Wah-wah wah-wah wah-wah wah-wah." That is exactly what students hear when teachers warn, threaten, lecture, or nag. Those four take class time, create a negative class tone, position the student as a combatant against the teacher, and have no positive effect on student behavior—or on teacher attitude.

Teacher Choices to Head Off and Redirect Undesirable Student Behavior

The following situations are framed with YOU as the teacher.

Beside each situation, jot down your thoughts on the best choice of a proactive teacher response that will do the following:

What will you choose to do?

1. Keep the lesson going.

2. Keep the class tone positive.

3. Don't waste your time and energy.

(Refer back to page 103 for ideas.) Then note one or more poor, counterproductive, and possibly reactive teacher response choices. (And we've all been there and made one or more of them.) When finished, you may wish to refer to R: Heading Off/Redirecting/Dealing With Undesirable Behavior in the Appendices for a discussion of some possible teacher choices.

VIGNETTE*	PROACTIVE RESPONSE CHOICE	COUNTERPRODUCTIVE RESPONSE CHOICE(S)
1. As class begins, Mateo pulls out a comic book and slips it into his lap. You . . .		
2. As you explain how to fill in the top of a state test, Rashid is staring into space and has not put pencil to paper. You . . .		
3. In silent reading time, Sofia passes a note to Adana. You . . .		
4. As you are reviewing key points of the Revolutionary War, Boone opens his backpack, takes out toy soldiers, and lines them up on his desk. You . . .		
5. As you monitor seatwork, Amir takes out his wallet, checks the contents, returns the wallet to his pocket, and continues on the assignment. You . . .		
6. After talking with Jamie three times about walking back from lunch and not running and shoving, he flies down the hall and tackles his friend Rob. The boys wrestle. You . . .		
7. For the fifth time in five minutes, Malika calls out when you have called on another student to respond. You . . .		
8. After asking Tomar three times to quit playing with the staple remover on your desk as he stands in line to leave for lunch, you hold out your hand and say, "Please give that to me." The boy closes its jaws on your first finger. Blood drips. You . . .		
9. In lab, Tony connects his Bunsen burner to the water line (blue handle) instead of the gas line (red handle), holds a lighted match over the burner, and turns on the water. Water squirts to the ceiling and drenches Tony and nearby students. You . . .		
10. Write a vignette from your own experience.		

Source: Adapted from Evertson and Harris (2003).

*All vignettes except #4 are from the classroom of one of the authors; #4 occurred next door.

Treating Everyone Exactly the Same

Ever pondered the question "How can I be fair if I don't treat every student exactly the same?" The answer is that *equal* is not the same thing as *fair*. If a surgeon has two patients—one needing a tonsillectomy and the other an appendectomy—the *equal* thing to do would be to compromise and remove the gallbladder of each. While this might be *equal*, it would not be *fair* for either patient!

In keeping with the medical analogy, consider that two people may show up at a doctor's office after each has accidentally stepped on a glass shard. Both will need a Band-Aid, and one or both may need stitches and/or a tetanus shot. The doctor is the professional and makes the decision of what is needed in each case. The fair thing to do is give each patient what is needed—the appropriate amount of intervention that will result in the desired cure.

It has been said that the definition of *teacher* is "professional decision maker." On average, a classroom teacher will make more than 1,500 educational decisions every school day—in an average six-hour school day, that equals more than four decisions every minute (Goldberg & Houser, 2017). The teacher is the professional, and just like the doctor in the previous paragraph, the teacher must decide what is needed in a given situation.

Teacher-Student Relationships

No significant learning occurs without a significant relationship (Garwood & Van Loan, 2019). As you interact with students at whatever age, remember that the most important thing your students need in you is a caring *teacher* rather than a friend—they have friends their own age. You as their *teacher* bring something to them that their peers cannot bring. They need an adult to whom they can relate in a positive way, and you can be that adult.

Both children and adolescents need attachment to adults—for children, we are caregivers and role models; for adolescents, we are role models and mentors. Because of their need for independence, adolescents shift away from adult-dependent relationships to ones where both parties' needs are considered (Clark-Lempers, Lempers, & Ho, 1991; Davis, 2003).

Secondary teachers sometimes distance themselves intentionally from their students in an effort to allow them the independence and separation they believe adolescents desire (Davis, 2003). However, adolescents still need adult attachments—just not the same types of attachments as when they were younger children (Clark-Lempers et al., 1991).

One way to begin to gauge the quality of teacher-student interactions with one or a group of students is by using the TAN framework presented in Area One (Garwood & Van Loan, 2019). Within this framework, a teacher is asked to consider the degree to which his or her actions in the classroom help movement *toward* or *away from* a student and to question how both parties' *needs* are being met.

The following chart can be used to reflect on interactions with a student that move you toward the student and meet both student and teacher needs. Think about that one student who is a major challenge. Use the following chart to reflect on your interactions and attitudes with this student, and consider which of the items you rate SOMETIMES or below you might choose to work on to address more consistently.

REFLECTING ON A SPECIFIC Teacher-Student Relationship	ALWAYS	USUALLY	SOMETIMES	SELDOM	NEVER
I daily greet this student by name as he or she enters the classroom.					
I listen thoughtfully to this student in our verbal interactions, as opposed to just waiting for my turn to talk.					
My interactions with this student create a feeling that I can be trusted.					
My verbal feedback statements to this student are predominantly positive.					
I look forward to seeing this student as opposed to avoiding him or her intentionally.					
In working with this student, I seek cooperation rather than compliance.					
Rather than providing an immediate solution to a problem or concern, I sometimes just listen to the student and allow him or her to express concerns.					
After verbal interaction with this student, I feel more rejuvenated than worn out.					
I provide this student with opportunities for choice in the classroom.					

You may wish to duplicate this chart and use it for multiple self-assessment inventories, focusing individually on one or more of your more challenging students. You may find that a liberal application of what you discover can make a major difference in your classroom.

Despite your best efforts, students may (will) still misbehave. Again, human behavior is human behavior. To prevent undesirable behaviors from getting out of hand, we suggest a three-stage de-escalation sequence (Jones & Jones, 2016): (1) Validate students' feelings. Communicate that you understand where they are coming from while also helping them understand why their behavior is not helpful to themselves or the class as a whole. (2) Give them a choice. Ask them if they can think of a different behavior they could choose to engage in and to predict what the outcome would be if they made that better choice. Finally, (3) invite students to brainstorm with you the best way to end the conflict and move to a more positive outcome.

Some Dos and Avoids in Choosing and Using Consequences

DO separate the deed from the doer.

AVOID any expiative punishment!

DO link failure to follow an expectation to a disciplinary consequence—not to a punishment.

AVOID yelling and sarcasm.

DO choose negative consequences thoughtfully, and use them as disciplinary and not punitive measures.

AVOID praising a student for a personal quality (such as "being good") or ability ("being smart").

DO link failure to perform a procedure correctly to a practice consequence.

AVOID sending a student to the office unless you have previously met with the administration and provided an objective data behavior log.

DO link nearing or achieving a goal to appropriate and encouraging praise.

AVOID tangible rewards unless they represent a legitimate achievement and are paired with encouraging praise that links effort and outcome.

DO praise a student for effort and/or choice, and when possible, link effort and choice to outcome.

AVOID trying to be buddies with students or win a popularity contest.

DO use a hierarchy of proactive intervention strategies when you notice budding misbehavior.

Key Takeaways: New and/or Reinforced Ideas on Behavior and Consequences

Possible Applications: Things I Plan to Try in My Classroom

Please use the following space to jot down (1) key ideas you want to remember—whether new or a reinforcement of your current knowledge and beliefs—and (2) ideas you want to remember to try in your classroom. In the second column, it may help to keep track if you consecutively number the ideas so you can check them off as you try them.

KEY TAKEAWAYS: New and/or Reinforced Ideas	POSSIBLE APPLICATIONS: Things I Plan to Try in My Classroom

STUDENTS' ENGAGEMENT IN ACADEMIC LESSONS

"I would rather have one day of authentic student engagement than a career of handing out worksheets."

—Sean Jenkins
Middle school instructional coach

Thus far we have considered (1) your students' perception of you as their teacher, (2) physical arrangement of the classroom and materials, (3) rules and procedures by which your class will run, and (4) consequences—including positive, negative and corrective—you will choose to use. Now we come to the purpose of these four: that students will be positively engaged—dare we say enjoying?—the lessons you provide for them.

The *what* of this area is student lesson engagement, and this involves three components that must *all* be activated (Fredricks, Blumenfeld, & Paris, 2004). The first is easily observed; the other two are not:

Behavioral engagement refers to a student's (1) positive conduct (such as following rules and procedures) and (2) effort toward learning and academic assignments (such as persistence).

Emotional engagement refers to a student's (1) sense of belonging and (2) valuing of success in school-related activities.

*Cognitive engagement r*efers to a student's mental investment and effort to learn, understand, and master the knowledge and skills and crafts being taught; it includes self-regulation, strategic planning, and reflection (Newmann, 1992).

Consider that a student may appear behaviorally engaged (and not causing any problems) but lack a sense of belonging and/or or a desire to master the content. Without these two components, there is no lasting learning and little or no measurable academic achievement.

Student engagement relates to motivation—to a student's desire and ability to stay engaged with a lesson. Student motivation is a subject on which there are thousands of publications—and no definitive single answer. Yet, there are several factors now known through research that influence student motivation and its resulting academic success. We offer three of these key factors for your consideration:

1. Things to which students attribute their success or lack thereof

2. A teacher's communication of academic expectations and how to be successful in meeting them (and teacher actions to encourage success)

3. Lesson design elements proven to engage students

Consider the following after-school conversation. To which of these three factors does it relate?

"My teacher's really tricky."

"What do you mean?"

"Last week I really studied, and the test she gave was easy."

"So . . . ?"

"So this week I didn't study so much—and the test she gave was hard."

"Yeah, just like my teacher—he does the same thing."

The *why* of this area includes our desire for our classrooms to be positive places of learning; for our students to gain knowledge, skills, and the ability to apply these; and for our own personal sense of accomplishment as a teacher—and our sanity.

What do we know from research that relates to students staying engaged with instruction and learning activities? Looking in classrooms reveals the following:

- Engagement is a multidimensional construct consisting of behavioral, emotional, and cognitive components (Fredricks et al., 2004).

- Behavioral engagement is typically observed when students display positive conduct (such as following rules, adopting classroom norms) and demonstrate effort toward learning and academic tasks (such as persistence, contributing) (Fredricks et al., 2004).

- Emotional engagement involves both a sense of belonging in the classroom and school community and a value for one's success in school-related activities (Finn, 1989).

- The source of emotional engagement will vary among students because different students value different things in different ways that may impact their emotional engagement. Some possible sources of emotional engagement include student interest, desire to do well, perceived importance, and cost (i.e., negative consequences of not doing the task) (Eccles et al., 1983).

- "Engagement is associated with positive academic outcomes, including achievement and persistence in school; and it is higher in classrooms with supportive teachers and peers, challenging and authentic tasks, opportunities for choice, and sufficient structure" (Fredricks et al., 2004, p. 87).

- In order to engage, students need a sense of relatedness to teachers and peers (Furrer & Skinner, 2003).

- In order to engage, students need to feel competent, to believe that they determine their own success, to understand what is needed to succeed, and to reach that success (Connell & Wellborn, 1991; Fredricks et al., 2004).

- Student attention span correlates with age and ability, and long lectures are boring at any age. Limiting direct instruction to a few minutes interspersed with audio, visual, and/or physical activities helps students stay engaged (Cienkus & Ornstein, 1997).

- Lesson variety increases lesson engagement, and student "doing" beats student listening when it comes to engagement (Deng, 2002; Gregory & Kaufeldt, 2015).

- Optimal learning occurs when lessons include knowledge-, student-, assessment-, and community-centered aspects. A learner-centered pedagogy results in more engaged and energized students (Bransford, Brown, & Cocking, 2000; Strahan & Layell, 2006).

- Teacher wait time of three to five seconds (as opposed to the typical less-than-a-second) results in students' increased academic confidence, willingness to respond, and more detailed responses at a higher level of thinking (Gage & Berliner, 1992).

Please reflect on each of the previously given items for a few moments, and think about things these findings suggest you might do or do differently to help students maintain lesson engagement. Use the Reflections on Area Five page at the end of this area to jot down your thoughts.

What RESEARCH Tells Us About Student Motivation (and Achievement)

Student lesson engagement strongly relates to student motivation. What do we know from research that relates to student motivation for learning? Looking in classrooms reveals the following:

- Teacher movement in the classroom and the use of varied participation structures support student motivation and learning (Anderman, Andrzejewski, & Allen, 2011).

- Choice plays a critical role in promoting students' intrinsic motivation and deep engagement in learning. Across a range of academic outcomes and student populations, positive impacts have been seen when student autonomy is promoted through meaningful and personally relevant choice (Evans & Boucher, 2015).

- Students are more motivated to try when they believe academic performance is linked to factors under their own control (such as note-taking, study habits) (Murayama, Pekrun, Lichtenfeld, & vom Hofe, 2013).

- Low-achieving students tend to believe factors beyond their control (such as bad luck, teacher ill will) determine their grades. For these students, teachers must make visible the effort-outcome link (Ames & Ames, 1985; Seligman, 2002; Urdan, Midgley, & Anderman, 1998).

- Specifically teaching students the relationship between effort and achievement increases their academic achievement more than teaching strategies for comprehension and time management (Van Overwalle & de Metsenaere, 1990).

- Intrinsic motivation is a better predictor of student performance quality; extrinsic incentives are used best in connection with intrinsic motivators (Cerasoli, Nicklin, & Ford, 2014).

- A review of cooperative learning reveals that cooperative structures enhance students' intrinsic motivation, leading them to learn more in small groups than in large groups (Shachar & Sharon, 1994).

- Students are more motivated when they receive signs from peers that they are safe and valued (Wasserman & Danforth, 1988).

- "Opportunities to play can be a terrific motivator. . . . Knowing that there is a fun, clever (and sometimes a student-chosen) activity to look forward to can be a great motivator." Play is a crucial developmental element that stimulates brain growth in the cerebellum, now known to be responsible for attention and language processing (Gregory & Kaufeldt, 2015).

- Choice is a powerful motivator for students with emotional and behavioral disorders (EBDs). Furthermore, by allowing students choices, teachers show students they trust them to make good decisions, and trust is a cornerstone of an effective teacher-student relationship (Brown, 2009; Jolivette, Sticher, & McCormick, 2002; Van Loan & Garwood, 2020b).

Please reflect on each of the previously given items for a few moments, and think about things these findings suggest you might do or do differently to encourage student motivation. Use the Reflections on Area Five page at the end of this area to jot down your thoughts.

Self-Assessment #5a:
Analyzing Factors Influencing Student Lesson Engagement

Check where you fall in each of the items that follow. Any one of these items can make a definite difference in academic engagement. A YES for each item means you have addressed an important component of student lesson engagement. Anything less than YES is an area where a change could improve engagement.

Enhancing Engagement!

Concerning Student Academic Engagement for My Classroom . . .	NO		SOMEWHAT		YES
1. I clearly present (visually and verbally) the lesson goal(s) in student-friendly language.	○	○	○	○	○
2. I begin a lesson by activating students' prior knowledge and causing them to link the current lesson to that prior knowledge.	○	○	○	○	○
3. Before giving directions, I wait until all students are listening, including making eye contact with me, before beginning.	○	○	○	○	○
4. After giving directions, I check multiple students' understanding of how to do an academic task before allowing them to begin.	○	○	○	○	○
5. I use instructional activities that include a good mix of visual, auditory, and tactile/kinesthetic modalities.	○	○	○	○	○
6. My timing and arrangement of instructional activities take into account students' attention span.	○	○	○	○	○
7. I repeatedly walk among all students during class.	○	○	○	○	○
8. I make eye contact with each student multiple times during class.	○	○	○	○	○
9. I use a system that assures all students an equal opportunity to respond (OTR).	○	○	○	○	○
10. I allow from three to five seconds of wait time (or more) before calling on a student and expecting a response.	○	○	○	○	○
11. Students transition smoothly and with little downtime between activities.	○	○	○	○	○

Check where you fall in each of the items that follow. Application of any one of these items can positively influence student motivation. A YES for each item means you have addressed an important component in this area. Anything less than YES is an area where a change could enhance motivation. Note that four of these items are also on the previous self-assessment.

Influencing Motivation!

5-4

Concerning Student Academic Engagement for My Classroom . . .	NO		SOMEWHAT		YES
1. I have surveyed my students to gain a knowledge of their interests.	○	○	○	○	○
2. I design and include lesson elements that build on students' natural curiosity.	○	○	○	○	○
3. I design lessons that allow some student choice in ways to gain knowledge and to demonstrate learning.	○	○	○	○	○
4. I make sure my students see the links between what we are studying and real life.	○	○	○	○	○
5. I make visible the link between student effort (such as habits both of behavior and of mind, organization strategies, study strategies) and academic outcome, and I teach my students to self-assess in these areas.	○	○	○	○	○
6. I provide formative assessment opportunities that involve elements of play (such as academic games for review).	○	○	○	○	○
7. I design lessons that involve opportunities for small-group academic interactions and peer coaching.	○	○	○	○	○
8. I repeatedly walk among all students during class.	○	○	○	○	○
9. I assess and teach as needed the social skills required for positive small-group interactions, and I actively monitor to see that students use them.	○	○	○	○	○

Lesson Engagement Key Factor #1:
Why Students Believe They Succeed—or Don't

You've probably heard the term *mindset*. Henry Ford stated the concept long before any educational experts gave it a name.

> *Whether you think you can or you think you can't—you're right!*
>
> —Henry Ford

In Area One we talked about adjusting our own teacher mindsets. Now we look at adjusting those of our students. Student motivation is radically influenced by students' beliefs about why they do or do not succeed. Perhaps the most powerful of these beliefs is the one called *mindset*, and it concerns a person's view about the nature of intelligence.

Student Mindset: What It Is and Why It Is Powerful

Students' mindsets play a key role in their motivation and achievement (Dweck, 2015). What students believe about the nature of intelligence determines their perception of their own abilities.

GROWTH MINDSET STUDENTS	FIXED MINDSET STUDENTS
Growth mindset students understand that the brain is like muscle, and with effort and practice, it becomes stronger and more intelligent with use (Dweck, 2010).	Fixed mindset students believe that the brain is born with a certain amount of intelligence, and this fixed amount cannot be changed no matter what you do (Farrington et al., 2012).
Because they believe they can "get smarter," growth mindset students see academic difficulty or errors as opportunities to learn and develop their brains (Dweck, 2010).	Because they believe they cannot "get any smarter," fixed mindset students are more likely to give up when they are faced with academic difficulties (Farrington et al., 2012).

We know three things about student mindset (Dweck, 2015):

1. Students who believe their intelligence can be developed (a *growth mindset*) outperform students who believe their intelligence is fixed (a *fixed mindset*).

2. Students can be taught to change from a fixed to a growth mindset.

3. When students make this change and learn that they can "grow their brains" and increase their intellectual ability, they do better. (And with lower-achieving middle and high school students, "better" includes both academics and behavior [Blackwell, Trzesniewski, & Dweck, 2007; Yeager et al., 2016].)

Changing Student Mindset From Fixed to Growth

So how can you encourage a "growth mindset" in your classroom? Consider the following five steps (Garwood & Ampuja, 2019):

1. **Gather baseline data.** Find out where your students are in terms of their mindsets. (See S: Mindset Quiz and T: Scoring the Mindset Quiz in the Appendices for a sample mindset quiz. Note that depending on student age, you may wish to modify some vocabulary.)

2. **Teach the two mindset concepts.** Tell students there are two ways of thinking about intelligence; explain the definitions of growth and fixed mindsets.

3. **Provide examples.** Give students examples of growth mindset, using a variety of instructional formats. A video from the University of California at https://www.youtube.com/watch?v=El-VUqv0v1EE could be one useful tool for this.

4. **Create a culture that fosters growth mindset.** Ask students to give examples of both growth and fixed mindsets, and create a bubble map of their ideas. Post this in the class for reference. (Posting U: Student Self-Talk to Help Develop a Growth Mindset from the Appendices can help guide students in using growth mindset self-talk.)

5. **Model growth mindset.** Incorporate growth mindset in classroom activities. Show students growth mindset in action through your word choice (for example make a mistake of your own, and identify it as an opportunity to learn; when a student makes a mistake, identify it as a growth opportunity.)

What you say to students make a difference. For a moment, put yourself in the place of a student struggling with a math problem. Pick an age—any age. Whether learning how to carry in an addition problem or how to solve for x in an equation, it works the same. How do each of the possible teacher statements below influence your attitude and willingness to try?

TEACHER STATEMENTS FOSTERING A GROWTH MINDSET	TEACHER STATEMENTS FOSTERING A FIXED MINDSET
"When you learn to solve a new math problem, you increase your brainpower."	"That's okay. You tried. Not everybody is good at math."*
"I heard you say you're just not a math person. Please add the word *yet* to the end of that sentence."	"Just keep trying. You'll eventually get there."*
"The goal isn't how fast you solve a problem, but if you understand the steps to get there. So what might you try next?"	"Don't worry—you tried your best."**
"Recognizing you made a mistake means you know more now than you did. So, what might you try next?"	"Looks like you still don't get it."

*But if the student is using the wrong strategies, his or her efforts may not work . . .

**And the message is "Your best isn't good enough. . . ." (Dweck, 2015).

Source: Adapted from Dweck (2015).

Lesson Engagement Key Factor #2a:
Making Visible What Students Can Do to Be Successful

And so you tell your students just what your academic expectations are—what assignments are due when and how much they count. But it's not just about students believing they can learn and be successful, it's also their knowing how to go about it. And here is another area where you as the teacher can make a lifelong difference for these students.

The term is *attribution theory* (Kelley, 1967), and it refers to the cause to which one attributes success or failure. A fixed mindset attributes failure to the mental inability to do any better; a growth mindset attributes success to potential ability and effort. But often students—even those with a growth mindset—need help in making the link between just exactly what efforts are needed to achieve the desired outcome. They may believe they have the ability to succeed but not understand what choices and behaviors will help them get there.

Remember the little fellow with the tricky teacher on the first page of this area—the student who saw no link between his effort and test difficulty? Chances are you have one or more students not reaching their potential for academic success because they think the same way. They fail to see the link between their choices and actions and the results thereof.

The form you see here was developed by a middle school teacher to help her students see these links. She reported that the percentage of passing grades steadily increased each grading period until she felt no need to continue using the form—whereupon her students demanded copies because they wanted "to mark on the good side!"

PREDICTING A GRADE I WILL EARN	ALWAYS	USUALLY	SOMETIMES	SELDOM	NEVER
1. I come to class.	○	○	○	○	○
2. I am seated and ready to begin when the bell rings.	○	○	○	○	○
3. I bring books and all needed materials with me to class.	○	○	○	○	○
4. I stay awake in class. (I get enough sleep the night before.)	○	○	○	○	○
5. I look at my teacher's face when she speaks to our class.	○	○	○	○	○
6. I take notes in class.	○	○	○	○	○
7. I ask questions if I don't understand.	○	○	○	○	○
8. I keep my notes well organized in my folder.	○	○	○	○	○
9. I review my notes before the next class.	○	○	○	○	○

PREDICTING A GRADE I WILL EARN *continued*	ALWAYS	USUALLY	SOMETIMES	SELDOM	NEVER
10. I write down assignments in a special place.	○	○	○	○	○
11. I complete my assignments.	○	○	○	○	○
12. I turn my assignments in on time.	○	○	○	○	○
One thing I choose to work on for improvement in the next six weeks is _____ _____.					

A lower elementary teacher used the same idea in a more visual way:

BECOMING A GOOD STUDENT

1. I come to school.	☺	😐	☹
2. I listen to my teacher.	☺	😐	☹
3. I stay at my table.	☺	😐	☹
4. I do my work.	☺	😐	☹
5. I share materials at my table.	☺	😐	☹

Keep in mind that statements on such checklists must be *objective* things over which a student has control to choose to *do*. For example, "I bring a positive attitude to class" is neither objective nor something over which a student has control—you have no idea what happened to a student before he or she arrived in your classroom.

In addition to the statements you find in these two examples, what other items might you put on a self-assessment list for *your* students? Work within the following guidelines to develop several that are specific to *your* class:

1. Make each statement a behavior that a student can easily evaluate. This is best done by beginning each statement with *I* and then an *action* verb. Review the statements in the previously given charts for examples.

2. Work to make each statement as objective as possible. Objective statements help students have a clear image of what they are—or are not—doing. "I bring a pencil, paper, and my book to class" *is* objective; statements such as "I am responsible" or "I care about being prepared" is NOT. Avoid words such as *responsible* and *care* as they are subjective, value-laden terms, and therefore, they are not helpful in this activity.

1. _____

2. _____

3. _____

4. _____

5. _____

6. _____

7. _____

Is there anything that you as the teacher can do to help your students stay on top of things and be academically engaged? Yes! By creating a system that sets the stage for them to be successful (think *design*) and then following through (think *maintenance*), you support their efforts.

There is an old saying about horses and water. You no doubt know it well: You can lead a horse to water, but you can't make him drink. True—BUT what if you put salt in his oats the night before? There are five things you can do to "salt the oats" before leading your "student colts" to drink. These are in the first column of the following teacher self-check list. Also, there are five things you can do as your students are learning that will help keep them drinking. These are in the second column. Self-assess yourself on both sides to discover how you might be more effective in supporting student lesson engagement.

PREDICTING MY STUDENTS' SUCCESS

DESIGN	ALWAYS	USUALLY	SOMETIMES	SELDOM	NEVER	MAINTENANCE	ALWAYS	USUALLY	SOMETIMES	SELDOM	NEVER
1. **Assignment location:** I have designated ONE VISIBLE SPOT where I write daily assignments, and I have students copy down their assignments in their notebooks as part of the daily closing routine.						1. **Consistency:** I follow through on the deadlines I set.					
2. **The *what*:** I clarify the specific work students should complete (all items, odds only, specific pages, etc.).						2. **Efficient time use:** I avoid having downtime in my lessons and make plans that anticipate potential interruptions.					
3. **The *how*:** I clarify how students should do work (collaboratively, complete sentences, show all work, etc.).						3. **Fair grading:** I assign more points to assignments that last three weeks than those that last three days.					
4. **The *when* and *where*:** I clarify when and where students should turn in work (as finished, at the end of the period, by midnight; into a basket, electronically, etc.).						4. **Next-day, detailed feedback:** I provide specific notes on *what* is good and *why* and *what* needs improvement and *how*, sooner rather than later.					
5. **Absentee makeup work:** I have a system for clearly communicating what, how, when, and where students should make up and turn in missed work from absence.						5. **Student self-tracking:** I teach my students to self-monitor by teaching them to self-track their progress/grades/accomplishments.					

Source: Adapted from Harris and Tomick (2016, p. 68).

Remember the reading and work on positive consequences you completed in Area Four? Please take a few minutes to turn back and review pages 91 through 94.

After reviewing the four pages, what thoughts do you have on how this type of praise might encourage a student to stay engaged in a lesson?

It takes effort to change praise patterns (it took one author of this book two years!), but the effort can be well worth it. The following story illustrates the power of such statements—even with adults.

True Story: 40 Percent!

We were five weeks into the semester of a weekly, three-hour graduate course, "Classroom Management and Effective Teaching," and the lesson topics had included the elements of more effective praise. Class ended with a challenge to students to begin changing ingrained praise habits by starting with their social comments. To illustrate this challenge, I asked students what they might say to a friend who was wearing a piece of clothing they thought attractive, and they offered comments such as "I like your hat," "Sharp shoes," I really like your necklace," and "Lovely scarf." I then asked a student wearing a patterned aqua and navy scarf with a navy top if she would help me with a teaching example; she agreed, and I delivered the following monologue:

> "You know, I really do like the scarf Sarah is wearing today, and I can say—" and I turned and made eye contact with her "—Sarah, I really like that scarf." Sarah smiled a bit, and I paused to look over the class and let the statement sink in. "Or I can say—" again I made eye contact with Sarah "—Sarah, the scarf you chose to wear today looks sharp with that navy top." Sarah smiled a lot, and I asked her if she felt any difference in being the recipient of those two statements.

> "Yes!" she replied. She paused for a moment as she searched for the right words and then continued, "The first one was nice—but the second one validated something I had done, and it left me feeling affirmed." And so the challenge to students before class next week was to try a minimum of five praise comments to friends that focused on a *choice* or *effort* the person had made.

> The next week Sarah bubbled into class, grinning from ear to ear. "You won't believe it!" she cried exultantly, and she gleefully shared the following before I ever had an opportunity to call class to order: "That thing about statements to validate a person's choice? It works! You know I work part-time as a bartender at (here she named an upscale boutique hotel near campus)? Well, I used it with customers this past week, and my tips went up 40 percent! Forty percent!! Am I ever a believer in praise for choice and effort!"

Ever been on the receiving end of a less-than-stellar lesson? We all have. Perhaps we found it boring because of one or more of the following:

- We lacked enough prior knowledge to make any connections or identify with the topic in any way—and we saw no logical link to anything useful and nothing activated our curiosity.

- We felt we had no options of what was required of us—and we felt little interest in or chance of success in the given requirements.

- We felt that this was just doing more of the same thing.

- We felt we were in a vacuum with no opportunity to interact and share ideas with others.

- The lesson moved so quickly that we were unable to grasp what was going on.

- We had no way of verifying what we did or did not understand.

If any of these resonate with our own experiences with boring lessons, you are in good company. The previous list represents the absence of the six common elements of an engaging lesson:

1. An initial challenge relating the coming topic to the real world and arousing curiosity in the topic (activation of curiosity)

2. Some learning activities options for engaging in the lesson (choice)

3. A variety of learning activities (variety)

4. Opportunities to share ideas with others (whole-class brainstorming, learning partners, small groups)

5. An appropriate lesson pacing (time)

6. Periodic checks for understanding (formative feedback)

Curiosity

Studies show that lessons that stimulate curiosity engage students. "Curiosity . . . is a motivator for learning" (Kidd & Hayden, 2015, p. 449). But what is *curiosity*? George Loewenstein (1994), an educator who studied human decision-making for over thirty years, describes curiosity as "a cognitive induced deprivation that arises from the perception of a gap in knowledge and understanding" (p. 76). In other words, when students realize they don't know and understand something, it creates an intellectual hunger. And that's when they are ready to engage with an academic lesson.

So how can we harness the value of curiosity in lesson design to cause students to be hungry for knowledge—and thus be motivated to seek out that knowledge? A recent term for a type of lesson designed to engage curiosity is *upside-down teaching* (Seeley, 2017). Consider the following chart.

TRADITIONAL TEACHING	UPSIDE-DOWN TEACHING
1. The teacher explains the concept or procedure—such as how to solve a math problem.	1. Students attempt to solve a problem that they may not yet know how to solve.
2. Teacher and students work examples together.	2. The teacher then talks with them about their thinking processes.
3. Students use what was just learned to solve a new problem.	3. The teacher then works to connect students' thinking with the correct process for solving the problem.

Source: Adapted from Seeley (2017).

But wait! Won't that cause students to struggle and get frustrated and give up? No. Here's why:

- When students constructively struggle with mathematical ideas, it engages their thinking and helps them persevere in problem-solving (Leinwand et al., 2014).

- The brain grows when a person struggles in a productive way with something difficult (Dweck, 2007).

- New neurons formed in the hippocampus of the brain require effortful learning experience if they are to survive and be incorporated into brain circuits used for learning (Shors, Anderson, Curlik, & Nokia, 2012).

More and more, teachers are confirming that students benefit from wrestling with problems they have not specifically been taught how to solve. In the process of the struggle, they "learn about the power of effort and persistence, become more confident problem solvers, and even grow their intelligence" (Seeley, 2017, p. 33).

So do you have to throw out lessons plans you already have? No way! But think of how you can preface them with something that makes your students curious about what is to come. Try creating a "challenge scenario" that puts your students into it. Here are some sample challenges that could create interest:

Before an elementary science lesson on life requirements	You are a tadpole living in a pond, and you'd like to grow up to be a frog. What things do you need to make it?
Before an elementary math lesson on fractions	You and your three friends want to share a large square pan pizza. But it arrived cut in six same-size pieces. How can you share it equally?

Before an elementary social studies lesson on maps	Imagine that a new student has just joined your class, and he does not yet speak English. You realize he needs to know how to get from your classroom to the restroom and to the lunchroom. You want to help him—but you cannot tell him with words and you cannot go with him. How might you help him?
Before a secondary language arts lesson on persuasive writing	The school principal is considering cutting lunchtime from thirty minutes to twenty minutes. You and your friends think this is a bad idea and decide to write her a letter. What might you say—and why?
Before a secondary language arts lesson on point of view	Imagine someone you don't know is hired to write "A Day in the Life" about your life. How might this differ from your own version of this day? How might the reader's opinion of you differ in these two versions?
Before a secondary math lesson on calculating combinations	Suppose you are ordering a pizza. You have a coupon for a two-topping pizza, and the restaurant offers five toppings (pepperoni, sausage, mushrooms, olives, and bell peppers). How many different kinds of pizza could you get with your coupon?

Student Choice

As human beings, we love autonomy. We are much more motivated to do a thing when that thing has the blessing of being our choice. We know this from personal experience—and from many studies over the past sixty-plus years: Choice enhances intrinsic motivation (Patall, Cooper, & Wynn, 2010). Well-designed and structured choices lead to increased student academic engagement (Ramsey, Jolivette, Patterson, & Kennedy, 2010). Furthermore, choice reduces problem behaviors of almost every population of students and especially of students with EBDs (Garwood & Ampuja, 2019; Kern & State, 2009). It works like this:

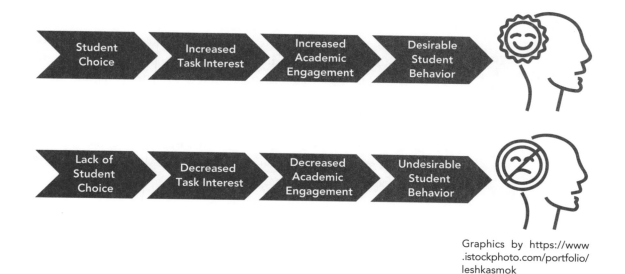

Graphics by https://www .istockphoto.com/portfolio/ leshkasmok

So how do we provide opportunities for student decisions of self-direction in our classrooms? There are six common choice areas a teacher can use. You see them in the first column and some examples after each.

CHOICE OF . . .	EXAMPLES	
	ELEMENTARY	SECONDARY
Task activity	Draw letters on colored paper or trace letters on personal whiteboard.	Interview ornithologist, and write up interview or write paper about birds.
Task sequence	Complete spelling assignments of writing words, creating sentences, and doing crossword in any order.	Complete homework assignments of any given secondary subject area in any order.
Materials	Use colored crayons or markers or pencils.	Use pen or pencil or computer.
With whom to work	Work with self, peer(s), teacher, or aide.	Work with self, peer(s), or teacher.
Where to work	Work at own desk, teacher's desk, table, in special area, or on floor.	Work at own desk, table, special area, or in library.
When to complete work	Finish in current period, next period, study hall, or next day.	Finish in current period, next period, or next day.

Source: Adapted from Kern and State (2009).

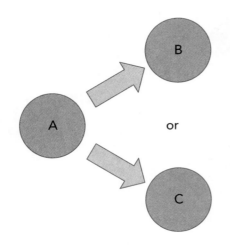

Regarding tasks or activities, some teachers combine choice within a required assignment—for example, all students must do item A and then can then choose to do either item B or C. Teachers report this is also a type of choice students appreciate on a test—students must answer item A and may then choose to answer any three of the four following items B, C, D, and E.

If you decide to involve student choice into your lesson plans, where do you start, and how much choice do you offer? Consider the following steps as a useful plan of action (Kern & State, 2009):

1. Decide *what* choices are appropriate for your lesson plan—which ones do and do not fit within the lesson.

2. Decide *where* the choices fit best in your lesson plan.

3. Incorporate your selections into the lesson plan.

4. Present the choices to students as the lesson unfolds.

5. Seek feedback from students on choices to help in the future.

> When you tell students they have different options to complete a project, You shift the focus away from "Am I going to do this project?" to "How am I going to do this project?"
>
> —Ari Mosquera (2015)

Choice of task is the most common option teachers use, and it is well documented for positive effects:

- Giving elementary students a choice among types of academic activities results in a positive impact on motivation and participation (Iyengar & Lepper, 1999; Kosky & Curtis, 2008).

- When offered a choice of two homework assignments on the same content, secondary students (1) report they are more motivated to do the work, (2) do it more completely and accurately, and (3) score higher on the unit test compared to when they had no choice (Patall et al., 2010).

- For students with EBDs, providing a choice of reading activities increases academic engagement (Garwood, Ciullo, & Brunsting, 2017).

- For students with EBDs, even a choice between two nonpreferred activities increases on-task behavior and decreases problem behavior (Vaughn & Horner, 1997).

Not all choices are equally motivating to all students. Consider your students and your lessons—and the choice to incorporate choice in the classroom is yours. Please take a few minutes to reflect on the six common choice areas, and consider choice options you would be willing to incorporate into your lessons. Briefly journal your thoughts in the following space.

1. Which one(s) would you be more likely to try in your classroom? Why?

   _____

2. Which one(s) would you be less likely to try? Why?

   _____

3. What "support structures" can you think of that might help students follow through once they have made a choice, especially with task activity and task sequence?

   _____

4. How might you introduce choice options to your students?

   _____

Lesson Variety

Often we get in a rut of providing the same types of learning activities. Something has worked well before, and so we repeat it and repeat it and repeat it. Now chocolate cake is good, but chocolate cake at every meal soon becomes monotonous no matter how good the cake. Variety in diet improves our eating pleasure and nutrition—and variety in instructional activities increases lesson engagement (Deng, 2002; Gregory & Kaufeldt, 2015).

There are three pathways of learning (called *modalities*) leading into the brain: visual, auditory, tactile/kinesthetic. A common error with modalities has been to identify a student's preferred modality and focus on teaching in that way. But wait! Students need to learn to process with all three modalities. Each modality stimulates a different set of neurons, and with the more neurons engaged through using multiple modalities, the faster and greater the learning (Frank, Slemmer, Marcus, & Johnson, 2009; Kirkham, Rea, Osborne, White, & Mareschal, 2019).

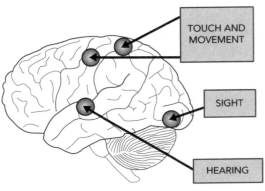

Graphic via Pixabay.com.

Consider the following list of possible learning activities (Tate, 2007). You might initially assume they are best used at kindergarten and lower elementary levels. However, brain research indicates that these strategies are just as appropriate for all grade levels and all content areas (Hannaford, 1995; Jensen, 2000; Wolfe, 2010). By the time a teacher has used all of them, that teacher has not only engaged all of the learning modalities (visual, auditory, tactile/kinesthetic) but also addressed all eight of Howard Gardner's (2006) eight multiple intelligences (logical/mathematical, linguistic, musical, spatial, bodily-kinesthetic, naturalistic, interpersonal, intrapersonal) (Tate, 2007). Which strategies do you currently use? Which ones would you be willing to add to your repertoire?

1. Brainstorming, discussion
2. Drawing, Artwork
3. Field trips
4. Games
5. Graphic organizers, word webs
6. Humor
7. Manipulatives
8. Metaphors, analogies, similes
9. Mnemonic devices
10. Movement
11. Music, rhyme
12. Project or problem-based instruction
13. Cooperative learning
14. Role-play, drama, pantomime
15. Storytelling
16. Technology
17. Visualization, guided imagery
18. Visuals
19. Work study
20. Writing

Note that Howard Gardner did NOT suggest—as is often mistakenly believed—that teachers should identify a student's specific intelligence and then tailor a lesson to the student's preferred modality. NO! Instead, Gardner suggested there are, in fact, multiple ways to learn new information, and the implication for teachers is a need to be sure lessons include multiple methods for students to acquire knowledge. In other words, teachers must differentiate their lesson plans! Allowing students multiple means of engagement, expression, and representation of their knowledge and skills is referred to as *universal design for learning* (UDL) (CAST, 2018).

So what options are available for engaging students in learning? The following chart offers thirty-one possibilities that include modalities, formats, and strategies. Try using it as a checklist to reflect on past lessons you have taught and/or in planning future lessons.

Note: As you use the various modalities, formats, and strategies in designing lessons, consider three types of task value:

1. Intrinsic value—experiencing interest or enjoyment from engaging in a task

2. Attainment value—anticipating achievement, notice, or influence through task attainment

3. Utility value—experiencing benefits to personal goals as a result of task completion

Include at least one of these to stimulate and engage student motivation (Eccles, 2005).

OPTIONS IN INSTRUCTIONAL VARIETY

1 = not used, 2 = used slightly, 3 = used moderately, 4 = used extensively

Modalities					ITEM #
1. Visual modality	1	2	3	4	1
2. Auditory modality	1	2	3	4	2
3. Tactile/kinesthetic modality (hands-on)	1	2	3	4	3
Formats					
4. Whole-group instruction	1	2	3	4	4
5. Teacher-led small-group instruction	1	2	3	4	5
6. Cooperative small-group work	1	2	3	4	6
7. Noncompetitive small-group work	1	2	3	4	7
8. Student pairs	1	2	3	4	8
9. Individualized instruction	1	2	3	4	9
10. Centers and/or stations	1	2	3	4	10

(Continued)

(Continued)

Strategies					ITEM #
11. Academic game	1	2	3	4	11
12. Art activity	1	2	3	4	12
13. Audio tape or CD	1	2	3	4	13
14. Brainstorming	1	2	3	4	14
15. Computer	1	2	3	4	15
16. Discussion (critical thinking)	1	2	3	4	16
17. Graphic organizer or cognitive maps	1	2	3	4	17
18. Lecture	1	2	3	4	18
19. Note-taking	1	2	3	4	19
20. Oral drill	1	2	3	4	20
21. Oral reading	1	2	3	4	21
22. Problem-solving	1	2	3	4	22
23. Project	1	2	3	4	23
24. Role-playing	1	2	3	4	24
25. Silent reading	1	2	3	4	25
26. Simulation	1	2	3	4	26
27. Student collaboration	1	2	3	4	27
28. Student presentation	1	2	3	4	28
29. DVD or overhead projector	1	2	3	4	29
30. Worksheet	1	2	3	4	30
31. Writing activity	1	2	3	4	31

Social Opportunities

If you have ever been a student in a class or taught a class of students, you know that human beings are basically social creatures. We like to talk with one another. Unfortunately, student conversation in any classroom is often to the detriment of student academic learning. But what if that natural inclination to communicate could be channeled into something academically constructive? Sound good? Yes! And, of course, the next question is *how*. If you've not used group work before—or if your prior experiences with it have been less than stellar and left you a bit leery of student groups, how can you provide social opportunities and still maintain order in your classroom?

Start small. Academically oriented social opportunities can be something as simple as a student-paired request from the teacher to do something like the following: Turn to a partner and . . .

- Explain in your own words what you think you are to do in this next activity.

- Compare and contrast how you tackled word problem number four.

- Predict what you think might happen if X occurred and tell why.

- Come up with three questions you would like to ask Dr. Martin Luther King Jr.

Note that each of these provides all students with opportunities to respond (OTRs). Often we think of OTR strategies as teacher-delivered questions, prompts, or cues to which students respond either individually or as a class. But students may also provide OTRs for one another. Whether from you or from peers, OTRs serve to increase both appropriate social behavior and academic performance (MacSuga-Gage & Simonsen, 2015; McMaster, Fuchs, & Fuchs, 2006).

Once students clearly understand the concept of taking turns in a partnered oral activity, consider teaching them the skills involved in truly *listening to understand* what the other person is saying—things such as making eye contact and paraphrasing. Too often in this type of activity students rapidly verbalize their own ideas without ever hearing what the other person is saying. Teaching students the four focus strategies below (Friermood, 2014) can help them learn to listen to one another.

CARE about UNDERSTANDING your Partner

·· **Four Focus Strategies** ··

FACE: Look your partner in the eyes. Lean in. Smile.

FEEDBACK: Nod your head. Give caring cues.

FOLLOW-UP: Ask a question. Try to find out more.

REPHRASE: Try saying back your partner's thinking.

Social skills impact academic achievement, academic achievement affects motivation, and motivation affects lesson engagement. The importance of social skills on academics has come to the attention of many US school districts to the point that they are now implementing social-emotional learning standards into curriculum (Gresham & Elliott, 2014).

In the space provided, please briefly record your thoughts on two things you would be willing to try in your classroom to provide academically focused social opportunities.

1. _____

2. _____

Note: Some teachers find that a useful motivational social activity for review is the small-group activity of Numbered Heads Together (Kagan, 1994). (See V: Numbered Heads Together in the Appendices for the steps in this activity.) With this activity, no one student is ever put on the proverbial spot.

A final thought on providing opportunities for students to talk with one another about academic content: Oral communication is a crucial social skill that some students—especially those with disabilities—need opportunities and guidance to practice and develop. When students possess social skills needed to interact positively with peers, they tend to be more engaged in learning, which improves their academic achievement (Wentzel, 2009), and "tend to be more engaged" equals more motivated. Note that you may need to provide coaching in social skills for social opportunities to be optimally motivating, for not all students come into class with the ability to speak in a respectful tone, ask appropriate questions, and disagree respectfully.

As you move past student pairs to groups of three to five, consider using flexible grouping as opposed to static grouping. Flexible grouping means that groups (or pairs) do not stay the same but are intentionally and frequently (for example, weekly) reorganized by different criteria and for different purposes. Flexible grouping is recognized as an important element in creating inclusive classrooms, especially for students with disabilities (National Association of Elementary School Principals [NAESP], 2020). Consider how many criteria you could use to group students for learning activities other than student academic performance. Note that we do NOT use the term *student academic ability*, for you have no way of knowing a student's ability—only his or her performance on a given day.

Beyond putting students together for instructional activities for academic remediation or academic enrichment, consider the following possible criteria for forming groups of students:

interests	shared culture
social skills	need for multicultural experience
prior experiences	English language proficiency
desired experiences	

If you have other ideas you have for forming student pairs and/or small groups, please jot them down for future reference.

_____

_____

_____

To help small groups work successfully . . .

1. **Group students carefully.** Groups work better with three to five students and when the teacher decides what students go in which groups (Mitman, Megendoller, Ward, & Tikunoff, 1981; Slavin, 1990).

2. **Clearly explain what is to be accomplished**, and check students' understanding (for example ask each group to agree on a one-sentence statement of what they are to do).

3. **Teach needed social skills for collaboration as needed.** Help students understand (1) the reason for using the skill (telling), (2) what the skill looks and sounds like in action (modeling) and when to use the skill, and (3) what the skill feels like in action (role-play) (Johnson & Johnson, 1990).

4. **Walk around among all students.** Your physical presence helps keep students on task; plus, it allows you to listen in and hear how students are thinking.

5. **Avoid group grades.** Students have higher academic achievement in collaborative work when team members work together to earn recognition, but each student is graded on his or her work (Slavin, 1990).

Formative Assessment

Consider two types of assessment: formative and summative:

Formative Assessments	Summative Assessments
Inform students' and teachers' understanding *during* the learning process	*Sum up* students' learning at the end of the learning process or school year
Are almost always *ungraded*	Provide a *grade* for the gradebook
Are *numerous* throughout a course of study	Are *only a handful* throughout a course of study
When the cook tastes the soup	*When the food critic tastes the soup*

If the cook tastes the soup along the way, the final product and the food critic's assessment will be much better. The same is true of our students and of us as teachers.

Students often do not realize what they do and do not know. Formative assessment gives them an opportunity to see and to correct incomplete understandings and misthinkings. Teachers often do not realize that the beautiful lesson we just taught did not connect with some students. Formative assessment gives us the opportunity to realize this and to revise and reteach.

Why use formative assessment? Grant Wiggins (2012), coauthor of *Understanding by Design*, gives this equation:

Less teaching + more feedback = better learning.

In other words, the more formative assessment students do, the better summative assessment teachers get.

So when should you plan to use formative assessment? First, consider the great value of *pre-assessment*. Finding out up front what your students already understand and *misunderstand* about a concept or topic before you begin does three things:

1. It saves you instructional time by not going over things students already know.

2. It allows you to catch and correct misunderstandings before students try to build on them.

3. It causes students to recognize what they do and do not yet know—and what they are going to need to know. (Also, it can allow you to identify possible peer tutors for later lessons.)

Next, consider the great value of *quick daily formative assessment* to see where students are. A class set of anonymous, brief one-sentence summaries written by each student at the end of a lesson takes little time for you to read through and even less time for your students to write. This allows you to take the daily academic pulse of what students are understanding, and it can inform your instruction for the next day. An exit card with the four sentence stems has provided useful formative feedback for some teachers of middle school through college level:

1. An important thing I learned or had reaffirmed in class today is . . .

2. Today's class experiences have left me feeling . . .

3. I wish that in class today we had . . .

4. Something I am left wondering after today's class is . . .

Finally, consider the value of *pretest formative assessment*. Some teachers find that a game format review (more about this later) shortly before the final summative assessment is something that students enjoy and that reduces test anxiety.

Games can be a powerful tool for formative assessment. They give students an opportunity to use what they have learned and to figure out for themselves what they know and don't know. Games can also give the teacher significant insight into what students understand and misunderstand—or just flat out have no clue.

Not all game experiences are created equal, however. Here are four key guidelines for using games in ways that most increase student achievement (Marzano, 2010):

1. **Use inconsequential competition.** Students typically enjoy a bit of within-the-game competition. BUT points earned from games should *NEVER* be factored into students' grades. This creates anxiety and discourages students from taking risks and learning from their mistakes.

2. **Target essential academic content.** Make as many questions or activities as possible relate to key terms and essential concepts, *NOT* on minutiae and details that are not essential to students' understanding. Game questions can include higher-order thinking as well as lower-order regurgitation.

3. **Debrief the game.** Instead of tallying the points and moving on, have students stop and reflect after a game. Ask them which questions or categories were the easiest and which were the hardest—and why. This can help clarify what students need to review.

4. **Have students revise their notes.** Create time and space for students to go back to their notes or previous assignments to review and correct any misunderstandings, add any missing information, or simply clarify a definition or an example. *This step is most often skipped or overlooked.*

Students are most engaged when they are involved. Academic games using student pairs ensure no one is left out. Academic games that use small groups of three to four (five at the very most) tend to hold students' interest. Academic games that involve large class "teams" with only one team representative actually engaged (for example one student from each team is up at the board doing something) set the stage for student misbehavior among those students who are sitting and watching. Choose game formats thoughtfully to keep students engaged.

Some Thoughts on Engaging Students in Virtual Instruction

As technology continues to change our world faster than teacher preparation and professional development organizations can determine what is research-based practice and what is just *tech du jour*, teachers across the nation are being asked (and sometimes forced through circumstance) to deliver more online and hybrid instruction. The cornerstones of effective online teaching are similar to those in face-to-face instruction (for example, scaffolded lesson design, content area expertise) (DiPietro, Ferdig, Black, & Preston, 2008; Notar & Sorbet, 2020). However, delivery strategies may vary between primary and secondary students. For example, elementary students require more audio directions, as they are less able to digest large chunks of text-heavy instructions posted to an online platform (Oliver, Kellogg, Townsend, & Brady, 2010). Also, in the digital domain, how to build or maintain positive relationships with students remains a valid concern.

Both elementary and middle/high school students enjoy opportunities to communicate with their peers in an online platform. Peer-to-peer interactions are often fostered during in-person instruction, and teachers should work to provide these opportunities in a digital world as well. A platform used by one author of this book to facilitate relationships in his online teaching is Flipgrid, which provides free and accessible video discussion with and between students.

Although the research on relationship-building in online learning environments is minimal, we offer three suggestions:

1. **Instructional immediacy.** Instructional immediacy, as defined by Anderson (1979), refers to the verbal and nonverbal communicative behaviors that occur between teachers and students in face-to-face learning environments. These behaviors can increase motivation to learn by reducing the social and psychological distance between teacher and student (Song, Kim, & Luo, 2016). In an online environment, researchers have coined the term *e-immediacy* to refer to the extra importance placed on verbal behaviors in a digital platform where nonverbal cues (such as eye contact, head shakes, smiles) are not always an option (Al Ghamdi, Samarji, & Watt, 2016). Effective verbal cues for building relationships in online teaching include (1) always using students' first names in communication, (2) being humorous, and (3) including appropriate emojis in email and text messages.

2. **Teacher self-disclosure.** Teacher self-disclosure refers to a teacher's sharing appropriate personal information (such as educational background, prior experiences, hobbies, personal stories relevant to the content behaving taught) (Cayanus & Martin, 2008). "Students need to know their instructor is a human being rather than a computer who simply processes and grades their work" (Dupin-Bryant, 2004, p. 2). Teacher self-disclosure has been found to improve teacher-student relationship quality, which in turn improves students' satisfaction with the class and perceptions of how much knowledge they gained in the course. The effect of self-disclosure is actually stronger in online environments than in face-to-face classes (Song et al., 2016).

3. **Flexibility.** Interviews with sixteen highly qualified K–12 online teachers (DiPietro et al., 2008) revealed several traits deemed key to effective online instruction:

- Maintaining an interest and willingness to explore new technology and not staying stuck in one way of doing things

- Accepting that the school day is no longer a defined period of time (A willingness to respond to student requests during off-hours sends a message of care and attention to students' needs. However, you may wish to clarify that student requests after 10:00 p.m. will be addressed the following day.)

- Providing students multiple ways to access content and to demonstrate their mastery of learning (i.e., implementing instruction based on UDL principles; for detailed information about UDL, check out http://www.cast.org/)

- Engaging students in discussion about content- and non–content-related topics

- Communicating with students via multiple technologies, such as phone calls, email, and texts

In addition to these suggestions, we include the following tips for building quality relationships with your students in an online environment:

- Include a mix of synchronous (i.e., live) and asynchronous learning sessions. There are many platforms for both options, but be sure all students can see and hear each other for synchronous sessions and be sure to record screencasts (i.e., audio of your voice over a visual presentation, like a PowerPoint) for asynchronous sessions.

- Email students as a class every day and as an individual at least once per week to provide important updates and reminders and simply to ask them "How are you doing?"

- Set up blocks of time where you are available for a live video chat session, and invite students to join and talk with you. Offer optional participation to all students.

- Aim to grade all work within one week of submission, and be sure to provide some personal feedback for each assignment (i.e., don't just give students a grade with no feedback).

- In email communications, make reference to current events (staying apolitical) to keep the course feeling fresh and to let students know you are living in the same world they face day in and day out.

Some Dos and Avoids to Encourage Student Lesson Engagement

Consider what things you can do to help students stay actively engaged in in any lesson.

DO teach students how to have a growth mindset.

AVOID teaching the same way all the time.

DO follow through with teacher actions that support your students' success.

AVOID assuming your students know the academic behaviors that lead them to success.

DO make visible to students the academic habits that will help them succeed, and then teach them how to self-assess their efforts.

DO convince your students that you believe in their ability to learn.

DO allow your students some opportunities to work together.

DO allow your students some choice in lesson activities.

DO provide your students with opportunities to engage in formative assessment—especially in playing academic games.

Key Takeaways: New and/or Reinforced Ideas on Student Lesson Engagement

Possible Applications: Things I Plan to Try in My Classroom

Please use the following space to jot down (1) key ideas you want to remember—whether new or a reinforcement of your current knowledge and beliefs—and (2) ideas you want to remember to try in your classroom. In the second column, it may help to keep track if you consecutively number the ideas so you can check them off as you try them.

KEY TAKEAWAYS: New and/or Reinforced Ideas	POSSIBLE APPLICATIONS: Things I Plan to Try in My Classroom

CLASSROOM CLIMATE AND COMMUNICATION

"Without a sense of caring,
there can be no sense of
community."

—Anthony J. D'Angelo

Author and founder of
Collegiate EmPowerment

Developing a Positive Classroom Climate

Your classroom climate is a reflection of students' opinions of their experience there, including (1) their perceptions of what is required academically, (2) their interactions with the teacher, (3) their interactions with other students, and (4) their involvement in the class (Barr, 2016). This means that positive classroom climate is most likely to develop when the following occur:

> **You've already covered a lot!**

- Students understand what is required to be academically successful and how to meet those requirements—and the teacher is consistent in expectations and in following through.

- Students see the teacher as a person and have frequent and equal opportunities to experience positive interactions with their teacher.

- Students have opportunities to interact safely and positively with one another.

- Students have opportunities to participate in the class and to be involved in their own academic experiences.

Because in previous five areas you have already considered multiple ways to support each of these items just listed, this area is the briefest of the six. Several of these are listed for each category in the following chart. As you review your notes, you can probably add to this list.

TOPIC	PREVIOUS AREAS OFFER IDEAS TO . . .
Students understand class academic standards and how to meet them.	Help students self-assess academic habits that lead to success. Self-monitor teaching habits that support student success. Identify important class procedures to support academics. Design and implement a lesson plan to teach students a procedure.
Students have frequent and equal opportunities to experience positive interactions with the teacher.	Better understand students' perception of you. Assess your own attitude toward your students. Assess your actions that influence students' perception of you. Assess your communication patterns with students. Deliver negative consequences in ways to discipline rather than punish. Better provide students with equal opportunities to respond (OTRs).
Students have opportunities to interact safely and positively with one another.	Develop and teach class rules and expectations that provide a safe classroom in which interactions may occur, especially teaching what "respect" will look, sound, and feel like in your classroom. Develop and teach (with rehearsal and practice) class procedures that create a safe classroom.
Students experience opportunities to participate and to be involved in their own academic experiences.	Employ elements of lesson design proven to engage and motivate student interest. Use equity cards to ensure all students have fair turns. Provide students with choices within a lesson.

What do we know from research that relates to classroom climate, teacher-student relationships, and effective classrooms? Looking in classrooms reveals the following:

- The three dimensions of "climate" in any human environment are (1) relationship (nature and intensity of mutual support between and among members), (2) personal development (personal growth of members), and (3) system maintenance (extent to which environment is orderly, clear in expectation, and responsive to change) (Moose, 1979, as cited in Adelman & Taylor, 2005).

- Classroom climate is a recognized major determiner of student behavior and learning (Adelman & Taylor, 2005; Bucholz & Sheffler, 2009).

- An extensive review of studies on school climate shows the influence of classroom climate starts in kindergarten, where the climate a kindergartner experiences through negative teacher-student relationships is likely to result in behavior and academic problems in later grades. Climate influence continues through middle school and high school to affect students' self-perception, academic engagement, and likelihood of graduation (Hamre & Pianta, 2001; Quin, 2016; Thapa, Cohen, Guffey, & Higgins-D'Alessandro, 2013).

- Students in classrooms with positive teacher-student relationships exhibit a more positive attitude toward school as well as increased academic achievement (Bernt & Keefe, 1995; Goodenow, 1993; Poling, Van Loan, Garwood, Zhang, & Riddle, 2020; Skinner & Belmont, 1993).

- An analysis of forty-six studies found strong teacher-student relationships were associated with improvement in student academic engagement and attendance and also with a reduction in disruptive behaviors and suspensions. These strong effects remained even after controlling for differences in students' individual characteristics, family, and school backgrounds (Quin, 2016).

- A teacher's relationship with students is the best predictor of how much the teacher experiences joy versus anxiety in class (Hagenaur, Votet, & Hascher, 2015).

- In classrooms where teachers deliberately increased the ratio of positive-to-negative verbal interactions with students to a five-to-one ratio, students' academic engagement increased and misbehavior decreased (Cook et al., 2017).

- Calling students by name, both in and out of the classroom, signals to students they are important (Glenz, 2014).

Please reflect on each of the previously given items for a few moments, and think about things these findings suggest you might do or do differently to build and maintain a positive classroom climate. Use the Reflections on Area Six page at the end of this area to jot down your thoughts.

Creating a Positive Classroom Climate Through Safety

The phrase *classroom climate* refers to the prevailing mood, attitudes, standards, and tone that you and your students feel when they are in your classroom. A negative classroom climate feels hostile, chaotic, and out of control; a positive classroom climate feels safe, respectful, welcoming, and supportive of student learning. A positive classroom climate improves a student's ability to learn; a negative climate impedes it (Bucholz & Sheffler, 2009). "The good news is that a classroom climate does not just happen—it is created" (Kamb, 2012).

Note the word *safe* and the phrase *it is created* in the first paragraph. The place to begin is with safety. Students need to feel safe. They need to feel physically safe from bodily harm by external elements (such as extreme weather), other students, the teacher, and surrounding elements of the classroom (such as a nearby teetering bookshelf or a tarantula in a terrarium). They need to feel emotionally safe from embarrassment—from themselves, other students, and the teacher, as well as safe from bullying by other students and adults in authority. "When students feel safe both emotionally and physically, they are able to focus better on learning" (Kamb, 2012).

You can contribute to students' feelings of physical safety by how you set up the classroom and teach emergency procedures. Also, you can take note of interactions among students to determine if there are any group dynamics that could cause a student to feel physically threatened (for example, seating a single student between two others who have been known to come to blows can create a fear of physical threat of being caught in the middle) and arrange the classroom to avoid the possibility of harm.

Emotional safety begins with teaching class expectations and rules that make clear what respect looks like, sounds like, and feels like in your classroom. Recognize that some students may come with language, intonations, and nonverbal ways of reacting that are unacceptable

in class. If so, you must specifically teach and have students practice more acceptable communication.

> Climate makes a huge difference!

Emotional safety also includes defusing the fear of making mistakes. Mistakes are things we learn from. Help students understand that recognizing a mistake just means you are smarter now than you were then. Students with this fear, especially adolescents, may act out in undesirable ways to avoid a public response that could be seen as a mistake. Their mantra here is "better to be thought cool than a fool," and acting out is a defense mechanism to sidetrack the teacher into dealing with behavior and thus to avoid having to give a possibly wrong response and be thought dumb.

Maslow (1943) identified a hierarchy of seven universal human needs. The bottom four "deficiency needs" must be met before the top three "growth needs" can flourish. We meet students where they are. If basic physiological needs are not met, schools provide free breakfasts and clothes closets. Now move up one. How do we make sure students' safety needs—both physical and emotional—are met? The self-assessment checklist on the next page provides some ideas.

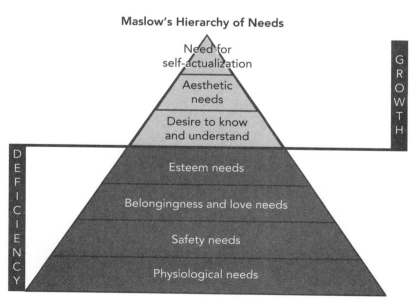

Maslow's Hierarchy of Needs

Check where you fall in each of the items that follow. All of these items contribute to a student's sense of personal safety in your classroom. A YES for each item means you have addressed an important component of creating a positive classroom climate. Anything less than YES is an area where an action on your part could help create a greater sense of student safety and thus a more positive classroom climate.

> **Create a sense of safety!**

Concerning Students' Safety Concerns in My Classroom, I Have . . .	NO		SOMEWHAT		YES
1. Gone over safety drills and taught students what they should do in the case of a tornado, fire, or building threat	○	○	○	○	○
2. Arranged the room so pathways are clear and students can easily exit in case of an emergency, either school-wide or personal	○	○	○	○	○
3. Provided students new to the building with a building map and either talked them through the map or walked them through the building	○	○	○	○	○
4. Developed classroom expectations and rules that made clear that respect includes both physical safety (such as "keep hands, feet, and objects to yourself") and emotional safety (such as expectations that students will accept one another without put-downs, laughter, ridicule)	○	○	○	○	○
5. Specifically taught and had students practice acceptable communication in word choice, intonation, and body language	○	○	○	○	○
6. Worked on defusing students' fear of making mistakes	○	○	○	○	○
7. Avoided the "emotional fear factor" and made clear that respect includes physical and emotional safety with me as well as with other students	○	○	○	○	○
8. Made intentional efforts to establish myself as a "4-F" teacher—one who is fair, friendly, and firm and also follows through	○	○	○	○	○
9. Made it a policy never to discipline a student when I am frustrated or angry	○	○	○	○	○

*There is nothing so useful as
a good theory!*

—Kathleen Hoover-Dempsey, PhD,
Professor of Psychology and Human
Development, Vanderbilt University

Maslow's hierarchy of needs suggests students must first have physiological needs met, feel safe, and have a connection with the classroom and its members before they are able to engage in higher-order thinking. We build on this theory to create a positive classroom climate in which students can and do learn. Along with food and clothing, we provide adequate restroom breaks, clean air, and good lighting. We address safety concerns in a variety of ways, and we strive to provide opportunities for students to be an integral part of small groups and of the class as a whole in ways that their voices are heard respectfully by others. The theory informs our actions.

Bronfenbrenner's (1976) ecological systems theory suggests the development of a human being—and that is each of your students—is influenced by four distinct systems that can be thought of as concentric circles with the child or adolescent in the middle.

- First, the *microsystem* is the child's immediate setting (such as a classroom, the home) where a child or adolescent participates and engages with others.

- Second, the *mesosystem* encompasses connections between and among the microsystems (for example, neglect by caregivers in the home plays out in a struggle to form meaningful connections with teachers).

- Third, the *exosystem* represents the microsystems of which the student is not a member, but those that do have an indirect influence on a student's development (such as parent's work setting, school board, public transportation, mass media).

- Finally, the *macrosystem* encompasses cultural contexts (such as socioeconomic status, race, ethnicity).

In this ecological theory, the student's microsystem (i.e., your classroom) may be most important in emotional and behavioral development (Doyle, 2006). According to Bronfenbrenner (1976), personal interactions between children and adults in the microsystem are the driving forces of development (Tudge, Mokrova, Hatfield, & Karnik, 2009). This tells us that if the classroom climate is not supportive of positive interactions between students and the teacher, it is likely to exacerbate rather than remediate the problems of those students at risk for school failure. And if the classroom climate is built on a predominance of positive teacher-student interactions, our struggling students have a much better chance of survival and success. Again, the theory informs our actions.

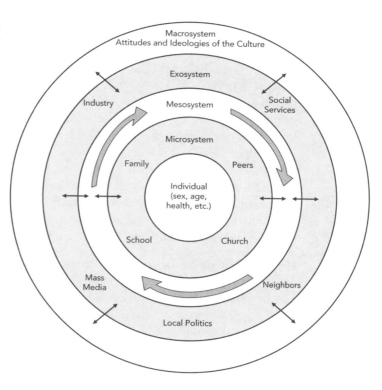

Maintaining Positive Classroom Climate Before, During, and After a Crisis

Life happens. And so, sometimes, does a crisis situation in the classroom. The first goal, of course, is to avoid the crisis, and the greatest contributor to success here is positive relationship-building before the opportunity for crisis arises. The second goal is to de-escalate the crisis quickly, and the third is to help the student reflect and make a better choice in a future similar situation.

Before a Crisis Situation. One of the best ways to maintain a positive climate is to focus on delivering more positive feedback (such as acknowledging students' desirable behavior when performed) than negative (such as reprimands, ultimatums) (Nelson & Roberts, 2000). Unfortunately, the students most likely to receive more negative feedback than positive are students with EBDs (emotional and behavioral disorders) (Sprouls, Mathur, & Upreti, 2015). (Consider self-recording for a half hour or more to discover your own positive-to-negative statements ratio.)

All students benefit from meaningful teacher-student relationships, but students with EBDs are the ones whose disability is in part defined by an inability to form meaningful relationships with others (Wery & Cullinan, 2013). Relationships are built through a continuing series of interactions throughout the school year, and students with EBDs especially need your intentional help in relationship-building. Remember the TAN framework from Area One (see page 17)? Consider that every interaction with a student is moving you either toward or away from that student and meeting or not meeting the needs of both teacher and student. With positive and intentional interactions, you build a good teacher-student relationship, and that relationship "is the best method for preventing undesirable behaviors and reducing the escalation of negative behaviors during a crisis situation" (Van Loan & Garwood, 2020a, p. 254).

During a Crisis Situation. If a crisis situation does occur, one of the most important things you can do is maintain self-control as you self-monitor words, tone, and body language (Van Loan & Garwood, 2020a). But, how do you do this in the heat of the moment? If you find yourself experiencing anger and/or frustration, then recognize your feelings but do *not* act on them. Work to stay calm, to imagine what feelings the student is experiencing at that moment (Long, Morse, Fecser, & Newman, 2007), and to respond in a normal tone of voice. Above all, avoid falling into the trap of responding in the same emotional way as the student—which is counterproductive for the student, for you, and for the climate of your entire class.

After a Crisis Situation. After a crisis, it is important to guide a student to understand how choices made can result in both natural and imposed undesirable consequences (for example, choosing not to brush your teeth results in cavities [natural]; choosing to drive too fast results in a speeding ticket [imposed]) (Van Loan & Garwood, 2020a). Help the student explore other choices he or she could have made and will commit to making if a similar situation arises again. As you consider what consequence is appropriate for a student (depending on the crisis, student age and/or maturity level, and your ultimate goal for that student), it may be simply an oral or written self-reflection on what better choices the student plans to make if a similar situation arises.

Keep in mind that students with EBDs often have little or no control of what happens to them in school or in their personal lives (Cefai & Cooper, 2010). If this is the case, a negative consequence of losing yet one more thing they value may be counterproductive. Instead of taking something away, spending time explaining the big picture of a student's actions and resulting consequences may preserve the teacher-student relationship and help the student see the teacher as an ally (Van Loan & Garwood, 2020a).

If you cannot think of an appropriate consequence at the time, Van Loan and Garwood (2020a) suggest saying something like "I noticed that you _____ [insert observed behavior in specific objective terms]. I need to think about how we are going to address that, and I will get back to you." This lets the student and other class members know that the behavior is unacceptable, and it allows you time to come up with an appropriate consequence without overreacting. By taking this step, you maintain a quality teacher-student relationship and foster a positive classroom climate (Fay & Funk, 1995).

Three Examples of Crisis Prevention and a Question

As the principal entered and sat at the side to observe a rural Tennessee second-grade classroom, two students began an animated exchange over crayons at their table. Looking at one another, both gave the "time-out" signal and walked toward the back of the room. As they passed the principal, one turned and said, "'Scuse me, ma'am. We got to go to the cussin' table." The look of shock on the administrator's face turned to relief when she saw them sit at a small table with the word *DISCUSSION* taped to the front where they verbally ironed out their differences, shook hands, and then returned to their desks.

Jared was a fifth grader with anger management issues who came with the warning of periodic explosion. He was hyper, he was sensitive, and he was angry. For two weeks, the teacher briefly journaled the boy's behavior and then looked for patterns. His conclusion was that when he felt frustrated, Jared lashed out. In an effort to help him gain self-control, the teacher offered the option of using a three-by-twenty-foot empty floor space in the back of the room as his "personal pacing space." Whenever he felt he was about to blow, he could remove himself from whatever or whoever was the source of frustration, walk to the back of the room, pace back and forth until he felt in control again, and return to his desk. About once each week, the boy could be seen striding to the back of the room and walking rapidly back and forth, with his pace gradually slowing and his demeanor growing calmer until at the end of three to five minutes he returned to his desk.

To encourage students to achieve a class goal of "Think and make wise choices," an eighth-grade teacher designated a "Thinking Space" by hanging a four-foot length of soft blue cloud-print fabric on the two walls next to a desk in a corner. She invited students to use it for brief periods (up to fifteen minutes) as an alternate seating space if they felt they were about to make an unwise choice in their current space or if they needed a change of space to focus better. He found four students made frequent use of the space—three for whom he had created it and one he would never have guessed felt a need for it.

An ISS (in-school suspension) teacher found the same slim tenth grader returning to his classroom about every two weeks during the third-period class. During each two-day class suspension, the boy sat quietly, did his work, turned it in, and the teacher passed it on to the third-period teacher. On the boy's third return, the ISS teacher spoke with him, expressing surprise at his repeated visit, especially when he was obviously capable of doing good academic work and caused no problems at all in ISS. The boy responded that he did his best work in ISS and really preferred it to his third-period class. He felt safe in ISS class because no other students ridiculed him, and the teacher never embarrassed him. He *liked* ISS. What advice would you give his third-period teacher?

Developing Community

Develop class community!

Looking at Maslow's hierarchy of human needs, just above the bar of "safety needs" you see "belongingness and esteem needs." One of the ways we strengthen students' feelings of safety is through their sense of belonging to a special group—and in this case, it is being an integral part of your classroom.

Your goal is to create a classroom culture where students experience a sense of membership and influence, have personal needs fulfilled, and share satisfying connections with others (Jennings & Greenberg, 2009). In other words, students need to (1) feel they belong, (2) feel they make meaningful contributions, (3) have their physiological and safety needs met, and (4) have opportunities to work in positive ways with other students and with the teacher.

Developing positive classroom community can start with something as simple as using students' names—calling students by their preferred names and pronouncing them correctly. (Note that some students prefer a nickname and are insulted by use of the given name; others are affronted if you shorten their names in any way—check students' preferences!) The simple act of calling students by their names repeatedly surfaces as a way that students perceive respect from their teachers (Glenz, 2014). Also, providing some way for students to know the names of all of their classmates and to know a little bit about one another contributes to a positive class community. A "question of the day" attendance procedure observed for several years in a chemistry teacher's classroom offers a two-birds-one-stone opportunity both to keep accurate attendance records required by the school and to allow students to learn more about one another as you learn more about them—and it begins a class on a positive note. (See W: Procedures Lesson Plan Outline for Taking Roll and X: Possible Questions for Roll Call "Question of the Day" for Students in the Appendices for a teacher lesson plan for this procedure and possible questions for both elementary and secondary classes.)

Ideas to Develop Class Community. What else can you think of to help fulfill these four student needs that help build community and a positive climate in your classroom? Jot down your ideas here.

1. Students feel they belong.

2. Students feel they make meaningful contributions.

3. Students have their basic physiological and safety needs met.

4. Students have multiple opportunities to work in positive ways with others.

To see ideas for each of these items that other teachers have shared with the authors in past years, see Y: Developing Class Community: Ideas From Teachers in the Appendices. Read through the lists, and add to your own list those that you think you would like to remember to try. Then use your list as a checklist to keep track of your implementation of various ideas for building a positive climate and community in your classroom.

Home-School Communication Influences Classroom Community

The students who come to your classroom bring with them the influences of their home. If adults in the home are positively disposed to education and to a child's teacher, the student is more likely to come with a positive disposition as well. What can you do to encourage this?

Just as *location* is the three most important things in real estate, so is *clear and positive communication* in home-school relationships. All parents love their children (and as a teacher was once overheard to say, "Parents are sending us the best kids they've got."). A principal once gave a first-year teacher a wise piece of advice:

> It's really hard for parents not to like you
>
> if they feel you truly care about their child.

Reach Out With Positive Communication. Going on the offensive to contact parents with something positive rather than wait for them to contact you with something less than positive results in greater parent appreciation and cooperation. Consider with the next report card including a brief printed and signed note along the lines of what you see here:

> *Just a note to say that this past grading period we have covered X, Y, and Z. In the coming weeks we will be studying A, B, and C. Thank you for trusting me with the education of your child.*

If your class load is no more than twenty-five, consider adding a line of something positive about the student, using the child's name. If your class load is between 25 and 150, the lines that were just given will still provide a positive contact.

Reach Out With Two-Way Communication. Provide parents and guardians with an easy way to communicate things that might help you better understand your students. In Z-1: Help Me Know Your Child (Elementary) and Z-2: Help Me Know Your Son or Daughter in the Appendices, you'll find two versions of a "Help Me Know . . ." form developed by a first-year teacher hired in December to take over a set of ninth-grade classes that had run off another first-year teacher midyear. She tells her story here:

> When in my second week of teaching, my principal called over the PA asking me to stop by his office after school, I was petrified. I could think of nothing I'd done to be called to his office. When the last bus departed, I entered the school's inner sanctum with trepidation. He turned to me and boomed, "Well done!"
>
> Relieved and shocked, I replied, "Uh . . . *what* was well done?"
>
> "That form you sent home," he replied. "Well done! I've had five parents call me in the last three days expressing thanks for the opportunity to share about their kids. From where I sit, that's a groundswell."

If you choose to send a brief note with the next report card, consider adding the following sentence and attaching a version of the "Help Me Know . . . " form: *As we continue into the school year, please help me know more about your son or daughter by completing and returning the attached page.*

The more you know about the home situation in which a student lives, the better you can understand that student. The better you understand a student, the better you can make choices that will help build a positive relationship. The "Help Me Know . . ." forms in the Appendices (see pages 199 and 200) can provide useful information—*if* the parent completes and returns it. But if a completed paper does not show up, avoid assuming the parent just doesn't care. There could be a variety of reasons for its absence. Perhaps the parent never got it, the student lost it, English is not the parent's first language, or there are other crucial and pressing family matters that push such forms to a back burner where they melt into oblivion. (Indeed, often when you learn what students are dealing with outside of school, you wonder how they are functioning as well as they are.) Don't give up! Follow up. Work to identify the cause of the communication breakdown, and try again.

Community includes families!

Multiple points of communication throughout the school year can help build positive relationships with parents, including notes, phone calls, emails, videoconferencing such as Zoom, TeamViewer), and parent conferences. For building relationships, the best of these are the face-to-face ones that include both verbal and nonverbal communication. Mehrabian (1971) found that the words a person speaks (or types) have the least amount of impact on the perceived meaning of a message, with intonation and facial expression accounting for over 90 percent of interpreted message meaning. Thus, email communication carries the greatest possibility for misinterpretation. (Remember this when you read a parent's email that offends at first reading!) In responding to a parent's email, sooner is better, but be sure to take time to think through and proofread any response before sending.

When you conference with a parent, whether live or online, be aware to monitor your non-verbal expressions and make sure they are a match for the message you wish to convey. If your face is an open book, then make sure what page it is turned to during a conference. The expression a parent reads on your face will convey much more than the words you say, and facial expressions of emotions are interpreted the same across cultures (Dunning, 1971). Your body sends a message as well. Rigid posture, crossed extremities, and feet pointing away from the other person send a negative message of an unwillingness to communicate; a slightly relaxed posture, with open chest, and feet planted facing the other person sends just the opposite message. With which person at right would you feel most comfortable in a conference?

Finally, consider the power of a positive handwritten note in developing a positive teacher-parent relationship. In a day when letter writing is becoming a lost art, a handwritten note from a child's teacher can be a thing to treasure. It need not be long—again, a note of one to three sentences is enough to make a lasting impact. (As a teacher, do you keep a file of positive written notes and pull them out every now and then to bring up good memories and feelings?)

Home-School Communication and Phone Calls

Phone Call
Suggestions!

One of the ways to maintain positive communication and build rapport with parents is to call with something good. Indeed, if you have first made a contact reporting something positive about a student, you will be better received if later you call about something not so positive. Teachers tell us again and again that a positive phone call home has been a major relationship builder that provided great benefits. Such calls can be brief—one to three sentences. And since you are the one initiating the call, you are the one who may close it after your brief statement.

But sometimes you may be on the receiving end of a negative phone call from a frustrated parent. How you handle this type of call influences your home-school relationship. Start by planning ahead to avoid a "surprise attack."

- For calls from parents during class time, ask your school secretary to inform the parent you are in class and will return the call *and* to ask what would be a good time to return the call.

- For calls from parents during your planning period, ask your school secretary to take a message, say you will call back, *and* ask what would be a good time to return the call.

Both of these responses to a during-the-day call give you time to review any notes on the student and to collect your thoughts before talking with the parent (Weinstein, 2003).

Carol Weinstein (2003) offers some excellent practical tips for those tough phone conversations that have the potential to be detrimental to home-school relationships:

- If a parent is calling with a complaint, avoid getting defensive. Listen to understand the parent's frustration. Use active listening techniques, (for example, first listening to a speaker's words and then rephrasing them back to make sure you are interpreting correctly).

- Respond by expressing concern and assuring the parent you are committed to finding a solution.

- If a parent calls to complain a student is upset about something (such as you're picking on or embarrassing his or her child), acknowledge the student's perception and convey regret that the student has that perception—for example, "Oh, I am so sorry that she has that perception. What specifically has she said that could help me figure out what's going on? Please help me understand because I don't want her to feel that way." Avoid replying defensively that you have not picked on or embarrassed the student.

- If you think a call is one in which you might become defensive, ask a friend to be in the room with you to help you monitor your tone of voice. The person can tap you on the shoulder or make a face if you begin to get hostile or defensive.

- If a parent is out of control, calmly suggest you talk at a later time to allow you both a time to think and process.

A great deal has been written about school climates. We know that positive school climates can decrease students' antisocial behaviors (McEvoy & Welker, 2000) and increase teachers' sense of job satisfaction (Billingsley, Carlson, & Klein, 2004), while a negative climate diminishes students' motivation to engage in school (Lee & Burkham, 2003).

You make the difference!

The result of today's emphasis on high-stakes testing is often a school climate focused solely on academic rigor. Such tunnel vision typically overlooks the needs of students dealing with trauma and/or struggling with EBDs and thus results in failure to cultivate a school climate that supports these students (Mihalas, Morse, Allsopp, & McHatton, 2009).

True, some schools do choose to have greater emphasis on an environment defined by care rather than solely academic rigor. School-wide systems in line with this mode of thinking, such as enacting positive behavior interventions and supports (Eber, Sugai, Smith, & Scott, 2002), teaching students' social skills (Gresham, Sugai, & Horner, 2001), and fostering collaboration between educators and families (Osher & Hanley, 2001), are all useful steps in this direction. However, these are system-level approaches that do not directly address the teacher-student relationship, and it is the teacher-student relationship that makes all the difference. Indeed, the better the relationship quality between teacher and student, the better schools can successfully implement such school-wide practices (Mihalas et al., 2009).

Positive relationships between teachers and students are the building blocks of a positive classroom climate. Such relationships provide the solid foundation to establish a positive school climate. And such relationships are foundational for student learning. Just ask the students! In survey responses, students with EBDs indicated teacher care was critical in a teacher's being effective at his or her job (McIntyre & Battle, 1998). Hiam Ginott (1975) said it well:

I've come to the frightening conclusion

that I am the decisive element in the classroom.

It is my personal approach that creates the climate.

It is my daily mood that makes the weather.

As a teacher, I possess tremendous power

to make a child's life miserable or joyous.

I can be a tool of torture or an instrument of inspiration.

I can humiliate or humor. Hurt or heal.

In all situations, it is my response that decides

whether a crisis will be escalated or de-escalated

and a child humanized or dehumanized.

Some Dos and Avoids to Develop a Positive Class Climate

Consider what things you can do to develop and maintain a positive climate in your classroom and positive and supportive home-school communication. (Some of these may seem familiar from other areas.)

DO greet students at the door with eye contact and pleasant demeanor.

AVOID assuming all of the students in a class already know one another.

DO make periodic eye contact with students (pleasant, human-to-human eye contact).

AVOID allowing a student or set of students to dominate class participation.

DO call students by name—both in and outside of the classroom.

AVOID disciplining a student when you are frustrated or angry.

DO teach and have students practice what respect looks, sounds, and feels like in your classroom.

AVOID waiting until there is a problem before ever contacting a parent or guardian.

DO provide students with positive ways to interact with one another.

AVOID assuming a nonresponding parent does not care; there may be many legitimate reasons for a lack of response.

DO establish a way to ensure all students have equal participation opportunities.

DO make an effort to provide periodic positive communication with parents.

Key Takeaways: New and/or Reinforced Ideas on Student Lesson Engagement

Possible Applications: Things I Plan to Try in My Classroom

Please use the following space to jot down (1) key ideas you want to remember—whether new or a reinforcement of your current knowledge and beliefs—and (2) ideas you want to remember to try in your classroom. In the second column, it may help to keep track if you consecutively number the ideas so you can check them off as you try them.

KEY TAKEAWAYS: New and/or Reinforced Ideas	POSSIBLE APPLICATIONS: Things I Plan to Try in My Classroom

PLANNING, IMPLEMENTATION, AND ASSESSMENT

"If there is no struggle,
there is no progress. "

—Frederick Douglass

American abolitionist
and statesman

Pulling It All Together

You have reviewed six areas that each contribute to a smoothly functioning classroom. In each of these you have (1) self-assessed some items, (2) looked at the research and considered what the implications are for your own situation (you and your set of students in your school), (3) noted some takeaway ideas, and (4) noted some possible applications for your own classroom. Perhaps you are using A: A Chart to Keep Track in the Appendices to track your progress. Hopefully you have jotted down your thoughts and ideas on the Reflections page at the end of each area. Now is the time to pull it all together and plan how you will be intentional in revising and/or restructuring your classroom management system when you and your students return to school.

> Plan your work; work your plan!

Start by reviewing the self-assessment checklist(s) and the research findings in the beginning of each area, and then look over your notes at the end of the area. Next make a plan of action for each area in the charts that follow—a numbered list of things related to that area you think you would like to try. Be specific. Nothing is too small, for sometimes the smallest change can make the biggest difference. (Plus, it gives you a sense of accomplishment when you can look back at your list and say to yourself, "I did that.")

Then prioritize your list, make a plan, and outline a time frame. You can't do everything at once. Decide what you think might have the greatest cost-benefit ratio, and start there. Maybe it is something as easy to do as being at the door and making pleasant eye contact with each student as he or she enters; perhaps it is taking the time to make equity cards (see I: Equity Cards—Not Craft Sticks in the Appendices) to teach students their purpose and use and to use them at least three days each week.

Area One: Assessing and Enhancing My Students' Perceptions of Me as Their Teacher

Reviewed: ___ self-assessment chart ___ research findings ___ takeaways and possible applications		
Plan of Action (Ideas numbered for future reference)	Dates	
	INTENDED	IMPLEMENTED

Area Two: Arranging the Furniture, Equipment, and Materials in My Classroom

<table>
<tr><td colspan="3">Reviewed:

___ self-assessment chart   ___ research findings   ___ takeaways and possible applications</td></tr>
<tr><td rowspan="2">Plan of Action
(Ideas numbered for future reference)</td><td colspan="2">Dates</td></tr>
<tr><td>INTENDED</td><td>IMPLEMENTED</td></tr>
<tr><td></td><td></td><td></td></tr>
</table>

Area Three: Reaffirming/Revising and Teaching Expectations (Rules) and Procedures of My Classroom

<table>
<tr><td colspan="3">Reviewed:

___ self-assessment chart   ___ research findings   ___ takeaways and possible applications</td></tr>
<tr><td rowspan="2">Plan of Action
(Ideas numbered for future reference)</td><td colspan="2">Dates</td></tr>
<tr><td>INTENDED</td><td>IMPLEMENTED</td></tr>
<tr><td></td><td></td><td></td></tr>
</table>

Area Four: Choosing and Using Appropriate Consequences to Encourage Appropriate Behavior

Reviewed:

___ self-assessment chart   ___ research findings   ___ takeaways and possible applications

Plan of Action (Ideas numbered for future reference)	Dates	
	INTENDED	IMPLEMENTED

Area Five: Engaging My Students in Engaging Lessons

Reviewed:

___ self-assessment chart   ___ research findings   ___ takeaways and possible applications

Plan of Action (Ideas numbered for future reference)	Dates	
	INTENDED	IMPLEMENTED

Area Six: Developing a Positive Classroom Climate and Strengthening Home-School Communication

Reviewed:		
___ self-assessment chart ___ research findings ___ takeaways and possible applications		

Plan of Action (Ideas numbered for future reference)	Dates	
	INTENDED	**IMPLEMENTED**

What do you think?

Look four to six weeks forward in your planning calendar from the date you begin to implement ideas and make an appointment with yourself to review the results of your efforts. Begin the appointment by completing the following sentence stems—along with the reason why—and then use the checklist on the following page to identify specific effects of the implementation of your plan.

1. The most valuable thing I've learned from this experience is . . .

2. The one change I made that seems to have made the biggest difference is . . .

3. The one thing I yet plan to do to help students and myself is . . .

Twenty Reflection and Assessment Questions . . .

Assessment of Results Four to Six Weeks After Implementation	GOTTEN WORSE		STAYED SAME		GOTTEN BETTER
1. My students' perceptions of me as a fair teacher who cares about them have . . .	○	○	○	○	○
2. My perception of my students as capable human beings who may be lacking in various developmental skills has . . .	○	○	○	○	○
3. Students' civility to one another has . . .	○	○	○	○	○
4. Students' civility to me has . . .	○	○	○	○	○
5. Ease of movement throughout our classroom (accessibility) for both me and my students has . . .	○	○	○	○	○
6. Room arrangement support for instruction (visibility, distractibility, flexibility) has . . .	○	○	○	○	○
7. My own understanding of the differences among expectations/rules/policies and procedures and goals has . . .	○	○	○	○	○
8. Students' following class expectations/rules/policies has . . .	○	○	○	○	○
9. Students' success in understanding and following class procedures has . . .	○	○	○	○	○
10. My use of appropriate positive, corrective, and negative consequences has . . .	○	○	○	○	○
11. My ratio of positive to negative statements made to my students has . . .	○	○	○	○	○
12. Variety within my academic lesson plans has . . .	○	○	○	○	○
13. Students' opportunities for choice within a lesson have . . .	○	○	○	○	○
14. Equal participation opportunities for all students have . . .	○	○	○	○	○
15. Students' understanding and implementation of things they can do to be academically successful has . . .	○	○	○	○	○
16. My understanding and implementation of actions I can take to support student academic success has . . .	○	○	○	○	○
17. The general climate in my classroom has . . .	○	○	○	○	○
18. My communication with parents has . . .	○	○	○	○	○
19. My sense of satisfaction in teaching has . . .	○	○	○	○	○
20. My overall classroom management system has . . .	○	○	○	○	○

APPENDICES
Charts, Resources,
Reproducibles, and Keys of Possible Answers

Using the following chart can help you track your efforts as you move through the process of reviewing and revising various areas of your classroom management.

	ASSESSMENT OF RESULTS	IMPLEMENTATION OF MY PLAN	DEVELOPMENT OF MY PLAN	POSSIBLE CLASSROOM APPLICATION	RESEARCH REVIEW	SELF-ASSESSMENT
My students' perceptions of me as their teacher						
Physical arrangement of my classroom						
Expectations and procedures by which my classroom runs						
Consequences I choose to use—positive, corrective, and negative						
My students' academic engagement						
The climate and community of my classroom						

B: Communicating a Positive Perception of Yourself as a Teacher: Ideas From Teachers

Myself as a Teacher

- Share my reasons for being a teacher.

- Share about my academic background and experiences.

- Share about a past teacher who was influential in my life.

- Explain that I am not perfect and do not know everything, but I am open to continued learning.

- Provide some basic information about myself in the class syllabus (very short).

- Display credentials (make a copy of teaching certificate and diploma).

Myself as a Person

- Play "Two Truths and a Lie" with students (to convey personal interest).

- Tell students selected things about my life, including outside the classroom or school.

- Identify common interests with my students.

- Share a carefully curated timeline of my life on website/blog.

- Share a carefully selected personal story.

- Get involved with students' extracurricular activities.

- Use light humor.

- Share a picture of myself at my students' age (takes bravery).

My Enthusiasm for This School Year With This Class

- Share with the class my vision of our class purpose, or the big picture.

- Explain why I love teaching and/or my subject.

- Give a hint of what is coming for the remainder of the year—add suspense.

- Share adjectives about feelings for the remainder of the year, and invite students to do the same.

My Honesty and Fairness

- Make visible my policy on academic honesty.

- Share the grading rubrics I use.

- Make visible my late work policy.

- Share with students mistakes I typically make.

- Make very visible how I grade.

- Provide a class syllabus with clear expectations.

- Provide clear course expectations.

- Demonstrate respect for self and others and the course.

My Values for Students as Individuals

- Incorporate different learning styles.

- Know students' names—and use them.

- Create a "cooling down" space for students to self-monitor their own behavior.

- Greet each student at the door.

- Demonstrate an interest in students' experiences or activities.

- Talk with students outside of class.

- Smile at students as a class and as individuals.

My Values for Our Class as a Community

- Engage students in cooperative learning/reciprocal teaching.

- Demonstrate respect for others' opinions.

- Develop class rules and expectations with the class.

- Develop a class motto or identity.

Source: From the accompanying screencast of *Getting Off to a Good Start: The First Three Days of School* (Harris & Tomick, 2016).

C: Some Thoughts About Our Classroom (Early Elementary)

Directions: Circle the face that shows your opinion about each statement.

Circle the smiley face if you really agree.

Circle the neutral face if you are not sure.

Circle the frowny face if you really disagree.

STATEMENT	AGREE	NEUTRAL	DISAGREE
1. My teacher cares about me.	☺	😐	☹
2. My teacher is fair.	☺	😐	☹
3. My teacher is happy.	☺	😐	☹
4. My teacher listens to me.	☺	😐	☹
5. My teacher is helpful.	☺	😐	☹
6. My teacher calls on me.	☺	😐	☹
7. My teacher knows how to laugh.	☺	😐	☹
8. I feel safe in our classroom.	☺	😐	☹
9. My teacher never hurts my feelings.	☺	😐	☹
10. My teacher likes me.	☺	😐	☹

Directions: Here is a list of words and phrases. Please read and reflect on each word or phrase as you think it describes your teacher. Using your pencil, mark each word or phrase this way:

If always true, circle the word or phrase.

If often/most of the time true, place a check after the word or phrase.

If not often/seldom true, draw a single line through the word or phrase.

If never true, x out the word or phrase.

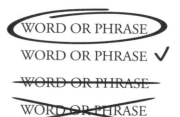

Likes me	Caring	Friendly	Fair	Helpful	Kind
Patient	Humorous	Calls on me	Gentle	Likable	Cheerful
Respectful	Looks at me	Generous	Creative	Listens to me	Loving
Exciting	Good ideas	Open-minded	Smiles	Pleasant	Organized
Enjoys our class	Polite	Interesting	Enthusiastic	Knows my name	Pleasant
Unfair	Cross	Cranky	Mean	Unkind	Grouchy
Boring	Impatient	Forgetful	Unprepared	Ignores me	Yells
Disorganized	Inconsistent	Cruel	Unpleasant	Loses temper	Doesn't know my name

E: Some Thoughts About Our Classroom (Secondary)

If our classroom were a basketball court, how would your teacher rate as a player? Please check the column that shows your opinion about each statement.

	MY TEACHER . . .	NEVER Personal Foul	ALMOST NEVER 0-Point Air Ball	SOMETIMES 1-Point Foul Shot	ALMOST ALWAYS 2-Point Basket	ALWAYS 3-Point Basket
1.	Is nice to me					
2.	Treats all students fairly					
3.	Has a sense of humor					
4.	Knows my name					
5.	Looks at me when she or he talks to me					
6.	Is enthusiastic about teaching					
7.	Likes me					
8.	Likes our class					
9.	Gives helpful feedback on my work					
10.	Is patient and understanding					
11.	Is willing to admit when she or he is wrong					
12.	Keeps his or her temper					
13.	Has a sense of humor					
14.	Encourages me					
15.	Thinks I can be a successful student					
16.	Never embarrasses me					
17.	Never lets other students embarrass me					
18.	Keeps order in class without yelling					
19.	Listens to me when I have something to say					
20.	Is someone I can talk to if I have a problem					

PROBLEM	POSSIBLE SOLUTION
Two students in each of five small groups of four sit with backs to the board and screen. Sometimes one tips over in the chair as he leans back trying to see; often, several of the students with their backs to the board ask a group member what is on the board while others are trying to listen.	➤ *If in a two-by-two student desks configuration where two students face front and two face back, turn the set of four desks from 45 to 60 degrees so that all students now look to the side to see the board.* ➤ *Rather than a two-by-two arrangement, use an "L-shape" configuration (see page 46) that faces the board.*
In alphabetical seating, the shortest student sits at the back of a row. With a basketball player seated in front of her, she has difficulty seeing you and the board.	➤ *Start the alphabet at the back of the room rather than the front.* ➤ *Move the girl to the front of that row (better to have a student out of place in alphabetical order than a student unable to see).*
The room is deep, and students seated far from the whiteboard and screen squint as they try to see what is there.	➤ *For the whiteboard, use extra-thick dry erase markers (see Artline products); for the screen, use large sans serif fonts such as Arial or Calibri.* ➤ *Request a large, double-sided, portable whiteboard; place it along a wide wall; and adjust student desks accordingly. (A double-sided board will give you twice the writing space!)*
Some students are unable to see the faces of other students speaking and have difficulty following a class discussion. (It's easier to engage in a class discussion with classmates' faces than with the backs of their heads.)	➤ *Develop an alternate student desk arrangement in which students can more easily see one another's faces. Then develop and teach a procedures lesson plan for students to move their desks in and out of that arrangement.* ➤ *Allow students to stand beside their desks so they can more easily turn to see a speaker.*
A student slips out of the door without your seeing her leave.	➤ *If this is an elusive student, move her away from the door.* ➤ *If allowed, keep the door closed to make it more difficult and noisier for her to leave.* ➤ *Work on your student observation skills— practice frequent scanning of the entire room.*

G: Avoiding Typical Physical Access Problems

2-5B

PROBLEM	POSSIBLE SOLUTION
Resource materials on a back shelf are inaccessible to everyone except students sitting in the back row; other students using them walk past one or more class members both there and back—sometimes detouring to drop off a note or speak to another student.	➤ Move the resource materials to a more suitable location. ➤ Reconfigure student desks so no students sit so close to the materials. ➤ Create a designated pathway to and from the resource materials—if space is narrow, use masking tape arrows on the floor to indicate a one-way traffic pattern.
The turn-in basket sits on a file cabinet behind the teacher's desk, and things periodically disappear from the top of his desk.	➤ Move the turn-in basket away from the teacher's desk.
At the pencil sharpener by the door, some students stand and sharpen pencils to a nub as they look out the door.	➤ Move the pencil sharpener—if possible. ➤ Add a battery-powered sharpener in a less distracting area of the room. ➤ Have a sharpen-pencils-only-before-class procedure along with a pencil pot for borrowing a fresh pencil.
There is frequent traffic congestion at the single wastebasket.	➤ Get a second wastebasket, and place it in another part of the room. If the custodian complains, have a class closing procedure where a designated student empties basket A into basket B. ➤ Have a procedure that limits the times or time during class that students may go to the wastebasket.
The tight space where students pick up and return calculators causes problems.	➤ Think one-way traffic. Use masking tape arrows to indicate the direction of traffic flow. Mark ENTRANCE and EXIT with signs to remind students.

STATEMENT	EXPLANATION
1. Think and make wise choices.	GOAL, both for teachers and students, throughout life
2. Use a purple crayon to correct your work in any class-checking session.	PROCEDURE, as it is a situation-specific "how to" do something
3. Speak at appropriate times, using appropriate voice and language.	EXPECTATION/RULE, as it governs a relationship between the student and others, and it is true all the time for everyone in the room, including the teacher Note: Multiple procedures will teach a student how to follow this expectation, rule, or policy in specific situations. Here are some examples: • In class discussion, speak loudly enough for everyone to hear. • In small-group work, use a quiet voice that does not travel beyond your group. • In partner activities, use a twelve-inch voice. • During a test, do not talk. If you have a question, raise your hand, and the teacher will come to you.
4. Sharpen pencils before class; if yours breaks, borrow one from the pencil pot.	PROCEDURE, as it is a situation-specific "how to" do something
5. Be in your chair and ready to begin when the bell rings.	EXPECTATION/RULE, typically found in secondary grades PROCEDURE, possibly for some elementary grades GOAL for lower elementary and kindergarten Note: If worded "Be at your desk," expect some students to be standing near the desk rather than seated.
6. In whole-class discussion, raise your hand and wait to be called on.	PROCEDURE that supports the rule in #3 Note: If this is always the procedure in your class, a student may escape participation simply by never raising a hand. See I: Equity Cards—Not Craft Sticks for an alternate procedure to use at times to avoid this possibility.

(Continued)

(Continued)

STATEMENT	EXPLANATION
7. Show respect to others and to yourself.	EXPECTATION/RULE, as it is always true for everyone in the room, including the teacher
8. Follow directions correctly the first time.	GOAL—one that both students and teachers may not always accomplish (Have *you* ever had difficulty following a set of directions?) Success in this goal depends on (1) the clarity of the directions given and (2) the frame of reference of the person receiving them. (Have you read any of the Amelia Bedelia books?) Student success here can be increased by checking student understanding and having students explain in their own words what it is they think they are supposed to do.
9. Bring all needed materials to class.	EXPECTATION/RULE, typically found in secondary grades BUT if a student comes without them, what is your ultimate goal? Student learning? Some students lack materials, others lose them, and still others may deliberately come without them to test you or to get out of work. Providing a couple of "borrowing sets" of writing materials and extra textbooks (clearly labeled as CLASS TEXT) can help achieve your ultimate goal of student learning. GOAL for lower elementary and kindergarten
10. Keep hands, feet, and objects to yourself.	EXPECTATION/RULE, typically found in lower elementary and kindergarten It is a statement to operationalize one aspect of what "respect" looks and feels like.
11. In computer lab, place the red plastic cup on top of the yellow and green ones to signal a need for assistance.	PROCEDURE, as it is a situation-specific "how to" do something This useful procedure requires each student have three same-size nesting paper cups—one red (stuck and need help now), one yellow (maybe need help), and one green (no help needed). Students stack the cups, rim down on the desk, with the color on top that indicates their need for assistance.
12. Bring a positive attitude to class.	GOAL, valuable for both teachers and students One or more students in a class may have had recent negative experiences over which they have had no control.

Using equity cards is a technique to ensure all students have equal opportunity to respond (OTR), which contributes to a teacher's being perceived as a fair teacher.

Make a class set of three-by-five-inch index cards, each with a single student's name on the front.

Introduce the cards as a procedure you will be using to make sure everyone has an equal and fair chance to be involved.

In a Q&A session, the process is to ask a question to the whole class, wait three to five seconds as you slightly shuffle the cards, then draw a card, and ask the student whose name is on that card to respond.

Once a name is called, turn that card upside down, and *keep it in the set*. This allows you easily to keep track of who has been called on. At least once (preferably a few times) after you shuffle the cards, "randomly" pull an upside-down card to call again on a previously designated student. This reinforces the idea that anyone can be called on at any time—it is not a one-and-done deal. Then turn that card backward as you return it to the set.

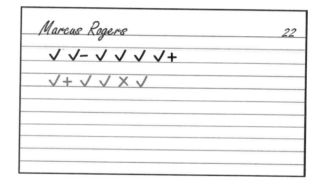

Use a different color pen each week to mark a check or plus or minus for a student's response. This allows you to keep track of who has and has not been called on. As you shuffle through cards to call "randomly" on a student, if after a week or so you see a card that has not been called, you can "randomly" select that card.

Note #1—Shy students: If you have a student who is shy and reticent to answer in class, this technique may seem threatening. For that student, one option is to meet privately and tell the student that in tomorrow's class you plan to call on her or him for question X—no one else knows this but the two of you, and if the student wants to check with you on a possible response via email or before class begins, that is fine.

Another option is to make clear to the class that there are many resources for information—including other people. If a student does not know the answer, she or he may turn and ask that same question of another student in the class, get an answer from that student, and rephrase that answer to you. (The student may not just repeat verbatim what another student said.)

Note #2—Overparticipating students: To control repeatedly raised hands and callouts, ask students to assume a "thinking position" with elbow on desk, head resting on thumb, and first finger over the mouth for the three to five seconds of thinking time.

Three Steps to _____

Graphic via Pixabay.com.

Four Steps to _____

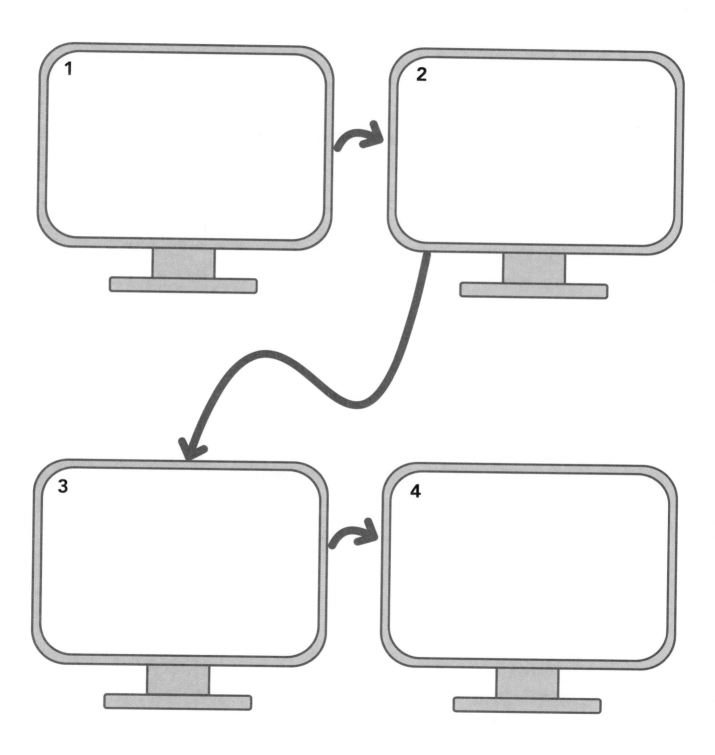

1

2

3

4

L: A Five-Step Graphic Organizer

Five Steps to _____

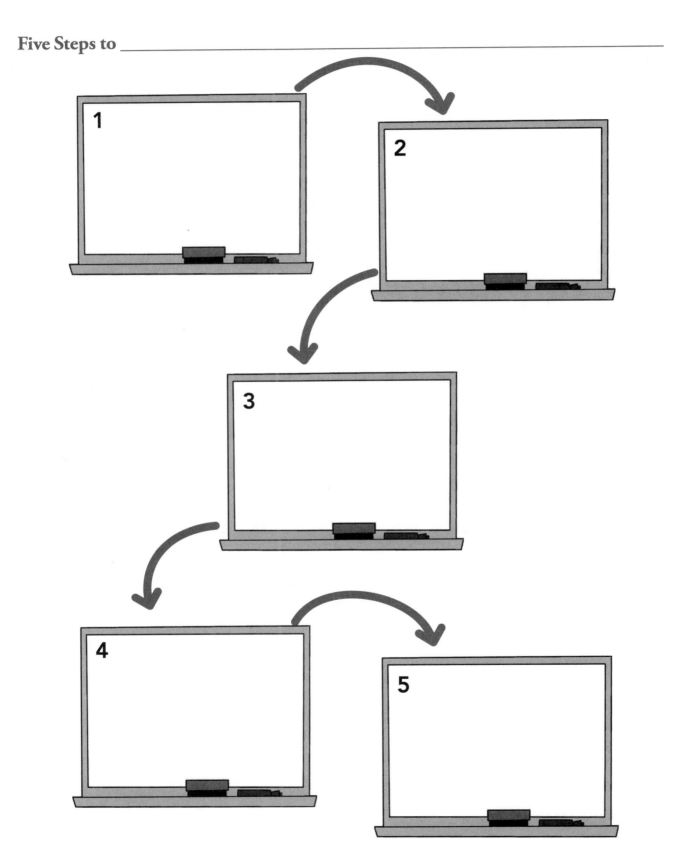

Six Steps to _____

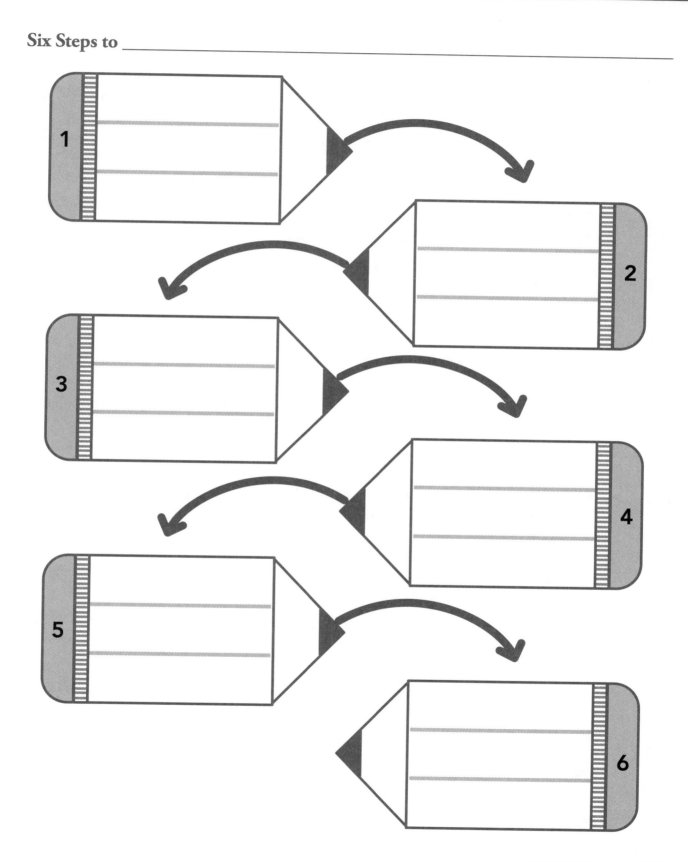

1. The most common reason students will challenge a teacher's authority is if they perceive the teacher as **unfair.**

2. The primary reason a teacher may be perceived as unfair is not clearly separating or distinguishing among **expectations (rules) and procedures and goals.**

3. Spending class time deliberately teaching class expectations (rules) and procedures *and* being consistent in in reinforcing these has been shown to produce three results: **(1) reduced off-task behavior, (2) more time to teach, and (3) higher student academic achievement.**

4. Relationships with others, time, space, and materials are addressed by **expectations (rules).**

5. Ways to get things done are addressed by **procedures.**

6. Statements that relate to desirable student attitudes and mental behaviors are **goals.**

7. An expectation is true (when?) **always.**

8. A procedure is true (when/where?) **depending on the situation.**

9. Classroom expectations generally number from **one to five or six**, while class procedures can number **over one hundred.**

10. The logical result of a student's not following a classroom expectation is a **disciplinary consequence.**

11. The logical result of a student's messing up on a procedure is a **reteaching.**

12. The logical result of a student's nearing or achieving a goal is **verbal praise.**

13. A major benefit of involving students in developing class expectations is **they tend to feel a sense of ownership and thus have a greater buy-in and are more likely to follow them.**

14. The most difficult behavior for a student to do is **the one he or she has never seen.**

15. Students can learn what following an expectation looks like and sounds like in your classroom by (doing what?) **observing and participating in role-play of specific situations.**

16. The steps for teaching a procedure are **EXPLANATION, including** *concrete definition, WIIFM rationale, demonstration, step-by-step analysis,* **and** *cue*; **REHEARSAL; FEEDBACK; and RETEACHING as needed.**

17. Students are much more likely to follow a procedure if they believe there is a **reason that is in their own best interest.** (WIIFM)

18. A **cue** lets students know *when* to do a procedure.

19. One value for students in using a graphic organizer to teach a procedure is that it **helps students see step by step how to be successful; also, it provides visual reinforcement.**

20. The only procedures students need to practice are **the ones you want them to do.**

O: Choosing Appropriate Practice Consequences

STUDENT BEHAVIOR The procedure is to . . .	POSSIBLE APPROPRIATE TEACHER RESPONSE AND REASON(S) TO DO THIS	POSSIBLE INAPPROPRIATE TEACHER RESPONSE AND REASON(S) NOT TO DO THIS
1. Pass papers to the left, and Paula passes hers to the right.	*Provide Paula with a visual cue—for example, that left means toward the windows wall and not the door.* *Ten percent of people cannot distinguish left from right.*	*Assume she deliberately did it wrong and call her out, ridicule her, give her a zero, and so on.* *Assume nothing negative. Seek the cause of the error and prevent it from happening again.*
2. Push chairs in before leaving for lunch, and Sam leaves his out.	*Pleasantly ask Sam to push up his chair, please. In the future, teach and use a verbal cue of "Please stand and push in your chairs so everyone can easily get by." Have the class practice this.* *This is most likely to result in the desired change.*	*Yell at Sam. Declare no one leaves until Sam pushes up his chair and make everyone wait. Berate Sam for being forgetful.* *Sam may be really hungry and chairs are not a priority, and teacher verbal bullying makes all students uncomfortable.*
3. Head papers in a certain way, and Juan writes his name on the wrong side.	*Provide Juan with a cue to know where the name goes—for example the name goes on the side with NO holes.* *Ten percent of people cannot distinguish left from right.*	*Refuse to take the paper and give Juan a zero. Fuss at Juan for doing it incorrectly. Take off points.* *Your ultimate goal is to see what content he puts on the paper, not where he writes his name.*
4. Sign your name, date, and time in and out on the bathroom pass sheet, and Maria forgets to write in the times.	*Pleasantly remind Maria to write the times, as a lengthy stay could signal she needs help. If this behavior repeats, ask her what could remind her to write in the times (such as if the headers TIME IN and TIME OUT were highlighted in yellow).* *Sometimes students can be more creative in solving their own problems than we can.*	*Suspend her bathroom privilege, or administer a negative consequence.* *It's possible Maria needed to leave in a hurry due to a call of nature and was in a hurry to return to her desk and finish her work.*
5. Close out all programs when leaving the computer station, and Roberto leaves some open.	*Pleasantly remind Roberto to close out all programs.* *Place a graphic organizer chart showing each step to do before leaving beside the computer.* *Roberto may not remember all of the steps.*	*Yell at Roberto. Take away his computer privileges for a day (which means he will likely fall behind in some of his work). Berate him for being forgetful.* *Roberto may not remember all of the steps, and teacher verbal bullying makes all students uncomfortable.*

(Continued)

(Continued)

STUDENT BEHAVIOR The procedure is to . . .	POSSIBLE APPROPRIATE TEACHER RESPONSE AND REASON(S) TO DO THIS	POSSIBLE INAPPROPRIATE TEACHER RESPONSE AND REASON(S) NOT TO DO THIS
6. Exchange a broken pencil with a sharp one from the pencil pot, and Sureka goes to the pencil sharpener and begins grinding away.	*Try to catch her eye, and motion toward the pencil pot. If that is not possible, say simply, "Sureka, pencil pot, please."*	*Yell at her across the room. Verbally berate her for sharpening her pencil.* *Teacher verbal bullying—any public humiliation of a student—makes all students uncomfortable.*
7. Place backpacks under the desks, and Mark leaves his in the aisle.	*Try to catch his eye, point at the bag, and motion putting it under his chair. If that is not possible, say simply, "Mark—backpack—under desk, please."* *Or, say, "Class, remember that clear aisles are a safety issue." This avoids singling out the student for correction.*	*Walk over and kick the backpack to send it under Mark's desk. Yell at him for leaving it in the aisle.* *Avoid modeling any behavior you do not want a student to repeat.*
8. Place your music folder on your music stand, and Carlos puts his under his chair.	*Try to catch his eye, point at the folder, and motion putting it on the stand. If that is not possible, say simply, "Carlos—folder—on the stand, please."*	*Disgustedly ask a student beside him to put Carlos's folder on his stand as he seems incapable of doing so.* *Any public humiliation of a student makes all students uncomfortable—and unsure if you can be trusted not to embarrass them in the future.*
9. _____ _____ _____ _____ (Fill in a procedure from your classroom.)		

P: More Effective Praise/Encouragement Statements

LESS EFFECTIVE AND/OR INEFFECTIVE PRAISE	MORE EFFECTIVE PRAISE/ ENCOURAGEMENT
Carmen wore a blue scarf. *"Carmen, I like your beautiful scarf."*	*"Carmen, the color of the scarf you chose today matches your outfit beautifully."*
Steve completed a difficult assignment (elementary). OR Steve correctly completed a complicated science lab experiment (secondary). 1. *"I'm so proud of you."*	*"Your thinking, efforts, and persistence paid off. You did it!"*
After receiving Cs on the last two math tests, Alene finally made an A. 2. *"You made an A? It must have been your lucky day."*	*"An A on the test—your study efforts are showing."*
Asim made the winning foul shot. 3. *"You're the best player on the team!"*	*"Your hard practice paid off."*
Laronda brought a finished art project to you, saying, "What do you think?" 4. *"Lovely!"*	*"Interesting use of color and texture."* *"You've really worked on that!"* *"Your creativity is definitely showing."*
Saul showed up at the ball game with his face painted in school colors. 5. *"Saul, I like that school spirit!"*	*"Now that's school spirit!"*
Kim stayed after school to help a returning absentee classmate catch up with lessons missed (elementary.) OR Kim stayed after school to help three new band members learn the music for an upcoming marching competition (secondary). 6. *"You are so good!"*	*"Your willingness to help a classmate catch up on what he missed shows you care about others"* (elementary). *"You went the extra mile to help a fellow band member and our band"* (secondary).

(Continued)

(Continued)

LESS EFFECTIVE AND/OR INEFFECTIVE PRAISE	MORE EFFECTIVE PRAISE/ ENCOURAGEMENT
Nancy *finally* turned in an assignment on time. 7. *"I like the way your work is on time for a change!"*	*"Your efforts to get work in on time were successful. Way to go!"*
The chorus stayed on key throughout the entire piece of music. 8. *"I enjoyed the way you were on key that time."*	*"Bravo on intonation! Your individual focus enabled the whole chorus to stay on key throughout the entire piece."*
Marcus was absent with the flu for a week and made up all of his missed work in three days. 9. *"Marcus, I appreciate you getting all your work made up quickly."*	*"Marcus, making up all your missed work in three days shows effort and focus."*
Every student in your class turned in a field trip permission slip on time (elementary). OR Every student in your class turned in a research paper on time (secondary). 10. *"Great! I'm so pleased everyone will get to go"* (elementary). OR *"Great! I'm so pleased that no one will lose points for being late"* (secondary).	*"Everyone remembered permission slips and will be with us on the field trip"* (elementary). *"You have each organized and prioritized and budgeted your time to complete this major project on time. Bravo!"* (secondary).

Source: Adapted from Evertson and Harris (2013).

Q: Developing a More Proactive Response

MISBEHAVIOR	WHY? PROBABLE CAUSE	WHAT? TEACHER GOALS	HOW? TEACHER ACTION *ALWAYS SPEAKING IN A CALM, NORMAL, RESPECTFUL TONE.*
A pencil rolls off student A's desk, and student B picks it up. Student A calls out, "Dirty thief!"	Typical pattern of interaction from past experience	Have the student substitute appropriate language in future similar situations. Keep the classroom climate positive. Don't waste class time or energy on anger.	*"A, let's practice using other words to get your pencil back. B was nice enough to pick up what you dropped. Please turn to B and say, 'Thanks for picking up my pencil. Please hand it to me,' and open your hand for B to place it there. Let's try it."*
A pencil rolls off student A's desk, and student B picks it up. Student A calls out, "Dirty thief!," grabs the pencil out of student B's hand, hits him with it, and smirks at the teacher.	Seeks to establish power and dominance over weaker student and over teacher	Bring home the facts that student A will treat others with respect, that hitting is never acceptable, and that the teacher is the one in charge in the classroom. Keep the classroom climate positive. Don't waste class time or energy on anger.	*Ignore the smirk, and add firmness to your tone.* *"A, hitting others is never acceptable in this classroom or in this school. We clarified that at the beginning of school, and we covered what would happen as a result."* *"As your teacher, it is my job to enforce the school policy, which is . . ."* *State the school policy, and then enforce it.*
Student C closes up her book and begins social chatting with a nearby student who is still working.	Has finished all assigned work—and has nothing to do	Redirect the student to an appropriate academic task. Keep all other students working. Don't waste class time or energy on anger.	*"B, I see you've completed the assignments. Would you please . . . ?"* *Finish the sentence to provide the student with some enrichment activity or ask the student to help another student or to do a classroom task to help you.*
Student C is making derogatory comments to a student sitting nearby.	Enjoys tormenting other students and getting them upset	Bring home the fact that unkind language and hurting other people's feelings are not acceptable. Cause other students to feel emotionally safe. Don't waste class time or energy on anger.	*"C, hitting others with unkind words is hurtful, and we do not hurt others in this classroom. If you have no kind words to say, then say nothing to others. If you have kind words, use them."*

(Continued)

(Continued)

MISBEHAVIOR	WHY? PROBABLE CAUSE	WHAT? TEACHER GOALS	HOW? TEACHER ACTION *ALWAYS SPEAKING IN A CALM, NORMAL, RESPECTFUL TONE.*
Student D is late for class, saunters in, and says with a grin, "Looks like I'm late again."	Has been goofing off in the hall and wants to be sent to the principal's office	Cause the student to get to class on time. Encourage all students to get to class on time. Don't waste class time or energy on anger, and don't let the student out of class.	*"Hello, D, we're glad you could make it. Please be seated." Go right on with the lesson.* *(If the student offers additional comments, try calmly repeating the phrase "Please be seated" after each offering. Repetition—aka the "broken record" technique—allows you NOT to be drawn into discussion.)*
Student D is late for class, comes in obviously upset, and mumbles an apology to you on the way to his seat.	Something happened between classes—causes the student to be upset and late	Help the student get emotions under control. Get class started and all other students engaged. Find a way to help or counsel or get help for the student.	*"Glad you made it, D. Take a minute to catch your breath, and join in when you're ready."* *If you have or can create a seatwork time, as you pass from student to student and look over shoulders and comment, stop at D's desk, and quietly ask if he or she would like to stop by and talk about anything sometime during the day or after school.* *For a superb resource for talking with students (and an easy read with specific examples), see* How to Talk So Kids Will Listen and Listen So Kids Will Talk *(Faber & Mazlish, 1980).*

R: Heading Off/Redirecting/Dealing With Undesirable Behavior

VIGNETTE*	PROACTIVE RESPONSE CHOICE	COUNTERPRODUCTIVE RESPONSE CHOICE(S)
1. As class begins, Mateo pulls out a comic book and slips it into his lap. You . . .	*EARLIER IN THE YEAR,* clarify *that if students bring something to class that will interfere with their or others' learning, because you value their learning, you will take up the item to remove the distraction and return it at the end of the day (assuming it is not contraband). Demonstrate that you will simply come to the student and hold out your hand to receive the item. Then, lock it in a desk drawer until the student retrieves it.* *Walk to Mateo's desk, point to the comic book, and extend your hand to receive it.*	*Ignore it, and allow the student to keep it.* *Make a big deal over confiscating it.* *Verbally reprimand him for bringing it to class.*
2. As you explain how to fill in the top of a state test, Rashid just stares into space. You . . .	*Walk to Rashid's desk, and tap gently on the top of the test to bring Rashid back from outer space.* *(Note: The student may be suffering from petit mal seizures. Be aware of medical possibilities.)*	*Ignore it, and allow him to miss out on instructions.* *Call him out for not paying attention.*
3. In silent reading time, Sophia passes a note to Adana. You . . .	*Move to intercept the note, and take it up. (If the student protests, you might say any written work in your classroom must surely be for that class.)* *Now what to do with the note? Students will ask if you are going to read it. You need not commit—just say it will be locked away.* *(Note: To read or not to read—it's your choice. A teacher friend read intercepted notes, but students never knew this. She once read a potential suicide note this way and so was able to contact the school counselor and get the student help.)*	*Ignore it, and allow note passing.* *Take it up, and read it aloud—or send it to the writer's parent—or post it on the bulletin board.*

(Continued)

APPENDICES **189**

(Continued)

VIGNETTE*	PROACTIVE RESPONSE CHOICE	COUNTERPRODUCTIVE RESPONSE CHOICE(S)
4. As you are reviewing key points of the Revolutionary War, Boone opens his backpack, takes out toy soldiers, and lines them up on his desk. You . . .	*Walk to Boone's desk (with a small container), and begin collecting the soldiers. (ASSUMING THIS IS A STUNT TO GET ATTENTION)* *OR* *Commend Boone for his interest in the Revolutionary War, and ask him which battle he'd like to demonstrate tomorrow using his toy soldiers. (ASSUMING HE HAS A GREAT INTEREST IN THE SUBJECT AND IS A TACTILE/ KINESTHETIC LEARNER)*	*Ignore it, and allow it to distract other nearby students.* *Make a big deal over his bringing toys to school and disrupting the class.*
5. As you monitor seatwork, Amir takes out his wallet, checks the contents, returns the wallet to his pocket, and continues on the assignment. You . . .	*Ignore it. Amir just wants to make sure he gets to eat today, and he quickly gets himself back on task.*	*Make any kind of comment about it.*
6. After talking with Jamie three times about walking back from lunch and not running and shoving, he flies down the hall and tackles his friend Rob. The boys wrestle. You . . .	*You've already conferenced with these students several times, and the behavior is physically dangerous both to the two students and possibly to others nearby. It is time to apply whatever negative consequence is appropriate to your school.* *This might start with a parent contact, expressing concern for the safety of the student.*	*Ignore it, and hope no one gets hurt (and you don't get called on the carpet for poor discipline).* *Yell at them, and send them to the office to deal with it.* *(Note: Sending a student to the office on the spur of the moment is the same as saying "I am not capable of handling this"—not a message you want to send.)*

VIGNETTE*	PROACTIVE RESPONSE CHOICE	COUNTERPRODUCTIVE RESPONSE CHOICE(S)
7. For the fifth time in five minutes, Malika calls out when you have called on another student to respond. You . . .	Pointedly ignore Malika (physically turn away from her if possible—make no eye contact), and again ask the original student the question. (Note: This behavior may require a behavior modification strategy. Such behavior will continue as long as it gains notice and attention.)	Accept Malika's callouts, and allow her to monopolize the class. Punish her for calling out.
8. After asking Tomar three times to quit playing with the staple remover on your desk as he stands in line to leave for lunch, you hold out your hand and say, "Please give that to me." The boy closes its jaws on your first finger. Blood drips. . . .	Question: Does Tomar look shocked—or satisfied? Say you will deal with him after lunch, and dismiss the class. This gives you time to consider if the wound was accidental or deliberate. It also gives him time to anticipate consequences. (Also, put the staple remover in a drawer.)	Yell at the student. Send him to the office. Make the whole class wait while you go off on the student.
9. In lab, Tony connects his Bunsen burner to the water line (blue handle) instead of the gas line (red handle), holds a lighted match over the burner, and turns on the water. Water squirts to the ceiling and drenches Tony and nearby students.	Question: Does Tony look shocked—or satisfied? Reality of the matter: Tony is color blind. Accidents just happen. Laugh, help the student clean up, and get on with it.	Yell at the student. Dock points from his grade. Berate him for being stupid. Send him to the office.
10. Write a vignette from your own experience.		

Source: Adapted from Evertson and Harris (2003).

*All vignettes except #4 are from the classroom of one author of this book; #4 occurred next door.

S: Mindset Quiz

Place a check in the column that best reflects how you agree or disagree with each statement.

	STRONGLY AGREE	AGREE	DISAGREE	STRONGLY DISAGREE
1. Your intelligence is something very basic about you that you can't change very much.	○	○	○	○
2. No matter how much intelligence you have, you can always change it quite a bit.	○	○	○	○
3. You can always substantially change how intelligent you are.	○	○	○	○
4. You are a certain kind of person, and there is not much that can be done to change that.	○	○	○	○
5. You can always change basic things about the kind of person you are.	○	○	○	○
6. Musical talent can be learned by anyone.	○	○	○	○
7. Only a few people will be truly good at sports—you have to be "born with it."	○	○	○	○
8. Math is much easier to learn if you are male or come from a culture who values math.	○	○	○	○
9. The harder you work at something, the better you will be at it.	○	○	○	○
10. No matter what kind of person you are, you can always change substantially.	○	○	○	○
11. Trying new things is stressful for me, and I avoid it.	○	○	○	○
12. Some people are good and kind, and some are not—it's not often that people change.	○	○	○	○
13. I appreciate when parents, coaches, and/or teachers give me feedback about my performance.	○	○	○	○
14. I often get angry when I get feedback about my performance.	○	○	○	○
15. All human beings without a brain injury are capable of the same amount of learning.	○	○	○	○
16. You can learn new things, but you can't really change how intelligent you are.	○	○	○	○
17. You can do things differently, but the important parts of who you are can't really be changed.	○	○	○	○
18. Human beings are basically good but sometimes make terrible decisions.	○	○	○	○
19. An important reason why I do my schoolwork is that I like to learn new things.	○	○	○	○
20. Truly smart people do not need to try hard.	○	○	○	○

Source: http://homepages.math.uic.edu/~bshipley/MindsetQuiz.w.scores.pdf

Circle the number in the box that matches each answer.

	STRONGLY AGREE	AGREE	DISAGREE	STRONGLY DISAGREE
1. Ability mindset—fixed	0	1	2	3
2. Ability mindset—growth	3	2	1	0
3. Ability mindset—growth	3	2	1	0
4. Personality/character mindset—fixed	0	1	2	3
5. Personality/character mindset—growth	3	2	1	0
6. Ability mindset—growth	3	2	1	0
7. Ability mindset—fixed	0	1	2	3
8. Ability mindset—fixed	0	1	2	3
9. Ability mindset—growth	3	2	1	0
10. Personality/character mindset—growth	3	2	1	0
11. Ability mindset—fixed	0	1	2	3
12. Personality/character mindset—fixed	0	1	2	3
13. Ability mindset—growth	3	2	1	0
14. Ability mindset—fixed	0	1	2	3
15. Ability mindset—growth	3	2	1	0
16. Ability mindset—fixed	0	1	2	3
17. Personality/character mindset—fixed	0	1	2	3
18. Personality/character mindset—growth	3	2	1	0
19. Ability mindset—growth	3	2	1	0
20. Ability mindset—fixed	0	1	2	3
Total				
Grand Total				

Strong Growth Mindset = 45–60 points

Growth Mindset With Some Fixed Ideas = 34–44 points

Fixed Mindset With Some Growth Ideas = 21–33 points

Strong Fixed Mindset = 0–20 points

Source: Diehl (2008). Adapted from http://www.classroom20.com/forum/topics/motivating-students-with.

What Can I Say to Myself?

INSTEAD OF . . .	TRY THINKING . . .
"I don't understand."	"I don't understand yet, but I can ask for help.
"I'm not good at this."	"What am I missing?"
"I can't do X."	"I'm going to train my brain to do X."
"I made a mistake."	"I didn't get it right, but I am still learning and getting better."
"This is too hard."	"It may be hard, but it isn't impossible."
"I give up."	"I don't know how to do this, yet, but I know there has to be a way."
"I can't make this any better."	"I can always improve. I'll keep trying."

Source: Adapted from Garwood and Ampuja (2019).

"Numbered Heads Together is a marvelous antidote to whole-class Q & A, which often boils down to a conversation between the teacher and the high achievers in the classroom, with the rest of the class between semi-interested and comatose" (Kagan, 1994, p. 10.3).

The strategy can be used in review or problem-solving. Students are grouped as equally as possible, with no more than five in a group. Groups may be preexisting or formed randomly as the moment.

Step 1 The students form groups.	Form groups of three to five students. Designate each group of students with a group number, beginning with group 1.
Step 2 The students number off.	Have students number off within each group from one to the highest number of the smallest group. For groups larger than the smallest number, some students will have two numbers; for example, if you have groups of four and five, the first two sets of students illustrate the student numbering; if groups range from three to five, all three sets illustrate the numbering:
Step 3 Teacher asks a question.	In asking a question, begin with the words "*Put your heads together and make sure everyone in your group can . . .,*" and then finish with the question, such as *explain how . . . , explain why . . . , describe . . . , figure out a way to . . .* , or *make a plan to . . . .* Questions may require either high or low agreement—for example, *"Put your heads together, and name the two elements in water"* would require high agreement. *"Put your heads together, and make sure everyone in your group can make several predictions about what might happen if X occurred"* would allow divergent thinking. To speed things up, some teachers add a time frame—for example, *"Put your heads together, and you have one minute to make sure everyone in your team can explain X."*
Step 4 Students put their heads together.	Students put their heads together to discuss and make sure everyone in the group knows the answer.
Step 5 The teacher calls numbers.	First, the teacher randomly calls a *student* number, and the student in each group with that number raises a hand. Then the teacher randomly calls a *group* number, and the student with his/her hand up in that group responds. *Note:* Using a die or spinner promotes students' perception of fairness—plus, a teacher does not have to keep track of what numbers have been called.

Source: Adapted from Kagan (1994).

Procedure to Be Taught:

How to sit quietly when I stand at the front of the class and participate in taking attendance by responding to a question asked of each student in the whole class

Benefit to the Teacher:

This procedure makes sure I have an accurate roll call and helps me learn more about my students.

Materials Needed/Prior Preparation:

Teacher: A question that can be answered with one word or brief phrase by every student in the class.

Students: No materials needed

1. Explanation

A. Concrete Definition

"Class, today we are going to learn how to participate in attendance. You may have never been asked to 'participate' in attendance before, but that is exactly what it is! As class begins, talking stops when I stand in front with my attendance chart. I'll begin by asking one question to our whole class. Then I'll go through the roster, and when I call your name, please answer the question with a single word or brief phrase—or say 'pass' if you wish. At the end I'll answer the same question."

B. Rationale

"This is an important procedure for several reasons! First, it's important that attendance is taken so that you get credit for being in class each day you are here. Second, imagine how well we will get to know one another as you answer a different question every day. And, of course, I'll answer the question, too, so you'll learn some things about your teacher as well!"

2. Demonstration

A. Step-by-Step Walking Through

"I'll ask two students to help me demonstrate. I'll ask 'What's your favorite ice cream flavor?,' wait five seconds, and call two names from the roll. I'll end by telling my favorite flavor."

B. Cue

"The cue for this procedure to begin is my standing at the front with the attendance chart in hand."

3. Rehearsal

As a rehearsal, I'll allow students to start conversations for about thirty seconds while I sit at my desk, then get up at the front of the class with the attendance chart and wait for the class to get quiet. If it takes too long, I will sit back at the desk, and we will try again. Once the class gets it right, I will ask the first question—"What is the best thing about high school so far?"—and go through the roll. Each student will answer the question, and that will be his or her first run at this procedure! After that, the procedure will become more routine every day, as this particular procedure will be practiced daily.

4. Feedback

If done right, I'll thank students for sharing and getting through the roll in a timely manner. If not, I'll reteach.

5. Reteaching

If some students use this as a "time waster," drawing out answers, I'll remind them to keep answers concise. If some tease or snicker, I'll remind students of our "respect" rule and that negative reactions to an answer will have consequences. If some take longer and longer to get quiet once I give my "cue" of standing at the front of the class with the attendance book, I'll rehearse that part of the procedure over again until they get it right.

*As observed in a senior chemistry class.

Learning About Your Students and Building Community While Taking Roll

More General/Lighthearted/Elementary

1. What's your favorite color?
2. What's your favorite ice cream?
3. What is your favorite sandwich?
4. What's your favorite dessert?
5. Who makes you laugh?
6. What's your favorite TV show?
7. What's your favorite movie?
8. Who's your favorite movie star?
9. What's your favorite Disney prince/princess?
10. Where's your favorite place to eat out?
11. Where's your favorite place to eat a hamburger?
12. Where's your favorite place to eat ice cream?
13. If you were a dog, what kind of dog would you be?
14. If you were a zoo animal, what animal would you be?
15. Would you rather ride in a boat, train, helicopter, or plane?
16. If you could meet anyone famous, who would it be?
17. If you could be famous for anything, what would it be?
18. What do you want to be when you grow up?
19. What's one thing I should know about you?
20. What do you do on a snow day (besides sleep!)?
21. What dish has to be on the table for it *really* to be Thanksgiving?

Possibly More Personal/Secondary

22. If you were stranded on a desert island, what three things would you take?
23. What's the first thing you remember wanting to be when you grew up?
24. Who is your favorite comedian?
25. If your life were a TV show, what kind of show would it be?
26. If you could have lunch with anybody, who would it be?
27. If you could spend the day as somebody else, who would it be?
28. What's your comfort food?
29. What was your happiest moment?
30. If you could have only one modern convenience, what would it be?
31. If you could pick an age and stay there, what age would it be?
32. What's the most important thing you've learned from your parents?
33. What's the most important thing you want to teach your children?
34. What's your New Year's resolution?
35. What would you name a son?
36. What would you name a daughter?
37. If you could change one thing about yourself, what would it be?
38. What's something that amuses you that most people don't find funny?
39. What was your best birthday?
40. What's the most important thing you've learned about yourself this year?
41. What scares you?
42. Who's your favorite music group?
43. If you could do anything for a career, what would it be?
44. If you could go anywhere for a weekend, where would it be?
45. Who's your hero?
46. What's one thing you've learned in this class that you'll remember?
47. The best thing about (your school) is _____.
48. The worst thing about (your school) is _____ (no names).
49. What gives you the creeps?
50. What sound/noise do you hate?
51. What's the strangest fact you'll remember from this school year?
52. What was your best April Fool's joke?
53. What's your favorite article of clothing?
54. What are your summer plans?

Source: Harris and Tomick (2016. p. 81).

Note that multiple secondary-level student teachers observed this procedure, described it to the authors, and reported that students listened attentively to hear how others would respond—including the teacher. It got each class off to a positive beginning.

Y: Developing Class Community: Ideas From Teachers*

Students feel they belong.

• Greet students as they enter.	• Know and periodically comment on students' interests/hobbies.
• Call students by name frequently (and in a positive manner).	• Acknowledge and celebrate student accomplishments.
• Make eye contact.	• Remember students' birthdays.
• Smile at students.	• Make a class quilt to show community.
• Provide adequate personal space.	• Find and acknowledge each student's strength.
• Create ways to help students learn one another's names.	• Display students' names within the room.
• Assign and rotate class jobs.	• Tell students they are missed when they return from being absent.
• Arrange it so everyone gets to be a leader at something.	

Students feel they have something to contribute and their ideas matter.

• Involve students in developing class expectations/rules/policies.	• Use a Paideia seminar (circle discussion).
• Involve students in developing procedures.	• Allow multiple options for contribution (verbal, written, etc.).
• Use equity cards for all students to contribute ideas.	• Teach students how to contribute appropriately in a class discussion.
• Allow students to express their point of view.	• Intro activity statements—such as "I am (name) and I am an expert at (insert something here)."

Students have basic needs (physiological and safety—both emotional and physical) met.

• Teach safety/emergency procedures.	• Have a safe seating arrangement.
• Keep the room at the proper temperature.	• Inform students how to get breakfast.
• Have good lighting.	• Teach—including practicing—what respect will look, sound, and feel like in your classroom.
• Have good air—fresh, not stale, pleasant smelling but not "perfumey."	• Allow appropriate water and bathroom breaks.
• Have enough desks and chairs.	• There is zero tolerance for bullying.
• Have furniture of appropriate size.	
• Have clear walkways.	

Students have multiple opportunities to work in positive ways with others.

• Use think-pair-share.	• Use Kagan strategies—for example, numbered heads together.
• Use multistudent workstations.	• Use a buddy system for makeup work.
• Use role cards for small-group work.	• Use small-group work, and periodically change up group members.
• Teach students procedures to turn into and out of groups.	

*From the accompanying screencast of *Getting Off to a Good Start: The First Three Days of School* (Harris & Tomick, 2016).

To the parents and guardians of my students: Would you please take a few minutes to complete the five items below? As we move into the remainder of the school year, your responses can help me better know and understand your son or daughter and thus be a more effective teacher for your child. Thank you for helping me better know my students.

(signature) _____

your child's _____ grade/subject area teacher

Student _____   Phone # _____

Parent/Guardian _____   Email _____

1. My child has special interests and/or abilities I'd like for you to know. They are . . .

2. If there is one area in school (reading, math, computer, etc.) where my child needs some extra coaching or practice, it is . . .

3. Because of his/her interests, I think school would be more interesting to my child if . . .

4. Something I think you, as a teacher, might benefit from knowing about my child is . . .

5. If you would volunteer your time and talents to our class, please tell me when you could visit. Also, please list any special talents you have (for example, storytelling, computers, baking, magic tricks) that you would be willing to share with our class.

To the parents and guardians of my students: Would you please take a few minutes to complete the five items below? As we move into the remainder of the school year, your responses can help me better know and understand your son or daughter and thus be a more effective teacher for him or her. Thank you for helping me better know my students.

(signature) _____

(subject area) _____

Student _____ Phone # _____

Parent/Guardian _____ Email _____

1. My son/daughter has special interests and/or abilities I'd like for you to know. They are . . .

2. If there is one area in this subject where my son/daughter needs some extra coaching or practice, it is . . .

3. Because of his/her interests, I think school and/or your class would be more interesting to my son/daughter if . . .

4. Something I think you, as a teacher, might benefit from knowing about my son/daughter is . . .

5. If you would volunteer your time and talents to our class, please tell me when you could visit. Also, please list any special talents you have (for example, computer, storytelling, graphic arts, baking, subject-related experiences) that you would be willing to share with our class.

Adelman, H. S., & Taylor, L. (2005). Classroom climate. In S. W. Lee, P. A. Lowe, & E. Robinson (Eds.), *Encyclopedia of school psychology* (pp. 304–312). Thousand Oaks, CA: Sage.

Alberto, P. A., & Troutman, A. C. (2016). *Applied behavior analysis for teachers* (9th ed.). Boston, MA: Pearson.

Al Ghamdi, A., Samarji, A., & Watt, A. (2016). Essential considerations in distance education in KSA: Teacher immediacy in a virtual teaching and learning environment. published online *International Journal of Information and Education Technology, 6,* 17–22.

Allday, R. A. (2011). Responsive management: Practical strategies for avoiding overreaction to minor misbehavior. *Intervention in School and Clinic, 46,* 292–298.

Alter, P., & Haydon, T. (2017). Characteristics of effective classroom rules: A review of the literature. *Teacher Education and Special Education, 40,* 114–127.

Ames, C., & Ames, R. E. (Eds.). (1985). *Research on motivation in education: Volume 2. The classroom milieu.* Orlando, FL: Academic Press.

Anderman, L. H., Andrzejewski, C. E., & Allen, J. (2011). How do teachers support students' motivation and learning in their classrooms? *Teachers College Record, 113,* 969–1003.

Anderson, J. F. (1979). Teacher immediacy as a predictor of teaching effectiveness. *Communication Yearbook, 3,* 543–559.

Arlin, M. (1979). Teacher transitions can disrupt time flow in classrooms. *American Education Research Journal, 16,* 42–56.

Barr, J. J. (2016). *Developing a positive classroom climate. IDEA Paper #61.* Manhattan, KS: The IDEA Center.

Bernt, T. J., & Keefe, K. (1995). Friends' influence on adolescent adjustment to school. *Child Development, 66,* 1312–1329.

Billingsley, B., Carlson, E., & Klein, S. (2004). The working conditions and induction support of early career special educators. *Exceptional Children, 70,* 333–347.

Blackwell, L. S., Trzesniewski, K. H., & Dweck, C. S. (2007). Implicit theories of intelligence predict achievement across an adolescent transition: A longitudinal study and an intervention. *Child Development, 78,* 246–263.

Bolick, C. M., & Bartels, J. T. (2015). Classroom management and technology. In E. T. Emmer & E. J. Sabornie (Eds.), *Handbook of classroom management* (2nd ed.). New York, NY: Routledge.

Boostrom, R. (1991). The nature and functions of classroom rules. *Curriculum Inquiry, 21,* 193–216.

Boysen, G. (2012). Teacher responses to classroom incivility: Student perceptions of effectiveness. *Teaching of Psychology, 39,* 276–279.

Brady, K., Forton, M. B., Porter, D., & Wood, C. (2003). *Rules in school. Strategies for teachers series.* Greenfield, MA: Northwest Foundation for Children.

Bransford, J. D., Brown, A. L., & Cocking, R. R. (2000). *How people learn: Brain, mind, experience, and school.* Washington DC: National Academy Press.

Bronfenbrenner, U. (1976). The experimental ecology of education. *Educational Researcher, 5,* 5–15.

Brookhart, S. M. (2008). *How to give effective feedback to your students.* Alexandria, VA: ASCD.

Brown, S. (2009), *Play: How it shapes the brain, opens the imagination, and invigorates the soul.* New York, NY: Penguin.

Bucholz, J. L., & Sheffler, J. L. (2009). Creating a warm and inclusive classroom environment: Planning for all children to feel welcome. *Electronic Journal for Inclusive Education, 2.*

Burke, K., & Burke-Samide, B. (2004). Required changes in the classroom environment: It's a matter of design. *The Clearing House, 77,* 236–239.

Capizzi, A. M. (2009). Start the year off right: Designing and evaluating a supportive classroom management plan. *Focus on Exceptional Children, 42,* 1–12.

CAST. (2018). *Universal Design for Learning Guidelines version 2.2.* Retrieved from http://udlguidelines.cast.org

Cavanaugh, B. (2016). Trauma-informed classroom and schools. *Beyond Behavior, 25,* 41–46.

Cayanus, J. L., & Martin, M. M. (2008). Teacher self-disclosure: Amount, relevance, and negativity. *Communication Quarterly, 56,* 325–341.

Castellucci, H. I., Arezes, P. M., Molenbroek, J. F. M., de Bruin, R., & Viviani, C. (2017). The influence of school furniture on students' performance and physical responses: Results of a systematic review. *Ergonomics, 60,* 93–110.

Cefai, C., & Cooper, P. (2010). Students without voices: The unheard accounts of secondary school students with social, emotional and behaviour difficulties. *European Journal of Special Needs Education, 25,* 183–198.

Cerasoli, C. C., Nicklin, J. M., & Ford, M. T. (2014). Intrinsic motivation and extrinsic incentives jointly predict performance: A 40-year meta-analysis. *Psychological Bulletin, 140,* 980–1008.

Chory-Assad, R. M., & Paulsel, M. L. (2004). Classroom justice: Student aggression and resistance as reactions to perceived unfairness. *Communication Education, 53,* 253–273.

Cienkus, R. C., & Ornstein, A. C. (1997). Distance learning: Teaching by lecture/explanation. *High School Journal, 80,* 247–253.

Clark-Lempers, D. S., Lempers, J. D., & Ho, C. (1991). Early, middle, and late adolescents' perceptions of their relationships with significant others. *Journal of Adolescent Research, 6,* 296–315.

Codding, R. S., & Smyth, C. A. (2008). Using performance feedback to decrease classroom transition time and examine collateral effects on academic engagement. *Journal of Educational & Psychological Consultation, 18,* 325–345.

Connell, J. P., & Wellborn, J. G. (1991). Competence, autonomy, and relatedness: A motivational analysis of self-system processes. In M. Gunnar & L. A. Sroufe (Eds.), *Minnesota symposium on child psychology* (Vol. 23). Chicago, IL: University of Chicago Press.

Cook, C., Grady, E., Long, A., Renshaw, T., Codding, R., Fiat A., & Larson, M. (2017). Evaluating the impact of increasing general education teachers' ratio of positive-to-negative interactions on students' classroom behavior. *Journal of Positive Behavior Interventions, 19,* 67–77.

Cothran, D. J., Kulinna, P. H., & Garrahy, D. A. (2003). "This is kind of giving a secret away . . .": Students' perspectives on effective class management. *Teaching & Teacher Education, 19,* 435–444.

Covington, M. V., & Müeller, K. J. (2001). Intrinsic versus extrinsic motivation: An approach/avoidance reformulation. *Educational Psychology Review, 13,* 157–176.

Cummings, C. (2001). *Managing to teach* (3rd ed.). Edmonds, WA: Teaching, Inc.

Davis, M. (2003). Addressing the needs of youth in transition to adulthood. *Administration and Policy in Mental Health, 30,* 495–509.

Deng, J. (2002). Unmotivated students—or unmotivating teachers? *Social Education, 66,* 133–134.

De Pry, R. L., & Sugai, G. (2002). The effect of active supervision and pre-correction on minor behavioral incidents and the sixth grade general education classroom. *Journal of Behavioral Education, 11,* 255–267.

Diehl, E. (2008, October 7). Motivating students with mindset coaching and how brains work (Dweck). Retrieved from http://www.classroom20.com/forum/topics/motivating-students-with

DiPietro, M., Ferdig, R. E., Black, E. W., & Preston, M. (2008). Best practices in K–12 online: Lessons learned from Michigan Virtual School teachers. *Journal of Interactive Online Learning, 7,* 10–35.

Dixon, J. P. (1995). Encouraging participation in a middle school classroom. In S. A. Spiegel, A. Collins, & J. Lappert (Eds.), *Action research: Perspectives from teachers' classrooms.* Tallahassee, FL: Southeastern Regional Vision for Education.

Doyle, W. (2006). Ecological approaches to classroom management. In C. M. Evertson & C. S. Weinstein (Eds.), *Handbook of classroom management: Research, practice, and contemporary issues* (pp. 97–125). New York, NY: Routledge.

Dreikurs, R. & Cassel, P. (1972). *Discipline without tears.* New York, NY: Hawthorn Books.

Drobnjak, L. (2017). Alternative seating for the classroom. *The Inspired Treehouse.* Retrieved from https://theinspiredtreehouse.com/alternative-seating-classroom

Dunning, G. B. (1971). Research in nonverbal communication. *Theory Into Practice, 10,* 250–258.

Dupin-Bryant, P. A. (2004). Strategies for teaching in online learning environments: Utilizing instructor immediacy behaviors. *Journal of Applied Research for Business Instruction, 2,* 1–4.

Dweck, C. S. (2015). Carol Dweck revisits the growth mindset. *Education Week, 35,* 20–24.

Dweck, C. S. (2002). The development of ability conceptions. In A. Wigfield, J. S. Eccles, A. Wigfield, & J. S. Eccles (Eds.), *Development of achievement motivation* (pp. 57–88). San Diego, CA: Academic Press.

Dweck, C. S. (2007). *Mindset: The new psychology of success.* New York, NY: Ballantine Books.

Dweck, C. S. (2010). Even geniuses work hard. *Educational Leadership, 65,* 16–20.

Eber, L., Sugai, G., Smith, C. R., & Scott, T. M. (2002). Wraparound and positive behavioral interventions and supports in the schools. *Journal of Emotional and Behavioral Disorders, 10,* 171–180.

Eccles, J. S. (2005). Subjective task value and the Eccles et al. model of achievement-related choices. In A. J. Elliot & C. S. Dweck (Eds.), *Handbook of competence and motivation.* New York, NY: Guilford Press.

Eccles, J. S., Adler, T. F., Futterman, R., Goff, S. B., Kaczala, C. M., Meece, J. L., & Midgley, C. (1983). Expectations, values and academic behaviors. In J. T. Spence (Ed.), *Achievement and achievement motivation* (pp. 75–146). San Francisco, CA: W. H. Freeman.

Emmer, R., T., Evertson, C. M., & Worsham, M. E. (2003). *Classroom management for secondary teachers* (6th ed.). Boston, MA: Allyn & Bacon.

Evans, M., & Boucher, A. R. (2015). Optimizing the power of choice: Supporting student autonomy to foster motivation and engagement in learning. *Mind, Brain, and Education, 9*, 87–91.

Evertson, C. M., & Emmer, E. T. (1982). Effective management at the beginning of the school year in junior high classes. *Journal of Educational Psychology, 74*, 485–498.

Evertson, C. M., & Harris, A. H. (2003). *COMP: Creating conditions for learning.* Nashville, TN: Vanderbilt University.

Faber, A., & Mazlish, E. (1980). *How to talk so kids will listen and listen so kids will talk.* New York, NY: HarperCollins.

Farrington, C. A., Roderick, M., Allensworth, E., Nagaoka, J., Keyes, T.S., Johnson, D. W., & Beechum, N. O. (2012). Teaching adolescents to become learners: The role of noncognitive factors in shaping school performance— A critical literature review. *Consortium on Chicago School Research.*

Fay, J., & Funk, D. (1995). *Teaching with love and logic.* Golden, CO: Love and Logic Press.

Finn, J. D. (1989). Withdrawing from school. *Review of Educational Research, 59*, 117–142.

Fovet, F. (2009). The use of humour in classroom interventions with students with social, emotional and behavioural difficulties. *Emotional & Behavioural Difficulties, 14*, 275–289.

Frank, M. C., Slemmer, J. A., Marcus, G. F., & Johnson, S. P. (2009). Information from multiple modalities helps 5-month-olds learn abstract rules. *Developmental Science, 12*, 504–509.

Fredricks, J. A., Blumenfeld, P. C., & Paris, A. H. (2004). School engagement: Potential of the concept, state of the evidence. *Review of Educational Research, 74*, 59–109.

Freeland, J. T., & Noell, G. H. (2002). Programming of maintenance: An investigation of delayed intermittent reinforcement and common stimuli to create indiscriminable contingencies. *Journal of Behavioral Education, 11*, 5–18.

Friermood, M. (2014). Retrieved from https://www.the thinkerbuilder.com

Furrer, C., & Skinner, C. (2003). Sense of relatedness as a factor in children's academic engagement and performance. *Journal of Educational Psychology, 95*, 148–162.

Gage, N., & Berliner, D. (1992). *Educational psychology* (5th ed.). Princeton, NJ: Houghton Mifflin Company.

Gardner, H. (2006). *Multiple intelligences: New horizons in theory and practice.* New York, NY: Basic Books.

Garwood, J. D., & Ampuja, A. A. (2019). Inclusion of students with learning, emotional, and behavioral disabilities through strength-based approaches. *Intervention in School and Clinic, 55*, 46–51.

Garwood, J. D., Ciullo, S., & Brunsting, N. (2017). Supporting students with emotional and behavioral disorders' comprehension and reading fluency. *TEACHING Exceptional Children, 49*, 391–401.

Garwood, J. D., & Moore, T. (2020). School connectedness insights for teachers educating youth with a severe emotional disturbance in residential treatment. *Residential Treatment for Children & Youth.* Advance online publication. doi:10.1080/0886571X.2019.1707145

Garwood, J. D., & Van Loan, C. L. (2019). Using social stories with students with social, emotional, and behavioral disorders: The promise and the perils. *Exceptionality, 27*, 133–148.

Garwood, J. D., Vernon-Feagans, L., & the Family Life Project Key Investigators. (2017). Classroom management affects literacy development of students with emotional and behavioral disorders. *Exceptional Children, 83*, 123–142.

Ginott, H. (1975). *Teacher and child: A book for parents and teachers.* New York, NY: MacMillan.

Glenz, T. (2014). The importance of learning students' names. *Journal on Best Teaching Practices*, 21–22.

Goldberg, G., & Houser, R. (2017, July 19). *Battling decision fatigue.* Retrieved from https://www.edutopia.org/blog/battling-decision-fatigue-gravity-goldberg-renee-houser

Good, T. L., & Brophy, J. E. (2008). *Looking in classrooms* (10th ed.). Boston, MA: Allyn & Bacon.

Goodenow, C. C. (1993). Classroom belonging among early adolescent students: Relationships to motivation and achievement. *Journal of Early Adolescence, 13*, 21–43.

Greene, R. W. (2008). Kids do well if they can. *Phi Delta Kappan, 76*, 272–283.

Greene, R. W. (2014). *Lost at school.* New York, NY: Scribner.

Gregory, G., & Kaufeldt, M. (2015). *The motivated brain: Improving student attention, engagement, and perseverance.* Alexandria, VA: ASCD.

Gresham, F. M., & Elliott, S. N. (2014). Social skills assessment and training in emotional and behavioral disorders. In H. M. Walker & F. M. Gresham (Eds.), *Handbook of evidence-based practices for emotional and behavioral disorders: Applications in schools* (pp. 152–172). New York, NY: Guilford Press.

Gresham, F. M., Sugai, G., & Horner, R. H. (2001). Interpreting outcomes of social skills training for students with high-incidence disabilities. *Exceptional Children, 67*, 331–344.

Grube, K. J. (2013). Detrimental effects of white valued walls in classrooms. *Educational Planning, 21,* 69–82.

Gulcan, M. G. (2010). Student perceptions regarding vocational high schoolteachers' problem solving methods against undesired behaviors in classroom management. *Education, 131,* 258–267.

Hagenaur, G., Votet, S., & Hascher, T. (2015). Teacher emotions in the classroom: Associations with students' engagement, classroom discipline and the interpersonal teacher-student relationship. *European Journal of Psychology of Education, 30,* 385–403.

Haichun, S., Haiyong, D., & Ang, C. (2013). Nothing but being there matters: Expectancy-value motivation between U.S. and Chinese middle school students. *International Education, 42,* 7–20.

Hamre, B. K. & Pianta, R. C. (2001). Early child-teacher relationships and the trajectory of children's school outcomes through eighth grade. *Child Development, 72,* 625–638.

Hank, O., Johnsonrude, I., & Pulvemuller, F. (2004). Somatotropic representation of action words in human motor and premotor cortex. *Neuron, 41,* 301–307.

Hannaford, C. (1995). *Smart moves: Why learning is not all in your head.* Arlington, VA: Great Oceans Publishers, Inc.

Harris, A. H., Shapiro, B. R., & Garwood, J. D. (2015). Space: Elementary and secondary classrooms. In W. G. Scarlett (Ed.), *The SAGE encyclopedia of classroom management* (pp. 567–570). Thousand Oaks, CA: Sage.

Harris, A. H., & Tomick, J. K. (2016). *Getting off to a good start: The first three days of school.* Nashville, TN: Ready to Teach.

Harris, A. H., Tomick, J. T., & Garwood, J. D. (2018). *Maintaining momentum: Building on a good start.* Nashville, TN: Ready to Teach.

Haydon, T., DeGreg, J., Maheady, L., & Hunter, W. (2012). Using active supervision and precorrection to improve transition behaviors in a middle school classroom. *Journal of Evidence-Based Practices for Schools, 13,* 81–94.

Haydon, T., & Musti-Rao, S. (2011). Effective use of behavior-specific praise: A middle school case study. *Beyond Behavior, 20,* 31–39.

Hill, S., & Nickels, M. (2018). It's elementary: Alternative seating engages students. *New Teacher Advocate, 26,* 2–3.

Hine, J. F., Ardoin, S. P., & Foster, T. E. (2015). Decreasing transition times in elementary school classrooms: Using computer-assisted instruction to automate intervention components. *Journal of Applied Behavior Analysis, 48,* 495–510.

Hirsch, S. E., Bruhn, A. L., Lloyd, J. W., & Katsiyannis, A. (2017). FBAs and BIPs: Avoiding common challenges related to fidelity. *TEACHING Exceptional Children, 49,* 360–379.

Horner, R. H., & Yell, M. L. (2017). Commentary on Zirkel: Judicial rulings specific to FBAs or BIPs under the IDEA and corollary state laws—An update. *Journal of Special Education, 51,* 57–79.

Horowitz P., & Otto, D. (1973). *The teaching effectiveness of an alternate teaching facility.* Alberta, Canada: University of Alberta. ERIC Document Reproduction Service No. ED 083242.

Hosinger, C., & Brown, M. H. (2019). Preparing trauma-sensitive teachers: Strategies for teacher educators. *Teacher Educators' Journal, 12,* 129–152.

Hunter, W. G., & Kittrell, J. R. (1966). Evolutionary operation: A review. *Technometrics, 8,* 389–397.

Ingram, C. (2006). *Effective parenting in a defective world: How to raise kids who stand out from the crowd.* Carol Stream, IL: Tyndale House Publishers.

Iyengar, S. S., & Lepper, M. R. (1999). Rethinking the value of choice: A cultural perspective on intrinsic motivation. *Journal of Personality and Social Psychology, 76,* 349–366.

Jennings, P. A., & Greenberg, M. T. (2009). The prosocial classroom: Teacher social and emotional competence in relation to student and classroom outcomes. *Review of Educational Research, 79,* 491–525.

Jensen, C. M., & Steinhausen, H. (2015). Time trends in incidence rates of diagnosed attention-deficit/hyperactivity disorder across 16 years in a nationwide Danish registry study. *Journal of Clinical Psychiatry, 76,* 334–341.

Jensen, E. (2000). Brain-based learning: A reality check. *Educational Leadership, 57*(7), 76–80.

Johnson, D. W., & Johnson, T. R. (1990). Social skills for successful group work. *Educational Leadership, 47*(4), 29–33.

Johnson, T. C., Stoner, G., & Green, S. K. (1996). Demonstrating the society model with classwide behavior interventions. *School Psychology Review, 25,* 199–214.

Jolivette, K., Sticher, J. P., & McCormick, K. M. (2002). Making choices—improving behavior—engaging in learning. *TEACHING Exceptional Children, 34,* 24–30.

Jones, V., & Jones, L. (2016). *Comprehensive classroom management: Creating communities of support and solving problems* (11th ed.). Boston, MA: Pearson.

Jones, M. G., & Vesilind, E. (1995). Preservice teachers' cognitive frameworks for class management. *Teaching & Teacher Education, 11,* 313–330.

Kagan, S. (1994). *Cooperative learning.* San Clemente, CA: Kagan Publishing.

Kamb, R. (2012). *Key factors in creating a positive classroom climate.* Retrieved from https://www.cfchildren .org/blog/2012/08/key-factors-in-creating-a-positive-classroom-climate

Kamins, M. L., & Dweck, C. (1999). Person versus process praise and criticism: Implications for contingent self-worth and coping. *Developmental Psychology, 35,* 835–847.

Kauffman, J. M., Bantz, R., & McCullough, J. (2002). Separate and better: A special public school class for students with emotional and behavioral disorders. *Exceptionality, 10,* 149–170.

Kelley, H. H. (1967). Attribution theory in social psychology. *Nebraska Symposium on Motivation, 15,* 192–238.

Kern, L., & Clemens, N. H. (2007). Antecedent strategies to promote appropriate classroom behavior. *Psychology in the Schools, 44,* 65–75.

Kern, L., & State, T. M. (2009). Incorporating choice and preferred activities into class wide instruction. *Beyond Behavior, 18*(2), 3–11.

Kidd, C., & Hayden, B. Y. (2015). The psychology and neuroscience of curiosity. *Neuron, 88,* 449–460.

Kirkham, N. Z., Rea, M., Osborne, T., White, H., & Mareschal, D. (2019). Do cues from multiple modalities support quicker learning in primary schoolchildren? *Developmental Psychology, 55,* 2048–2059.

Kosky, C., & Curtis, R. (2008). An action research exploration integrating student choice and arts activities in a sixth-grade social studies classroom. *Journal of Social Studies Research, 32,* 22–27.

Kostewicz, D. E., Ruhl, K. L., & Kubina, R. M. (2008). Creating classroom rules for students with emotional and behavioral disorders: A decision-making guide. *Beyond Behavior, 17,* 14–21.

Kounin, J. S. (1970). *Discipline and group management in classrooms.* Malabar, FL: Holt, Rinehart & Winston.

Kounin, J. S., & Gump, P. V. (1961). The comparative influence of punitive and non-punitive teachers upon children's concepts of school misconduct. *Journal of Educational Psychology, 52,* 44–49.

Lambert, N. M. (1995). Seating arrangements in classrooms. In L. W. Anderson (Ed.), *The international encyclopedia of teaching and teacher education* (2nd ed., pp. 196–200). Tarrytown, NY: Elsevier Science.

Lampi, A. R., Fenty, N. S., & Beaunae, C. (2005). Making the three Ps easier: Praise, proximity, and precorrection. *Beyond Behavior, 15,* 8–12.

Lee, V. E., & Burkham, D. T. (2003). Dropping out of high school: The role of school organization and structure. *American Educational Research Journal, 40,* 353–393.

Leinwand, S., Brahier, D. J., Huinker, D., Berry III, R. Q. Dillon, D. L., Larson, M. R., . . . & Smith, M. S. (2014). *Principles to actions: Ensuring mathematical success for all.* Reston, VA: National Council of Teachers of Mathematics.

Lewis, T., Colvin, G., & Sugai, G. (2000). The effects of pre-correction and active supervision on the recess behavior of elementary students. *Education and Treatment of Children, 23,* 109–121.

Little, S. G., & Akin-Little, A. (2008). Psychology's contributions to classroom management. *Psychology in the Schools, 45,* 227–234.

Loewenstein, G. (1994). The psychology of curiosity: A review and reinterpretation. *Psychological Bulletin, 116*(1), 75.

Long, N. J., Morse, W. C., Fecser, F. A., & Newman, R. G. (2007). *Conflict in the classroom.* Austin, TX: Pro-Ed.

MacDonald, J. M., Ahearn, W. H., Parry-Cruwys, D., Bancroft, S., & Dube, W. V. (2013). Persistence during extinction: Examining the effects of continuous and intermittent reinforcement on problem behavior. *Journal of Applied Behavior Analysis, 46,* 333–338.

MacSuga-Gage, A. S., & Simonsen, B. (2015). Examining the effects of teacher-directed opportunities to respond on student outcomes: A systematic review of the literature. *Education and Treatment of Children, 38,* 211–240.

Mader, C. E. (2009). "I will never teach the old way again": Classroom Management and External Incentives. *Theory Into Practice, 48,* 147–155.

Mancuso, J. C., & Allen, D. A. (1976). Children's perceptions of a transgressor's socialization as a function of type of reprimand. *Human Development, 19,* 277–290.

Marlowe, M. J., Garwood, J., & Van Loan, C. L. (2017). Psychoeducational approaches for pre-service teachers regarding emotional and behavioral disorders and the relationship-driven classroom. *International Journal of Special Education, 32,* 858–876.

Marlowe, M. J., & Hayden, T. L. (2013). *Teaching children who are hard to reach: Relationship-driven classroom practice.* Thousand Oaks, CA: Corwin.

Marshall, M. (2005). Discipline without stress, punishments, or rewards. *The Clearing House, 79,* 51–54.

Marzano, R. J. (2010). The art and science of teaching: Using games to enhance student achievement. *Educational Leadership, 67*(5), 71–72.

Maslow, A. H. (1943). A theory of human motivation. *Psychological Review, 50,* 370–396.

McEvoy, A., & Welker, R. (2000). Antisocial behavior, academic failure, and school climate: A critical review. *Journal of Emotional and Behavioral Disorders, 8,* 130–140.

McIntyre, T. (2011). What is "PsychoEd"? Retrieved from http://www.behavioradvisor.com/PsychoEdModel

McIntyre, T., & Battle, J. (1998). The traits of "good teachers" as identified by African-American and white students with emotional and/or behavioral disorders. *Behavioral Disorders, 23,* 134–142.

McLeskey, J., Landers, E., Williamson, P., & Hoppey, D. (2012). Are we moving toward educating students with disabilities in less restrictive settings? *Journal of Special Education, 46,* 131–140.

McMaster, K. L., Fuchs D., & Fuchs, L. S. (2006). Research on peer-assisted learning strategies: The promise and limitations of peer-mediated instruction. *Reading & Writing Quarterly, 22,* 5–25.

Mehrabian, A. (1971). *Silent messages.* Belmont, CA: Wadsworth Publishing.

Menendez, A. L., Payne, L. D., & Mayton, M. R. (2008). The implementation of positive behavioral support in an elementary school: Processes, procedures, and outcomes. *Alberta Journal of Educational Research, 54,* 448–462.

Mercer, S. H., & DeRosier, M. E. (2010). A prospective investigation of teacher preference and children's perceptions of the student-teacher relationship. *Psychology in the Schools, 47,* 184–192.

Mihalas, S., Morse, W. C., Allsopp, D. H., & McHatton, P. A. (2009). Cultivating caring relationships between teachers and secondary students with emotional and behavioral disorders: Implications for research and practice. *Remedial and Special Education, 30,* 108–125.

Miller, G. (2014). Data from a century of cinema reveals how movies have evolved. Retrieved from https://www.wired.com/2014/09/cinema-is-evolving/

Mitchell, M. M., & Bradshaw, C. P. (2013). Examining classroom influences on student perceptions of school climate: The role of classroom management and exclusionary discipline strategies. *Journal of School Psychology, 51,* 599–610.

Mitman, A. L., Megendoller, J. R., Ward, B. A., & Tikunoff, W. J. (1981). Ecological case studies of classroom instruction in a successful school. Verification Inquiry, Volume VI. *Ecological Perspectives for Successful Schooling Practice.* (Far West Lab Rep. No. EPSSP-81-15). San Francisco, CA: Educational Research and Development.

Morrow, L. M., & Weinstein, C. S. (1982). Increasing children's use of literature through program and physical design changes. *Elementary School Journal, 83*(2), 131–137.

Mosquera, A. (2015, March 29). 9 simple ways to provide choice in your classroom. Retrieved from https://thesciencepenguin.com/2015/03/9-simple-ways-to-provide-choice-in-your-classroom.html

Mueller, C. M., & Dweck, C. S. (1998). Praise for intelligence can undermine children's motivation and performance. *Journal of Personality and Social Psychology, 75,* 33–52.

Mundschenk, N. A., Miner, C. A., & Nastally, B. L. (2011). Effective classroom management: An air traffic control analogy. *Intervention in School and Clinic, 47,* 98–103.

Murayama, K., Pekrun, R., Lichtenfeld, S., & vom Hofe, R. (2013). Predicting long-term growth in students' mathematics achievement: The unique contributions of motivation and cognitive strategies. *Child Development, 84,* 1475–1490.

Muthyala, R. S., & Wei, W. (2013). Does space matter? Impact of classroom space on student learning in an organic-first curriculum. *Journal of Chemical Education, 90,* 45–50.

National Association of Elementary School Principals (NAESP). (2020). Flexible grouping for inclusivity. *Principal, 99*(3).

National Child Traumatic Stress Network. (2016). Symptoms and behaviors associated with exposure to trauma. Retrieved from http://www.nctsn.org/trauma-types/early-childhoodtrauma/Symptoms-and-Behaviors-Associated-with-Exposure-to-Trauma

Nelsen, J., Lott, L., & Glenn, S. (2000). *Positive discipline in the classroom: Developing mutual respect, cooperation, and responsibility in your classroom* (3rd ed.). New York, NY: Three Rivers Press.

Nelson, J. R., & Roberts, M. L. (2000). Ongoing reciprocal teacher–student interactions involving disruptive behaviors in general education classrooms. *Journal of Emotional and Behavioral Disorders, 8,* 27–38.

Newmann, F. M. (1992). Higher-order thinking and prospects for classroom thoughtfulness. In F. M. Newmann (Ed.), *Student engagement and achievement in American secondary schools* (pp. 62–91). New York, NY: Teachers College Press.

Nie, Y., & Lau, S. (2009). Complementary roles of care and behavioral control in classroom management: The self-determination theory perspective. *Contemporary Educational Psychology, 34,* 185–194.

Notar, C. E., & Sorbet, S. R. (2020). Withitness in the eLearning. *Technium Social Sciences Journal, 10,* 58–78.

Nucci, L. (2006). Classroom management for moral and social development. In C. M. Evertson & C. S. Weinstein (Eds.), *Handbook of classroom management: Research practice and contemporary issues* (pp. 711–731). Mahwah, NJ: Lawrence Erlbaum.

Obenchain, K. M., & Taylor, S. S. (2005). Behavior management: Making it work in middle and secondary schools. *Clearing House: A Journal of Educational Strategies, Issues and Ideas, 79,* 7.

Ogata, K. (2017). Maltreatment related trauma symptoms affect academic achievement through cognitive functioning: A preliminary examination in Japan. *Journal of Intelligence, 5,* 1–7.

Oliver, K., Kellogg, S., Townsend, L., & Brady, K. (2010). Needs of elementary and middle school teachers developing online courses for a virtual school. *Distance Education, 31,* 55–75.

Oram, L., Owens, S., & Maras, M. (2016). Functional behavior assessments and behavior intervention plans in rural schools: An exploration of the need, barriers, and recommendations. *Preventing School Failure, 60,* 305–310.

Osher, D., & Hanley, T. V. (2001). Implementing the SED national agenda: Promising programs and policies for children and youth with emotional and behavioral problems. *Education and Treatment of Children, 24,* 374–403.

Oswald, K., San Fran, S., & Johnson, G. (2005). Preventing trouble: Making schools safer places using positive behavior supports. *Education and Treatment of Children, 28,* 265–278.

Pappano, L. (2014). "Trauma-sensitive" schools: A new framework for reaching troubled students. *Harvard Education Letter, 30,* 1–5.

Parcells, C., Stommel, M., & Hubbard, R. P. (1999). Mismatch of classroom furniture and student body dimensions: Empirical findings and health implications. *Journal of Adolescent Health, 24,* 265–273.

Parker, R., Rose, J., & Gilbert L. (2016). Attachment aware schools: An alternative to behaviourism in supporting children's behaviour? In H. E. Lees & N. Noddings (Eds.), *The Palgrave international handbook of alternative education* (pp. 463–483). London, England: Palgrave Macmillan.

Patall, E. A., Cooper, H., & Wynn, S. R. (2010). The effectiveness and relative importance of choice in the classroom. *Journal of Educational Psychology, 102,* 896–915.

Phelan, P., Davidson, A. L., & Cao, H. T. (1992). Speaking up: Students' perspectives on school. *Phi Delta Kappan, 73,* 695–704.

Philipp, R. A., & Thanheiser, E. (2010). Showing your students you care: Seeing the individual trees in the classroom forest. *New England Mathematics Journal, 42,* 8–17.

Plank, S. B., McDill, E. L., McPartland, J. M., & Jordan, W. J. (2001). Situation and repertoire: Civility, incivility, cursing and politeness in an urban high school. *Teachers College Record, 103,* 504–524.

Poling, D., Van Loan, C. L., Garwood, J. D., Zhang, S., Riddle, D. (pending revision). A review of school-based teacher-student relationship intervention approaches. *Educational Research Review.*

Quin, D. (2016). Longitudinal and contextual associations between teacher-student relationships and student engagement: A systematic review. *Review of Educational Research, 87,* 345–387.

Ramsey, M. L., Jolivette, K., Patterson, D. P., & Kennedy, C. (2010). Using choice to increase time on-task, task-completion, and accuracy for students with emotional/

behavior disorders in a residential facility. *Education and Treatment of Children, 33*(1), 1–21.

Rathvon, N. (2008). *Effective school interventions: Evidence-based strategies for improving student outcomes* (2nd ed). New York, NY: Guilford Press.

Rock, M. L. (2004). Graphic organizers: Tools to build behavioral literacy and foster emotional competency. *Intervention in School and Clinic, 40*(1), 10–37.

Rohrkemper, M. M. (1984). The influence of teacher socialization on students' social cognition and reported interpersonal classroom behavior. *Elementary School Journal, 85,* 244–275.

Romi, S., Lewis, R., Roache, J., & Riley, P. (2011). The impact of teachers' aggressive management techniques on students' attitudes to schoolwork. *Journal of Educational Research, 104,* 231–240.

Ryan, R. M., & Deci, E. L. (2000). Intrinsic and extrinsic motivations: Classic definitions and new direction. *Contemporary Educational Psychology, 25,* 54–67.

Schaps, E., & Solomon, D. (2003). The role of the school social environment and preventing student drug use. *Journal of Primary Prevention, 23,* 299–328.

Schlosser, L. K. (1992). Teacher distance and student disengagement: School lives on the margin. *Journal of Teacher Education, 43,* 128–140.

Schunk, D. H., & Meece, J. L. (Eds.). (1992). *Student perceptions in the classroom.* Mahwah, NJ: Lawrence Erlbaum.

Searle, M. (2013). *Causes and cures in the classroom: Getting to the root of academic and behavior problems.* Alexandria, VA: ASCD.

Seeley, C. L., (2017). Turning teaching UPSIDE DOWN: Students learn more when we let them wrestle with a math problem before we teach them, how to solve it. *Educational Leadership, 75*(2), 32–36.

Seligman, M. E. P. (2002). *Authentic happiness: Using the new positive psychology to realize your potential for lasting fulfillment.* New York, NY: Free Press.

Shachar, H., & Sharon, S. (1994). Talking, relating, and achieving: Effects of cooperative learning circles. *Instructional Science, 19,* 445–466.

Shors, T. J., Anderson, M. L., Curlik II, D. M., & Nokia, S. M. (2012). Use it or lose it: How neurogenesis keeps the brain fit for learning. *Behavioural Brain Research, 227,* 450–458.

Simonsen, B., Fairbanks, S., Briesch, A., Myers, D., & Sugai, G. (2008). Evidence-based practices in classroom management: Considerations for research to practice. *Education & Treatment of Children, 31,* 351–380.

Sinha, S. P., Nayyar, P., & Mukherjee, N. (1995) Perceptions of crowding among children and adolescents. *Journal of Social Psychology, 135,* 263–268.

Skinner, E. A., & Belmont, M. J. (1993). Motivation in the classroom: Reciprocal effects of teacher behavior and student engagement across the school year. *Journal of Educational Psychology, 85*, 571–581.

Slavin, R. E. (1990). Research on cooperative learning: Consensus and controversy. *Educational Leadership, 47*(4), 52–54.

Smith, R., & Lambert, M. (2008). Assuming the best. *Educational Leadership, 66*(1), 16–21.

Sommer, R., & Olson, H. (1980). The soft classroom. *Environment & Behavior, 12*(1), 3–16.

Song, H., Kim, J., & Luo, W. (2016). Teacher-student relationship in online classes: A role of teacher self-disclosure. *Computers in Human Behavior, 54*, 436–443.

Sprouls, K., Mathur, S. R., & Upreti, G. (2015). Is positive feedback a forgotten classroom practice? Findings and implications for at-risk students. *Preventing School Failure, 59*, 153–160.

Sterling, D. R. (2009). Classroom management: Setting up the classroom for learning. *Science Scope, 32*, 29–33.

Stinson, S. W. (1993). Meaning and value: Reflections on what students say about school. *Journal of Curriculum and Supervision, 8*, 216–238.

Strahan, D. B., & Layell, K. (2006). Connecting caring and action through responsive teaching: How one team accomplished success in a struggling middle school. *Clearing House: A Journal of Educational Strategies, Issues and Ideas, 79*, 147–153.

Stronge, J. H., Ward, T. J., & Grant, L. W. (2011). What makes good teachers good? A cross-case analysis of the connection between teacher effectiveness and student achievement. *Journal of Teacher Education, 62*, 339–355.

Taba, H., Durkin, M. C., Fraenkel, J. R., & McNaughton, A. H. (1971). *A teacher's handbook to elementary social studies: An inductive approach* (2nd ed.). Reading, MA: Addison-Wesley.

Tate, M. (2007). *Shouting won't grow dendrites: Teaching for managing a brain-compatible classroom.* Thousand Oaks, CA: Corwin.

Thapa, A., Cohen, J., Guffey, S., & Higgins-D'Alessandro, A. (2013). A review of school climate research. *Review of Educational Research, 83*, 357–385.

Thorson, S. (1996). The missing link: Students discuss school discipline. *Focus on Exceptional Children, 29*(3), 1–12.

Tobin, K., Ritchie, S. M., Oakley, J. L., Mergard, V., & Hudson, P. (2013). Relationships between emotional climate and the fluency of classroom interactions. *Learning Environments Research, 16*, 71–89.

Tudge, J. R., Mokrova, I., Hatfield, B. E., & Karnik, R. B. (2009). Uses and misuses of Bronfenbrenner's theory of human development. *Journal of Family Theory and Review, 1*, 198–210.

Urdan, T., Midgley, C., & Anderman, E. M. (1998). The role of classroom goals structure and students' use of self-handicapping strategies. *American Educational Research Journal, 35*, 101–122.

US Department of Education, National Center for Education Statistics. (2015). Digest of education statistics, 2013 (NCES 2015-011).

US Department of Education, Office of Special Education and Rehabilitative Services, Office of Special Education Programs. (2018). *40th annual report to Congress on the implementation of the Individuals with Disabilities Education Act, 2018.* Washington, DC: Author.

van der Kolk, B. (2014). *The body keeps the score: Mind, brain, and body in the transformation of trauma.* London, England: Penguin Books Limited.

Van Loan, C. L., Cullen, J. A., & Giordano, K. (2015). *Shifting gears: Conflict avoidance through working partnerships.* Boone, NC: ASU.

Van Loan, C. L., Gage, N. A., & Cullen, J. P. (2015). Reducing the use of physical restraint: A pilot study investigating a relationship-based crisis prevention curriculum. *Residential Treatment for Children & Youth, 32*, 113–133.

Van Loan, C. L., & Garwood, J. D. (2020a). Facilitating high-quality relationships for students with emotional and behavioral disorders in crisis. *Intervention in School and Clinic, 55*, 253–256.

Van Loan, C. L., & Garwood, J. D. (2020b). Measuring relationships between adolescents with emotional and behavioral disorders and their teachers: A psychometric report. *Assessment for Effective Intervention, 45*, 144–150.

Van Overwalle, E., & de Metsenaere, M. (1990). The effects of attribution-based intervention and study strategy training on academic achievement in college freshman. *British Journal of Educational Psychology, 60*, 299–311.

Vaughn, B. J., & Horner, R. H. (1997). Identifying instructional tasks that occasion problem behaviors and assessing the effects of student versus teacher choice among these tasks. *Journal of Applied Behavior Analysis, 30*, 299–312.

Vidyarthi, N. (2011, December 14). Attention spans have dropped from 12 minutes to 5 minutes—How social media is ruining our minds [Infographic]. *Social Times.* Retrieved from http://socialtimes.com/attention-spans-have-dropped-from-12-minutes-to-5-seconds-how-social-media-is-ruining-our-minds-infographic_b86479

Walkley, M., & Cox, T. L. (2013). Building trauma-informed schools and communities. *Children & Schools, 35*, 123–126.

Wannarka, R., & Ruhl, K. (2008). Seating arrangements that promote positive academic and behavioural outcomes: A review of empirical research. *Support for Learning, 23,* 89–93.

Wanzer, M. B., Frymier, A. B., Wojtaszczyk, A. M., & Smith, T. (2006). Appropriate and inappropriate uses of humor by teachers. *Communication Education, 55,* 178–196.

Wasserman, H., & Danforth, H. E. (1988). *The human bond: Supporter groups and mutual aid.* New York, NY: Springer.

Way, S. M. (2011). School discipline and disruptive classroom behavior: The moderating effects of student perceptions. *Sociological Quarterly, 52,* 346–375.

Weinstein, C. S. (2003). *Secondary classroom management: Lessons from research and practice.* New York, NY: McGraw-Hill.

Weinstein, C. S. (2007). *Middle and secondary classroom management: Lessons from research and practice.* New York, NY: McGraw-Hill.

Wentzel, K. R. (1997). Student motivation in middle school; The role of perceived pedagogical caring. *Journal of Educational Psychology, 89,* 411–419.

Wentzel, K. R. (2009). Peers and academic functioning at school. In K. Rubin, W. Bukowski, & B. Laursen (Eds.), *Handbook of peer interactions, relationships, and groups* (pp. 531–547). New York, NY: Guilford Press.

Wery, J. J., & Cullinan, D. (2013). State definitions of emotional disturbance. *Journal of Emotional and Behavioral Disorders, 21,* 45–52.

Wiggins, G. (2012). Less teaching and more feedback? Retrieved from https://inservice.ascd.org/less-teaching-and-more-feedback/#:~:text=Learning%20is%20caused %20by%20learners,%2B%20more%20feedback%20 %3D%20better%20learning

Williams, C. E. B. (2020). *Evaluating the use of alternative seating with children at risk for emotional and behavioral disorders.* Ann Arbor, MI: ProQuest LLC.

Wlodkowski, R. J. (1983). *Motivational opportunities for successful teaching [Leader's guide].* Phoenix, AZ: Universal Dimensions.

Wolfe, P. (2010). *Brain matters: Translating research into classroom practice* (2nd ed.). Alexandria, VA: ASCD.

Wong, H. K., & Wong, R. T. (1991). *The first days of school: How to be an effective teacher.* Mountain View, CA: Harry K. Wong Publications.

Wong, H. K., Wong, R., Rogers, K., & Brooks, A. (2012). Managing your classroom for success. *Science and Children, 49,* 60–64.

Yeager, D. S., Romero, C., Paunesku, D., Hullemen, C. S., Schneider, B. Hinojosa, C., & Dweck, C. C. (2016). Using design thinking to improve psychological interventions: The case of the growth mindset during the transition to high school. *Journal of Educational Psychology, 108,* 374–391.

Yun-Jeong, S., & Kelly, K. R. (2013). Cross-cultural comparison of the effects of optimism, intrinsic motivation, and family relations on vocational identity. *Career Development Quarterly, 61,* 141–160.

CORWIN
A SAGE Publishing Company

CORWIN HAS ONE MISSION: to enhance education through intentional professional learning.

We build long-term relationships with our authors, educators, clients, and associations who partner with us to develop and continuously improve the best evidence-based practices that establish and support lifelong learning.